BOOKS BY PHILLIP LOPATE

*Against Joie de Vivre*

*Bachelorhood: Tales of the Metropolis*

*Being with Children*

*The Rug Merchant*

*Confessions of Summer*

*The Eyes Don't Always Want to Stay Open*

*The Daily Round*

# AGAINST JOIE DE VIVRE

*Personal Essays*

# PHILLIP LOPATE

POSEIDON PRESS

NEW YORK   LONDON   TORONTO   SYDNEY   TOKYO

**POSEIDON PRESS**
Simon & Schuster Building
Rockefeller Center
1230 Avenue of the Americas
New York, New York 10020
Copyright © 1989 by Phillip Lopate
POSEIDON PRESS is a registered trademark of Simon & Schuster Inc.
POSEIDON PRESS colophon is a trademark of Simon & Schuster Inc.
Designed by Barbara Marks Graphic Design
Manufactured in the United States of America
10  9  8  7  6  5  4  3  2  1
Library of Congress Cataloging-in-Publication Data
Lopate, Phillip, date
    Against Joie de vivre: personal essays/Phillip Lopate.
       p.   cm.
    I. Title.
PS3562.066A74   1989
814'.54—dc19                                        89-30363
ISBN 0-671-67679-2                                  CIP

Lyrics to "The Man I Love" © 1924 WB Music Corp. (Renewed). All rights
reserved. Used by permission.

"Samson and Delilah and the Kids" appeared in *Congregation: Contemporary
Writers Read the Jewish Bible*, edited by David Rosenberg (Harcourt Brace
Jovanovich).

"Against Joie de Vivre" appeared in *Ploughshares* and in *The Best American Essays of
1987* (Ticknor & Fields) and *The Pushcart Prize XII.*

"Art of the Creep," "Revisionist Nuptials," "A Passion for Waiting," "On
Shaving a Beard," and "Upstairs Neighbors" appeared in *Dallas Times Herald's
Westward Magazine.*

"A Nonsmoker with a Smoker" appeared in *New Age Journal.*

"What Happened to the Personal Essay?" and "Waiting for the Book to Come
Out" appeared in *The New York Times Book Review.*

"Never Live Above Your Landlord" appeared in *Columbia.*

"Anticipation of *La Notte*: The 'Heroic' Age of Moviegoing" appeared in
*American Film* in an abridged form and in *Columbia* in an expanded form.

"Modern Friendships" appeared in *Texas Monthly.*

"Chekhov for Children" appeared in *Teachers and Writers Magazine.*

"Only Make Believe: Some Observations on Architectural Language" appeared
in *Metropolis.*

Parts of "Houston Hide-and-Seek" appeared in *Cite* and *Houston Style.*

"Reflections on Subletting" appeared in *7 Days.*

"Suicide of a Schoolteacher" appeared in *Boulevard.*

TO MAX APPLE

AND

BILL ZAVATSKY

*the A to Z of friendship*

# CONTENTS

# AGAINST

# JOIE

# DE

# VIVRE

I

# SAMSON AND DELILAH AND THE KIDS*

I grew up in the era of the great Jewish lovers. *Samson and Delilah, David and Bathsheba, Solomon and Sheba* were burning up screens across the land. I never managed to see *David and Bathsheba* (though I knew the coming attractions by heart), because the movie industry in its wisdom decreed that I was too young for this adulterous tale. Inconsistently, they let me into *Samson and Delilah* when I was seven.

I still remember my excitement when I first saw the poster announcing its imminent arrival in our neighborhood. "See Sam-

---

* This essay was written originally for an anthology of essays about the Old Testament, *Congregation*, in which each author was asked to establish personal ties with a biblical text. I chose to focus on the Samson story, both because it seems to me one of the key narratives in the Bible (its richness attested to by the many plays, operas, epic poems, films drawn from it), and because I suspected the Samson and Delilah dynamic had helped to shape me as a man, like it or not.

son battle a lion with his own hands! See Samson tear down the Temple of Dagon! See Delilah tame the strongman!" I was so crazy about movies that I saw everything connected to them as a *promesse de bonheur:* lobby stills, newspaper ads on the entertainment pages, and especially the ten-foot billboards displayed outside the Commodore, where giants held at bay an encircling, ungrounded chaos of tempting panoramas.

My tolerance for celluloid had been built up over the long Saturday matinees that my siblings and I attended regularly, and which included a double feature, seven cartoons, newsreels, coming attractions, and a Flash Gordon or Hopalong Cassidy serial. "O dark, dark, dark, amid the blaze of noon!" *(Samson Agonistes)* By the time we had stumbled onto the street, sated with the blood of scalped cavalrymen, the highballs served by Veronica Lake, the dynamite set off by a Bugs Bunny in drag, it was already dinner time. We would walk under the El past the discount stores serving our ghetto in Williamsburg, Brooklyn; past Stevens Bakery, which specialized in white icing; past the fish restaurant with its grotesque lobster tank in the window; past the tough shoeshine boys on the corner; past the synagogue, quickly and guiltily, because it was *Shabbes;* and make our way back to the tenement where we lived, debating our favorite scenes all the while.

If you ask me what the Bible meant to me as a child, I can tell you it signified two things: those awkwardly drawn comic strips the *Brooklyn Eagle* would run (next to "Dick Tracy" or "Mary Worth") each Sunday, "Tales from the Scriptures," featuring stern, bearded patriarchs and women with pitchers on their shoulders, and the biblical spectacles we were constantly told cost "millions" and had "casts of thousands." Whatever possessed Hollywood to turn out all those biblical/Roman clinkers throughout the fifties? The postwar audience's abandonment of a neorealist aesthetic for the escapist anodynes of costumed bloodshed, the advent of wide-screen technologies that cried out for spectacle, the more conservative political mood, the irresistible formula of having one's cake (sin) and eating it too (piety), the collapse of the studio system and its replacement by international package deals—all must have contributed to the zenith of this ill-fated genre.

Cecil B. DeMille's *Samson and Delilah* (1949) was one of the first of the postwar biblical spectacles. Watching a VCR tape of it some thirty-five years later, I am struck by how dioramic and artificial (if entertaining in a kitschy way) it looks now, its drama as stylized as Kabuki, its sets like an old World's Fair made of endless lathe and temporary grandeur. The virtues of the biblical epic—which DeMille had a large hand in shaping—were mainly to be found in art direction, costumes, and special effects. DeMille began in the silent era, and there is an echo of Griffith's Babylonianism in the idol-gargoyled Temple of Dagon.

"Before the dawn of time . . ." intones the narrator in the opening shot; we see clouds, and marching feet, and are treated to a little lecture about the struggle between tyranny and freedom. Biblical epics tended to be made after both world wars, when America, as "leader of the free world," had a need to wrap itself in the sanctimonious mantle of previous Chosen Peoples. Curiously, the word "Jew" is never mentioned in the DeMille film, nor are the words "Hebrew" or "Israelite." Samson's people are referred to only as "Danites," in what may have been nervousness about anti-Semitism during the McCarthy era.

*Samson and Delilah* boasted one of those "international" casts: the star (Hedy Lamarr) spoke Viennese-scented English, her leading man (Victor Mature) hailed from Kentucky, and all the Philistine opponents of Judeo-Christianity had, in the curious convention of such films, British accents (George Sanders, Angela Lansbury, Henry Wilcoxin).

A DeMille scholar told me that the director had wanted to make *Samson and Delilah* ten years earlier but that he couldn't secure the financing. By the time the deal had come together with the actress he wanted, a certain freshness had gone out of Lamarr: she looked bruised by another decade's strain of holding together her glamour. But her worldly, mocking Viennese air had some of Dietrich's alluring melancholy, especially when it came up against the younger, oafish Mature: it was the Old World seducing the New World, yet again.

Hedy's basic Delilah costume consisted of a sleeveless halter that stopped just below her breasts, a long skirt, usually with a slit to show off her nice legs, and, anachronistically, a pair of pumps as well. After she becomes a Bad Woman she is never seen without a feather-duster plume, which she waves around to make her points, and which is color-coordinated to match her silver, turquoise, rose, and sapphire gowns. At times she seems to act mainly with her midriff (midriff eroticism being a staple of these epics, rendered more piquant by the code rule forbidding umbilici on-screen), or with her eloquent shoulder blades, as she leans against a wall, thrusting her breasts forward. Even though she seems rather diminutive next to Mature, she is altogether luscious with her upturned nose, saucy gazes, and spit curls.

Mature responds with a supercilious sneer like a country bumpkin who knows they are putting something over on him but isn't sure what, and hopes his cynicism will distract attention from his slowness. It was about this actor that David Thomson wrote, memorably if cruelly: "It is too easy to dismiss Mature, for he surpasses badness. He is a strong man in a land of nine-stone weaklings, an incredible concoction of corned beef, husky voice and brilliantine—a barely concealed sexual advertisement for soiled goods. Remarkably, he is as much himself in the cheerfully meretricious and the pretentiously serious. . . ." Here, however, he seems bewildered; his eyes look dead when he is called upon to say things like "You—daughter of hell!" He wears a green leather jerkin that leaves most of his chest uncovered, and his broad body, by our more stringent, Schwarzenegger standards of muscular definition, looks fat. (Incidentally, there is nothing in the Bible that says Samson was a brawny, muscular person. Since his strength came from God's spirit inhabiting him, the theological point might have been better made by casting Mickey Rooney or Arnold Stang.)

Yet, by that familiar phenomenon that makes it difficult to picture a story's characters afterward except in the physical shape of the actors who played them on-screen, however miscast they may have been, the past-her-prime Lamarr and the stalwart ham Mature will always remain in my imagination the quintessential, the *actual*, Samson and Delilah.

As a child I was a very forgiving moviegoer. If a picture had one or two scenes that excited my imagination, I would simply evacuate the duller parts from consciousness and concentrate on these privileged images, carrying them around like mental slides long afterward and consulting them solacingly in bad moments. Such a scene was the destruction of the Philistine hall in *Samson and Delilah*, where the pillars crumbled in sections like gigantic white Tootsie Rolls. For me, Samson was essentially a Superman figure. Just as I would jump off a chair and pretend to fly like the Man of Steel, so I used to play at tying my hands together and ripping the ropes off; eyes closed, I would grit my teeth and fantasize pulling a building down by straining with all my might. I had dreams of toppling P.S. 11, breaking everything I hated into rubble, like the newsreels of bombed Berlin. (As it happened, many blocks in Williamsburg already looked that way, torn down to make way for the future Brooklyn–Queens Expressway.)

I prayed to get back at everyone who had humiliated me in one blow, like poor Samson, the blind giant. Not that I had so many enemies, but every child suffers from powerlessness, bossed around by adults, older brothers, classroom bullies. There was one tormentor, Ronald, big for his age, who used to beat me up after school. I would imagine ways to torture him, a new one each night like Scheherazade. As I grew older I began to concoct more subtle revenge fantasies, sometimes even letting my prisoner go. Curiously, this reprieve gave me a greater *frisson*: I enjoyed the idea of playing cat and mouse with my victim, one day vicious, the next unexpectedly benevolent. Control, restraint, sadism, creativity. I was only a few years from eroticizing this fantasy with a chivalric twist.

In sixth grade I was attracted to a girl with a Roman nose named Felicia, as were all the boys, since she already had the curves of a woman. She was from a better family than ours; her father was a lawyer, and she carried herself rather haughtily. "She thinks she's Cleopatra—or Delilah!" we would say behind her back, because she knew all the boys fancied her. Secretly, I imagined myself drawing daily closer to the beautiful Felicia and impressing her with my intelligence. One afternoon when I tried to make friendly conversation she ridiculed me, saying that I wore the same clothes, the same ugly sweater, every day. It was true. I had taken no notice of what I had on, and neither, apparently, had my parents.

After she had humiliated me, I began to have dreams in which Felicia would knock on my door, completely naked and defenseless. Someone had stolen her clothing. Not only did I not take advantage of the situation, I would immediately throw a coat or blanket around her shoulders and escort her home. This chaperonage would sometimes take us down dank castle steps in which I would have to protect her honor by sword fight. Never did I ask her for so much as a kiss in payment—though sometimes she would reward me with a feast of kisses.

The closeness with which dreams of gallantry and revenge were tangled in my brain must be why, even today, when I remember to act in a polite manner (for instance, giving up my seat to a woman in the bus) and am thanked for being "chivalrous," I instantly feel a twinge of guilty conscience. But then, I am chronically guilt-ridden about my virtuous side, if you will. "You were always a good boy," my mother has told me so often. "You I never had to worry about." Even as a baby, before I had any choice in the matter, I was "good": when my mother was in the maternity ward, when all the other babies were wailing from the air-raid sirens, I quietly found her breast.

One of my earliest memories, from about the age of four, is of my older brother and younger sister experimenting with matches. "They shouldn't be doing that," I thought. Sure enough, the kitchen curtain caught fire. There was smoke, flames; my mother came home in the nick of time and doused the fire with pots of water. When it was over she demanded to know what had happened. My brother and sister pointed fingers at each other. "I didn't do anything," I kept telling her. Finally she said, "I know, cookie, I know you didn't." The question years later is, *Why* didn't I do anything? Why was I such a goody-goody? Was I good because I chose to be or because I was too timid, too programmed to do otherwise?

There were rewards for being the "good" boy, but sometimes it came as a mixed blessing; I was both my mother's favorite and the one to whom she paid the least attention, because I didn't cause her trouble. By nursery school, I had already developed a reputation for honesty. "Phillip never lies," my nursery teacher said. My mother, pleased to hear it, nevertheless insisted healthily, "Every child lies." "Not Phillip," said this woman, whom I had clearly managed to make fall in love with me.

One day, not long thereafter, I was jumping up and down on my parents' bed, using their mattress as a trampoline. I was no angel, I wanted to have a good time, to break the rules, to become an evildoer! (In Part 2 of *The Brothers Karamazov*, which Dostoevsky never got to write, the saintly Alyosha was supposed to turn into a great sinner.) In mid-jump I heard my mother coming. "What were you doing? Were you jumping on my bed like I told you not to?" "No, uh-uh," I protested. "I *saw* you do it!" she exclaimed. "Don't fib to me." Though I got a beating afterward we were both relieved: he lies!

In Judges, the story of Samson begins with his mother's barrenness. An angel appears to the wife of Manoah and tells her she is going to have a son, but she should drink no wine nor eat anything unclean, and "No razor shall come upon his head, for the boy shall be a Nazarite to God from birth; and he shall begin to deliver Israel from the hand of the Philistines." (Judges 13:5) She runs and tells her husband what the stranger has said, and Manoah gets the angel to repeat these instructions a third time. Then a puff of smoke, flames, and the couple realizes that the stranger is indeed an angel of the Lord; they fall on their faces to the ground. This angelic visitation to a barren woman is a recurrent biblical formula; only in the context of Judges, with its dense narrative style, does the incident's leisurely redundance surprise. Why is a whole chapter of twenty-five verses "wasted" on this business? Certainly no other judge is accorded such preliminary buildup; it is almost as though the whole Book of Judges were taking a breath before launching into the Samson story.

In a way, also, the chapter lets us know that before Samson is even born he is in God's debt. His body itself doesn't quite belong to him—it's a sacred weapon for God to inhabit with His spirit when He so desires. Moreover, without any choice in the matter, Samson is pledged to be a Nazarite: one who is consecrated, abstinent, separate from others, pure. No wonder Samson acts "bad": he is trying to make a space for his own life, inside the one already owed to his parents and God.

So he indulges in skirt-chasing. All his troubles—but also all his heroic deeds—stem from whoring and womanizing. He falls in love easily, and, it seems, purely on a physical basis. Like Portnoy, he is drawn to *shiksas*. In our very first encounter with the adult Samson, he has just seen a woman in Timnah, the daughter of Philistines, and wants her for a wife. His parents object: "Is there not a woman among the daughters of your kinsmen, or among all the people, that you must go to take a wife from the uncircumcised Philistines? But Samson said to his father, 'Get her for me; for she pleases me well.' " (Judges 14:3)

Now, this first time he is exonerated from blame, because the text immediately assures us that Samson's romantic entanglement was the doing of the Lord, who "was seeking an occasion against the Philistines." Later, in the Delilah episode, this cosmic alibi is withdrawn; Samson will be made to stand completely alone with his mistake. Everything in the Samson story happens twice, sometimes thrice; repetitions establish his character patterns. Thus, if he had let only Delilah wheedle a secret out of him, that would be one thing, but before he does so he gives the woman of Timnah the answer to his wedding riddle, "because she pressed him hard."

Samson is a man women nag. For all his strength, he seems not to engender their full respect, much less their obedience.

They know how to play on his guilt with tears and reproaches ("You don't really love me or you'd tell me your secret"), to twist him around their fingers. And ultimately, they betray him. Not only does the woman of Timnah broadcast the riddle's answer, forcing Samson to pay everyone the betting price, but she cuckolds Samson by giving herself to "his companion, who had been his best man." (Judges 14:20) Delilah does even worse: she ruins him. Sandwiched between these two women is the harlot in Gaza, who also endangers Samson by keeping him occupied while his enemies surround his house. He escapes by lifting the city gates on his shoulders, but he is clearly tempting fate.

Samson also is a man who seems to enjoy being righteously angry. "If you had not ploughed with my heifer, you would not have found out my riddle," he tells the wedding guests, kills thirty men, and stomps off "in hot anger." Later, when he returns to Timnah and finds his wife has been given to another man, he rejects the offer of marrying her younger sister. "This time I shall be blameless in regard to the Philistines, when I do them mischief," he says, then ties three hundred foxes together, attaches lit torches between their tails, and lets them burn up all the Philistine orchards and grain. The Philistines retaliate by torching his wife (who had already abandoned him) and her father. Samson retorts: " 'If this is what you do, I swear I will be avenged upon you, and after that I will quit.' And he smote them hip and thigh with great slaughter." The implication is that any destruction, however disproportionate, is "justifiable" if interpreted as retaliation. No wonder Samson allows himself so often to be betrayed: it frees him to do what he wants.

I grew up in a household where there was much arguing and yelling, even hitting. But it was necessary, as we learned from imitating my mother, always to lay a groundwork of self-righteousness before any explosion. "I am only doing this to you because you did X and Y to me first." Within the never-ending chain of injured feelings that is family history, it is not always easy to find the beginning of a causal series, which is why the person with the loudest voice or the longest memory is generally able to make the best tit for tat. My older brother, Hal, whose voice is very strong, was for a while the undisputed king of righteous explosions. Fortunately, Hal would fulminate so long on the heinousness of the wrong done him that it was possible to get out of the way of any serious physical harm before he swung into action. We were much more terrified of my father, who was phlegmatic, quiet, and withdrawn for the most part; but if he blew up you had less than a second's warning. When my father got physical the slaps and punches came hard and fast, as in a street fight. He had powerful, bony hands and sharp elbows, and in anger he seemed to lose control, with white spittle foaming at his mouth like a mad dog—or at least that was how it looked to a child. Curiously, he always tried to get out of spanking us; he had no heart for premeditated disciplining, leaving such beatings to my mother.

She would take out her ironing cord—a black-and-white fabric switch, which we thought of as a live creature. What was interesting about the way she beat us was that she would herself grunt and make awful faces each time she picked up her arm. "You had enough?" she would demand, after each blow. "Gonna try that again?"

It was a dialogue; we were supposed to respond correctly so that she would know when to quit. My brother would take his punishment like a man; howling only when he was in pain. I was more of a faker: very early I caught on that it was all symbolic, and I would scream and carry on from the first hand-raise so that she would let me go with next to nothing. My sister Molly, however, would laugh in my mother's face, would giggle or hum a tune to herself, refusing to concede even when I could see tears welling in her eyes, until finally my mother would stop, baffled, her arm exhausted.

I am struggling to find the pattern between all these pieces. I have the sense that the Samson story and my family story touch in odd ways; I try to put the stencil of one over the other, and, while they occasionally overlap, just as often the connection seems farfetched. Nonetheless, I am convinced that at the center of both is the mystery of power relations between men and women. I start to write "How did it come about that I started mistrusting women, or thought they would betray me?" But then I pause: Do I really? Aren't I often less guarded around women than I am with men? Let us say that a part of me still fears (hopes?) that women are treacherous creatures. I know that growing up, watching the unhappiness between my parents, watching my mother disparage my father every day and my father refuse to let her go, made me cautious toward the opposite sex. Then, too, my mother was very insecure as a young woman: we would climb into her lap and she would suddenly push us away, saying "Don't start that 'Mommy I love you' crap, you're only being lovey-dovey because you want something out of me. Okay, what is it this time? An ice cream? A quarter?" Naturally, I learned to be skeptical of affection, almost to *want* a barbed hurt to accompany love. As for my father, he had been treated wretchedly by his stepmother, who put him to work all the time, so he was both desperate for maternal warmth and suspicious of any feminine softness. When these two hurt, insecure people, the black sheep of both their middle-class families, came together to live in poverty and raise their own family, the results were not pretty.

My parents had a bookcase which held a few hardcovers and a library of Pocket Books, whose flimsy, browning pages would crack if you bent down the corners. I can still picture those cellophane-peeling covers with their kangaroo logo, their illustrations of busty, available-looking women or hard-bodied men or solemn, sensitive-looking Negroes; with titles like *Intruder in the Dust; Appointment in Samarra; Tobacco Road; Studs Lonigan; Strange Fruit; Good Night, Sweet Prince; The Great Gatsby; The Sound and the Fury.* . . .

Father brought home all the books, it was his responsibility; though Mother chafed at everything else in the marriage, she still permitted him at the time to be her intellectual mentor. I have often wondered on what basis he made his selections: he'd had only one term of night college (dropping out because he fell asleep in class after a full day in the factory), and I never saw him read book reviews. He seemed, all the same, to have a nose for decent literature. He was one of those autodidacts of the Depression generation, for whose guidance the inexpensive editions of Everyman, Modern Library, and Pocket Books seemed intentionally designed, out of some bygone assumption that the working-man should—must—be educated to the best in human thought.

My father had an awed respect for the power of good fiction, especially when it was able to mirror uncannily the conflicts in his own life. He would often marvel at Kafka's story "The Judgment," in which the patriarch tells his son to jump off a bridge— obviously because *his* father, my grandfather, had treated him like dirt. He never stopped praising *The Brothers Karamazov*, which had the status of the Bible in Brooklyn at the time. Again, I suspect its patricidal theme excited him more than Dostoevsky's philosophy. He did dip into one philosopher, Schopenhauer, and would occasionally read aloud one of the gloomy German's misogynistic aphorisms. These were usually to the effect that women had no capacity for ideas, that their only cleverness was in tricking men to perpetuate the species. (My mother gave an odd sort of credence to this theory by boasting that she had "seduced" my father into siring us—finagling away the contraception, I suppose—since he hadn't really wanted children. Four times she tricked him? Whether true or not, it was her way of making us feel indebted to her and opposed to him.)

In any event, Schopenhauer's *bons mots* were his single means —a delayed one, at that—of answering Mother's nagging. My father was one of those dependable Jewish workingmen of his generation who regarded housework or any physical task around the house as anathema. (In his case, the phobia may have been increased because of his chore-filled childhood.) He would not "lift a finger around the house, if it killed him!" my mother would say. It was she who had to bang the nails, unstick the windows, lay the linoleum, complaining while my father sat, the soul of passivity, reading a book or napping. It enraged her partly because she had to go to work, too, and partly because my father was so able-bodied. As a young man he was tall, wiry, and very strong, like Samson. In his factory he could lift huge bales; at carnivals he would ring the bell; he triumphed at arm wrestling. Yet he became a weakling as soon as he arrived home; his kryptonite was family life. If my mother said something sarcastic to him, like "Why don't you get off your bony ass and do something?" or "What do I need you for? You're not married to me, you're married to your easy chair and the goddamn ball game!" he would merely sink deeper into a defeated shrug. But I believe that behind his stoical, resigned mask there raged a fierce misogyny.

What I would call the *Blue Angel/Of Human Bondage* plot—the educated or sensitive man who is dragged down by a coarse, sluttish vixen—had a particular vogue with my father's generation. One of the books he often touted to us was Ludwig Lewisohn's novel, *The Tyranny of Sex.* When I was sixteen and still a virgin I read it, naturally, to find out what was in store. Its lumpy, post-Dreiserian naturalist style disappointed, and I remember feeling the author was weighting the scales a bit too unfairly against the wife. Nevertheless, the luridly compelling story remained with me: a man becomes attracted to a woman, wants to sleep with her, and the next thing he knows he is married, cuckolded, in debt, his dreams for himself have flown out the window, his wife has become a slattern, no longer even attractive, a nagging shrew—in short, woman as swamp, quicksand.

Given the atmosphere in my home, I found the Samson and Delilah story the most natural in the world. Already I had imbibed from my father his sense of sexuality as a nightmarish tyranny, robbing a man of his strength, just as I had absorbed from my mother a rebellious, defiantly flirtatious, erotic appetite for life.

My mother had bought a piano, and she practiced her songs on it, preparing for the far-off day when she would become a professional entertainer. She sang mostly torch songs, the kind Helen

Morgan made famous: "The Man I Love," "Just My Bill," "I Must Try to Make the Man Love Me," "Bewitched, Bothered, and Bewildered," "I Want a Sunday Kind of Love." With her pretty, tremulous voice, she would pour all her yearning and disappointment into these bittersweet verses. The message was unmistakable, even to a little kid: she was not happy with my father, she was still looking for something better, for "romance."

I loved to listen to her practice, glancing over her shoulder at the rising and falling syllables of the sheet music. All day in elementary school, her songs would go round in my head. At recess I would play tag or punchball to the rhythms of her longing.

One day, when it was too rainy to go outside, the teacher herded us into the auditorium and staged an impromptu talent show. Each child was urged to perform in front of the combined second and third grades. There were rampant cases of stage fright; some kids started to entertain, then giggled and hid their faces; others came on and rattled through a comic ditty or radio jingle so fast you couldn't make out the words. I wanted to sing. I faced the group and, hearing my mother's semitrained voice in my ears, I let her guide me through the melody.

> *Some day he'll come along, the man I love*
> *And he'll be big and strong, the man I love*

I could sense the teachers snickering, trading looks that said "We know how *this* one's going to turn out." My classmates started laughing. I realized too late that the song was for a girl, they would think me a sissy. I had no choice but to finish. At least I could try to sing on key and with feeling, as my mother did; maybe I would seduce them into liking it.

When the last contestant was finished, the teachers awarded me "first prize," a comic book. I, part Delilah, wondered if I would ever become a real man.

My mother was bawdy: she reveled in calling a spade a spade. She had a store of witticisms about excretory malfunctions, and she would tell smutty Hollywood stories—the scandals of her youth—about Fatty Arbuckle's Coke bottle and Mary Miles Minter, George S. Kaufman ("Oh, he must have been hot stuff!"), and Mary Astor's diary read aloud in divorce court. All this was a little hard for me to take. I particularly found it embarrassing when my mother let slip her physical appraisal of men. If we were watching a baseball game, say, on television, and Ted Kluszewski with his cutoff sleeves stepped up to bat, she would say, "Look at the shoulders on that guy! That's for me!" or "Boy, that Campy's built like a brickshit house. He's gor-geous." The drama of the baseball diamond would be spoiled; I would suddenly be forced to see it from a sexual perspective, and imagine Mother having trysts with the local butcher, the baker, the ballplayer, whoever possessed a massive physique. (It didn't help that we all knew my mother was having extramarital affairs. Later on, I came to see that she had done the right thing for herself in scraping together a little happiness by going outside a marriage that was irredeemably bleak and frustrating, but when I was coming into puberty myself I sympathized with my father and thought her "cheap," a Bad Woman.) These comments about male physique made me feel especially inadequate, since I had narrow shoulders and a scholar's untoned body. If being a man meant having a body like Victor Mature or Roy Campanella, then forget it, I would never make it. Fortunately, my mother had another erotic ideal besides the powerful bruiser: the sensitive, poetic "gentleman" with manners and an English accent—Leslie Howard, her favorite, or James Mason. I at least had an outside chance at this ideal. If I speak gently today, to the point of habitually mumbling, it is probably because I am still trying to be Leslie Howard for my mother.

Samson "loved a woman in the valley of Sorek, named Delilah." But nowhere does the text say anything about Delilah loving

Samson back. Indeed, immediately after this first sentence introducing Delilah, the Philistine lords approach and say: "Entice
him, and see wherein his great strength lies, and by what means
we may overpower him, that we may bind him to subdue him;
and we shall each give you eleven hundred pieces of silver." In
the Bible, Delilah is literally a *femme fatale*: she comes on, performs
her treacherous function, and disappears from the narrative. We
are left to guess whether she betrays Samson just for the money
or because it is her nature. Virtually all later adaptations soften
the harsh functionalism of the biblical Delilah, both by "human-
izing" her with ambivalent motives of love, jealousy, revenge,
and politics, and by having her visit Samson after he is in captiv-
ity. But the first Delilah is the pure Delilah, a dark female force
who destroys men with her sex. Like a dominatrix, she is remarkably straightforward about her intentions: "Tell me, I pray thee,
wherein thy great strength lieth, and wherewith thou mightest
be bound to afflict thee." (Judges 16:6)

Fair warning. Samson receives even more evidence of her
treacherous intent when, after fending her off with a false explanation of his strength, she calls in the soldiers, who had been
hiding in her inner chamber, to seize him. Any man with half a
brain would leave at this point. But no: three times Delilah en-
tices Samson to give her his secret, three times he puts her off
with fabrications, and three times she summons the Philistine
troops to ensnare him. (The fourth time works the charm.)

The mystery is: What happens to Samson's famous self-righteous anger during this period of the three wrong explanations?
Either Samson likes the danger, finds it spicy, or has come to
expect nothing from women other than constant betrayal. Or
does he simply overestimate his power to resist Delilah's coaxing
(which would be foolish, given his past history)?

His hanging around her obviously booby-trapped tent has a
comical side. Later dramatizations of the Samson story refrain
from showing all four of Delilah's interrogations about his
strength and his answers, partly because it would be dramatically
redundant, but also because it would get farcical, and Samson

would lose too much stature. Any man who puts up with that many consecutive betrayals is not a tragic hero but a *shlemiel*.

Although not necessarily. In fairy tales, it often happens that characters make the same mistake three times (for instance, misuse their wishes), and at the end of each mistake there is no accrual of wisdom. The point is made that human nature keeps screwing up the same way over and over. Seen from this perspective, Samson is Everyman: his continuing to stay with Delilah after he knows she will betray him is no more unusual than, say, a woman who remains with a husband who beats her, or a man who puts up with a wife who continually cheats on him.

Saint-Saëns's operatic Samson is so sexually fixated on Delilah, like Don José on Carmen, that he can't pull himself away, however much he realizes that she intends to ruin him. And she, for her part, betrays him because that seems the inevitable melodramatic outcome of all fatal passions. But this "fatal passion" explanation, so nineteenth century, seems incomplete. The biblical Samson takes too much active pleasure inventing the three lies about his strength for him to be seen as merely a passive moth drawn to the flame. Gradually, he himself allows Delilah to get a little "warmer," the third time actually referring to his hair, telling her that to tie up seven locks into a web would subdue his strength. In a way, the two are like children playing a game. Each time she notifies him "The Philistines be upon thee, Samson," she is in a sense calling out a ludic formula, such as "Tap, tap, Johnny, one two three!"

There is an undeniably playful element in this part of the Samson story. One could say that the strong man is experimenting with disarming himself and seeing how close he can come to being trapped, a Houdini who ties himself up in order to escape. After all, Samson delivers himself voluntarily into his captors' hands not once but twice: the first time was earlier in Judges, when his own people betrayed him to the Philistines and he ended up smiting a thousand with the jawbone of an ass.

The strong would seem to have a need to experiment with the limits of their strength—to experiment, indeed, with their weakness, as though it held a key to self-knowledge. Often in stories the great warrior "forgets" his duty to fight, detained in the arms of a beautiful woman: Samson and Delilah belong in the same company with Ulysses and Circe, Antony and Cleopatra, Lord Nelson and Lady Hamilton. Yet in these trysts, isn't the strong man measuring his fortitude against an opponent he recognizes as potentially more dangerous than an enemy general?

The strong man enters the erotic interior of the tent, the boudoir, with the understanding that other rules prevail than those on the battlefield. Here he hopes to be refreshed, but also tested in an intriguing manner. With a too-docile love slave, there would be no stimulating tension, no edge to the encounter. An experienced wanton like Delilah cannot offer the challenge of her virginity, so there must be another kind of advance-retreat. Like the geisha who are celebrated for their pert replies, wheedling, and jealous tantrums, the woman to whom the strong man surrenders must be in command of an entire repertoire of catlike capriciousness.

He enters the dark interior of her body to explore, to reconnoiter like a soldier moving laterally across a field; but by the end he has become soft and feminized, his ejaculated penis small. The strong man enters the tent, secretly, to become a woman. Lovemaking allows him to be tender, to loll about in bed, to be playful and "effeminate," to exchange sexual roles:

> *I yielded, and unlocked her all my heart,*
> *Who with a grain of manhood well-resolved*
> *Might easily have shook off all her snares.*
> *But foul effeminacy held me yoked*
> *To her bond-slave.*
>
> Milton, *Samson Agonistes*

Afterward, the man resents the woman, wanton or not, for several reasons: because she has witnessed his "weakness"; because he needed her in the first place; and because she can go much longer than he can, sexually speaking—she has no sword to break. Men take revenge for their dependency by projecting their sexual needs onto women, reviving the figure of the insatiable temptress, the castrating Delilah.* Proverbs warns "Give not thy strength unto women" and "The horseleach hath two daughters, crying, Give, give. There are three things that are never satisfied, yea, four things say not, It is enough: The grave; and the barren womb; and the earth that is not filled with water; and the fire that saith not, It is enough." (Proverbs 30:15, 16) The Bible is filled with a sexual-economic fear of women, not unlike the general in *Dr. Strangelove* who practices celibacy so as to hold on to his "precious bodily fluids." The Samson story would seem to admonish us that sex with women depletes the hero of his strength—if not through one "castration" (the postcoital shrunken penis; the depleted fluids), then indirectly through another (the cut-off hair).

Yet while the message of Samson's fall, like Adam's, would seem to be cautionary and misogynistic, underneath we experience his time with Delilah as a liberating fantasy. That is why the story has such continuing claims on us. Don't we secretly rejoice at his having the good sense to follow the route of his desire, to free himself from the "good-boy" Nazarite onus by putting himself in temptation's way?

After all, Samson has always been a loner. "If a leader, he was one from a distance. Almost everything he did was as a private individual," writes the Israeli Talmudist Adin Steinsaltz. And Robert G. Boling, in his Anchor Bible commentary, notes: "The whole structure of the Samson segment is different from that of the other judges. There is no participation by Israelites in his elevation to judge and no mention of Israelites taking the field behind him." He is so alone, he might as well be an artist. The

---

* Not that castration fear should be seen solely as a projection of male insecurity. There really are psychologically castrating women, analysts tell us. My mother belittled my father every day of their marriage. She was certainly provoked—he has a maddeningly taciturn, withdrawn, ungiving nature—but she took to provocation like a duck to water: "What are you good for? What do I need you for? You're like a mummy. Get lost, why don't you," she would say, "take a hike." One day he did, and jumped into the East River. Someone fished him out, fortunately, before he could drown. The police brought him home in his wet clothes.

first time he comes to grips with another human being and doesn't run, doesn't go off angry or bloodthirsty, but stays, is with Delilah. It is progress of a sort.

The retreat of lovers from the world has always been perceived as both an alluring ideal and a dangerous threat to society, which must be punished—if not by the authorities, then by the dynamic of romantic love itself. In the Japanese film Oshima's *In the Realm of the Senses*, a geisha and a bouncer run off together. They become so immersed in making love that they rarely go out, they forget to eat, they become mystics in the pursuit of higher and higher pleasure. But the logic of ecstasy seems to dictate ascending risk; normal intercourse is no longer enough, they experiment with short strangulations to intensify the orgasmic rush. In the end, the woman strangles her lover fatally and, realizing he is dead, cuts off his penis and runs through the streets with it. It is unclear from the film whether the man has submitted to the woman's homicidal castrating tendencies or whether she has been the instrument of his suicidal desires. They have reached a point of such fusion, such boundarylessness—the desideratum of lovers, according to poetry—that it is pointless to speak of one "doing" anything "to" the other.

I would like to offer the possibility that a similar sort of collaboration or collusion existed between Samson and Delilah. Not that "she done him wrong," but that together the lovers were able to bring about the desired fatalistic result, which they had been working up to in practice three times. This interpretation is, I realize, perversely revisionist; it has little support in the text. What the good book does say is that Delilah pressed Samson until "his soul was vexed to death." Finally he opened his heart to her. "A razor has never come upon my head; for I have been a Nazarite to God from my mother's womb. If I be shaved, then my strength will leave me, and I shall become weak, and be like any other man." (Judges 16:16) The irony is that Samson's great folly consists in nothing more than telling the truth—and telling it to one he loves.

"And she made him sleep upon her knees; and she called for a man, and she caused him to shave off the seven locks of his head; and she began to afflict him, and the strength went from him." (Judges 16:19) She places his head in her lap, that maternal gesture. He is finally "unmanned" by surrendering to his need for mothering. This is at the heart of the male fear of Woman: that she will touch him in that sore place and open up his bottomless need for mother-love, which he had thought he had outgrown, and he will lose his ability to defend himself."*

I hated getting haircuts. When my mother took me, it seemed that the barber would pay more attention to her than to me. And when I was big enough to go alone, I still felt invisible in the large barber chair, always imagining that the barber must be bored cutting a little boy's head, or annoyed that he would not be getting the full fee, or inattentive because he'd been working all day and wanted to close up early.

One time, when I was around eleven, I went to get my hair cut at a barbershop near the Havemeyer Street markets. I had heard that this particular barber was twenty cents cheaper than most, and I hoped to use the money I saved for a treat. The barber turned out to be a tiny old man with a *yarmulkah* and a palsied shake to his hands—no wonder he was so cheap. His fingers had liver spots on them, like my grandfather's; I was tempted to get up and run, but the cover sheet was already around my shoulders. He brought the scissors close to my head, trembling, stopping at an arbitrary point where he jabbed them into my temple. As he clipped he would make a hundred tentative approximations in the air, like the outlines in a Giacometti drawing, before he landed. When he shaved the nape of my neck, he nicked me. "Oh, did I cut you?" he said. "I'm sorry."

I couldn't wait to escape. The second after I paid him I darted

* Is it only my *mishegoss* that associates the Samson story with Oedipus? Both men dealt with riddles, both suffered ruin by sleeping with the wrong woman, both were blinded. Maybe the two legends came about in the same period or influenced each other.

out of the shop and ran several blocks. Finally I stopped in front of a luncheonette. I had twenty cents to spend: I read all the signs above the counter, grilled cheese sandwich, burger and fries, bacon lettuce and tomato . . . I had never tasted bacon. Though my parents did not keep a strict kosher household, we lived in an Orthodox Jewish neighborhood and eating pork was taboo, it just wasn't done. I ordered a BLT, feeling sinful but defiant, telling myself I deserved to break the rule because I had had to suffer that haircut; therefore my sin would be canceled out, I would be "blameless."

I wanted to say something earlier about tests of weakness. Even as a child, I had a strange experimental tendency to indulge a lassitude at the most inopportune moments. Once, when I was about nine, I let myself dangle upside down on a swing and refused, as it were, to exert the necessary muscle traction to grip my legs to the seat. I fell on my head and had to have several stitches taken. Superheroes fascinated me as much for their sudden enfeeblements as for their vast powers. I would picture being in the presence of kryptonite and the voluptuous surrender to weakness. All my childhood illnesses were rehearsals for this crumbling of the will, this letting go of the effort to be a little man.

As an adult, I still often experience the temptation to go weak as a babe, or to let my body get into incredibly clumsy positions, knowing full well that with a little extra effort I could manage the action better. I will forgo putting down one kitchen object before picking up another, and in my awkward maneuvering let food spill. Or I will go limp as a beanbag when having to extricate myself from the back seat of a car. Or sometimes, when I am helping several people lift a heavy piece up the stairs, I will suddenly become dreamy, forget to hold up my end. It isn't goldbricking exactly, because I'm not generally lazy about work. It's a way of resisting life on the physical plane.

A manly man will pick up a tool and perform a task with just the right amount of well-focused energy. I, on the other hand, view all implements as problematic, and all chores as a test of manhood that I am half-eager to fail. My mechanical ineptness is so fertile that it borders on creativity. I have no sooner to pick up the simplest can opener than I feel all vigor drain from my hands. I struggle to concentrate my sluggish fingers, to make a go of it; I tell myself "Even a child can do this." I force myself to grip the can opener and sink its sabertooth into the metal. Then, all too quickly, growing impatient, I bludgeon my way around the circle, starting half a dozen punctures. Soon the whole top is a twisted mess and I am tearing it off with my bare hands, cutting my flesh in the process. From lassitude to excessive force, with nothing in between. In all this feigned weakness and physical inattention, one sees a reluctance to leave the boy-man stage, as well as a perverse intellectual vanity, since what is not given to the body must be given to the mind.

Why does Delilah betray Samson? That is the problem all adaptations of the story have sought to solve.

The most complex answer, and the most noble Delilah, are found in Milton's *Samson Agonistes*. She is the secret hero of that great poem. First, the poet raises Delilah's status by making her Samson's wife. Though this allows Samson's father, Manoa, to quip, "I cannot praise thy marriage choices, son," and the blinded hero to roar when she visits him in prison, "My wife, my traitress, let her not come near me," she herself behaves with sympathy and dignity. She begs his forgiveness several times, offering a spectrum of explanations. The first is that, being a woman, she was subject to "common female faults . . . incident to all our sex, curiosity" and the urge "to publish" the secrets she learns. Then she says they were both weak, so they should both forgive each other. The strongman has very little sympathy for this excuse, retorting that "all wickedness is weakness." Then, more tenderly, she brings up the "jealousy of love"; she has seen his wandering fancies and wanted to hold him near her, to keep him from all his "perilous enterprises." She swears, too, that she was tricked by the Philistines, who assured her that no harm would come to her husband. He accuses her of betraying him for the gold. Dalila vigorously denies this, claiming that the magistrates had told her she had a "civic duty" to "entrap a common enemy," and the priest had appealed to her further on religious grounds, asserting that Samson was a "dishonorer of Dagon." He bats this argument away indignantly, saying that she had a primary duty to her husband, not her country. Dalila answers, abjectly, "I was a fool, too rash, and quite mistaken. . . . Let me obtain forgiveness of thee, Samson." She paints a picture of the life they could lead from now on: she thinks she could secure his release; true, he is blind, but "Life yet hath many solaces, enjoyed/ Where other senses want not their delights/ At home in leisure and domestic ease. . . ." He refuses to be caught again, ensnared by "Thy fair enchanted cup." Dalila: "Let me approach, at least, and touch thy hand." Samson practically jumps out of his skin. The extremity of his reaction, threatening to "tear her joint by joint," betrays how much feeling he has for her still. Sorrowfully, she notes: "I see thou art implacable. . . . Thy anger, unappeasable, still rages." It is a beautiful matrimonial scene; she understands full well the function and operation of his rage. When he tells her that her name will be notorious forever, she allows herself a proud parting shot: if she is to be infamous among the Israelites, her own people will commemorate her as a heroine. And she compares herself to Jael, who in the same Book of Judges, "with inhospitable guile/ Smote Sisera sleeping through the temples nailed."

Indeed, any judgment of Delilah is complicated by the fact that her behavior seems structurally not so different from Jael's, or from Judith's decapitation of Holofernes. All three actions occur in a tent, with a guileful woman bringing a warrior down while he sleeps. Yet Delilah's "sisters," narratively speaking, are admired and celebrated, while she is reviled as the epitome of sluttish perfidy. History is written by the winners.

The Saint-Saëns opera also makes Delilah a Philistine patriot, but adds the dimension that she is the apostle of Love and is jealous of Samson's primary devotion to God. She carries on like a forlorn Dido about to be jilted by her Aeneas (*Mon coeur s'ouvre à ta voix...*), weeping and appealing to his pity.

In the movie, DeMille's scriptwriters introduce yet another motive by conveniently making Delilah the younger sister of the woman of Timnah (played by Angela Lansbury). The tomboyish Delilah develops a schoolgirl crush on her older sister's fiancé, Samson. When he rejects her as the replacement for the errant Lansbury, she is a woman scorned, and vows to get even by becoming a great courtesan. But her anger fades away during the idyllic period after she has seduced Samson; indeed, the scenes of the lovers dallying by the stream and inside Delilah's commodious tent are so charmingly playful that it becomes difficult to believe her subsequent betrayal, except as the reemergence of some innate "Delilah" nature. The Hollywood version has the lovers reunited, and it is a contrite Delilah who leads Samson to the pillars, gladly volunteering to die with him!


Why do men want Delilahs? If not in their homes, then in their fantasy lives? Why is the Bad Woman, the deceitful betrayer in all her *film noir* guises, always able to sell movie tickets? Because she is beautiful and sexy? So might be a virtuous woman. Because one yearns to be swept away by a passion stronger than one's reason, which can only be proven if it goes against one's own best interests; because by losing control one can turn around later and blame her, *she* tempted me, she snatched away my willpower; because one never takes her seriously as a partner for life, and so there is no threat of having to make a commitment; because, while she may destroy you, she will not smother you with admiration or doting affection, which makes you feel like a fraud; because her treacheries are exciting in an operatic (if ultimately tiresome) way, they keep you feeling alive and angry, and anger is an aphrodisiac; because she confirms your worst ideas about women; because you want to feel alone, to guard your solitude; because she is full of surprises and that keeps you off-balance; because you who have hurt women so often dream of being a victim, of being punished for your crimes; because, while Delilah may lack the domesticity and compassion of the woman in Proverbs whose "price is far above rubies," she possesses other arts: the ability to sustain an appearance of glamour (which is a function of the imagination as much as good looks); the control of scents; the manipulation of interior spaces; the ability to keep the humdrum everyday world at bay; sometimes the art of dance and playing an instrument; a refreshingly candid lack of decorum; the naughtiness of a young girl or a kitten or anything but a fully adult woman (who would remind you of your own death); a touch of androgyny when called for; a keen insight into men; and a thorough knowledge of sex.

All my life I have been searching for a woman who will live up to—or down to—this bad-girl archetype. Instead I have met, on the one hand, a succession of kind, sweet, devoted women (worse luck), or, on the other, hassled, self-absorbed, remote women (worse still). I am still waiting to encounter Hedy Lamarr's Delilah, with the headband around her forehead and her many teases.

Actually, I did come close to finding a Delilah type. She was capricious, sexy, smart, crazy, abusive, and pretty, and she tortured me for seven years. We started with a strong erotic spark, which later grew to be rooted in mutual anger—mine at her infidelities, hers at my refusing to take her "seriously." During all this time I was very productive, managing to put her provocations and scenes in the back of my mind and working out of that bottomless pit of creative energy, the feeling of being unloved, le chant du mal-aimé. As it happened, Kay was a writer, too, but her work did not get published very often. She would become furious and throw tantrums when she saw my poems in magazines unless I placated her for half an hour about how much better her poems were—which I rarely did. Once she asked me point-blank: "How are you able to wield so much power in the world? Teach me, how does one get literary success?" I shuddered. It was Delilah's question: Where does your strength come from? I was tempted to say my literary prominence was hardly so grand as to merit envy; but I had to admit that, compared to her, I was "successful."

She felt that as a woman she had been kept in the dark about worldly power and now she wanted to become more like men, initially, perhaps, by sleeping with them. Myself, I was able to do very little for Kay as a poet—not that I tried very hard. She hated me at times with a palpable shocking openness that was, if nothing else, different: most people like me. My own feelings were a murk of pity, lust, and confusion, revulsion at her misconduct and disgust at myself for staying in the relationship. But I admit that, in a way, it kept me amused.

So Samson is captured and blinded, and made to grind wheat in the prison house, like a beast of burden. "Howbeit the hair of his head began to grow again after he was shaven." Odd that the Philistines, having paid so dearly to learn that the secret of Samson's strength resided in his hair, should let him grow it back again. In any event, the foreshadowing detail has been planted, and the stage is set for the final catastrophe. The rest we know well: the Philistines trot him out for sport on their feast day to Dagon, and Samson tells the lad who leads him: "Let me feel the pillars on which the house stands, that I may lean against them." It is a very satisfying narrative invention, this meeting of architectonics and apocalypse. Samson prays to the Lord for his strength to be returned, "only this once, that I may be avenged upon the Philistines for one of my two eyes." The Lord complies, and the house topples on everyone in it. "So the dead which he slew at his death were more than they which he slew in his life." (Judges 16:30)

A good death. To redeem a whole misspent life by the manner of one's dying—to take this inevitable poll tax, mortality, and turn it into a *tour de force* of accomplishment—has been a dream of many suicides through the ages, from Samson to Sydney Carton to Mishima. However, Samson redeems himself not just by destroying slews of Israel's enemies, which is nothing new for him, but by his self-awareness, contained in his words: "Let me die with the Philistines." He does not pray to God, as he might have: "Let me destroy them in such a way that I can get off harmless." His conscience considers his sins, his follies, his own betrayal of his potential, and logically asks for the death penalty. We tend to forget that Samson was also—in whatever sense we care to take it—a judge ("And he judged Israel twenty years"): his last judicial act is to pronounce sentence on himself. When he says "Let me die with the Philistines," he also seems to be alluding to his taste for Philistine women: I have eaten *trayf*, it is only just that I go down with the *trayf*-eaters. With his last noble words, he exiles himself from his own people and joins the Diaspora of the dead. A bitter ending, but he has come a long way from the young, self-righteous man who petulantly exclaimed, before wreaking havoc, Now am I blameless for the harm I will do them. Like a hero in a Greek tragedy, he has finished his journey from warrior pride to humility by taking responsibility for violating the tribal laws.

I have said that my father was a physically strong man; this made his inability to deal with my mother or manifest any ambition all the more puzzling to me as a child. It often seemed to me that, in another situation in life, he would have realized a heroic potential. Though he never went into the army (excused from service because he had too many children), he would have made a good soldier. He was intelligent and stoic and did not shirk duty. I am not romanticizing, I hope, when I say that he would have run into a burning building to pull us out, without giving any thought to his safety. I still get shivers remembering one occasion when he risked his neck. We were locked out of our house— someone had lost the keys during a family outing—and my father went next door to see if he could leap from the neighbor's fire escape to ours. It was no small distance; if he slipped and fell he would hit solid cement. We couldn't see how he was doing because the fire escapes were all on the back side of the building and we waited in the front vestibule. My brother Hal started whistling the Funeral March. "Hope you like being a widow. Was that a splat?" he said, cocking his ear. Ordinarily, sarcasm and gallows humor were the preferred family style, but this time my mother chewed her lips and stared through the locked glass door, holding her mouton coat closed at the throat. She had tried to talk my father out of the attempt, insisting they could call the police to break down the door, but my father wouldn't hear of it. This was his job. I remember my mother's terrified, tear-streaked face while she waited in suspense. Molly said, "Ma, I don't think this is such a good idea," and my mother slapped her across her face for saying what all of us were thinking. Eventually we saw my father's trousers coming downstairs, the whole of him shortly after. When he let us in, we kids cheered: "Our hero!" "Don't give me that bullshit," said my father, modestly and gruffly. It did not take my mother long to recover her acid tongue: "Big show-off! You could have gotten killed, dummy!" But her agitated concern during those few minutes he'd been gone was a revelation to me. Maybe she cared about him more than she let on.

My father is now seventy-six, my mother sixty-eight. Two years ago she finally gave herself a present she had been wanting for over forty-five years: a divorce. Not that I blame her: she was, as she said, tired of being a full-time unpaid nursemaid to someone she didn't love. She kicked my father out of the house, and he went to live in a less-than-desirable nursing home in Far Rockaway. He has been depressed and emaciated, and he misses the city streets. Recently, we heard of the possibility of an opening in a much better old-age home near Columbus Avenue, in the middle of Manhattan. There is a long admissions procedure; it is as complicated as getting into an exclusive prep school. My mother took him to his interview herself, crowing afterward that the director mistook them for father and daughter. So far his chances look pretty good: my father is not very outgoing, but he is ambulatory and in his right mind. We all have our fingers crossed. So far the home has raised only one objection, my mother tells me: they would want him to shave his beard.

# AGAINST JOIE DE VIVRE

Over the years I have developed a distaste for the spectacle of *joie de vivre*, the knack of knowing how to live. Not that I disapprove of all hearty enjoyment of life. A flushed sense of happiness can overtake a person anywhere, and one is no more to blame for it than the Asiatic flu or a sudden benevolent change in the weather (which is often joy's immediate cause). No, what rankles me is the stylization of this private condition into a bullying social ritual.

The French, who have elevated the picnic to their highest rite, are probably most responsible for promoting this smugly upbeat, flaunting style. It took the French genius for formalizing the informal to bring sticky sacramental sanctity to the baguette, wine, and cheese. A pure image of sleeveless *joie de vivre* Sundays can also be found in Renoir's paintings. Weekend satyrs dance and wink; leisure takes on a bohemian stripe. A decent writer, Henry Miller, caught the French malady and ran back to tell us

42

of *pissoirs* in the Paris streets (why this should have impressed him so, I've never figured out).

But if you want a double dose of *joie de vivre*, you need to consult a later, hence more stylized, version of the French myth of pagan happiness: those *Family of Man* photographs of endlessly kissing lovers, snapped by Doisneau and Boubat, or Cartier-Bresson's icon of the proud tyke carrying bottles of wine. If Cartier-Bresson and his disciples are excellent photographers for all that, it is in spite of their occasionally rubbing our noses in a tediously problematic "affirmation of life."

Though it is traditionally the province of the French, the whole Mediterranean is a hotbed of professional *joie de vivrism*, which they have gotten down to a routine like a crack *son et lumière* display. The Italians export *dolce far niente* as aggressively as tomato paste. For the Greeks, a Zorba dance to life has supplanted classical antiquities as their main touristic lure. Hard to imagine anything as stomach-turning as being forced to participate in such an oppressively robust, folknik effusion. Fortunately, the country has its share of thin, nervous, bitter types, but Greeks do exist who would clutch you to their joyfully stout bellies and crush you there. The *joie de vivrist* is an incorrigible missionary who presumes that everyone wants to express pro-life feelings in the same stereotyped manner.

A warning: since I myself have a large store of nervous discontent (some would say hostility), I am apt to be harsh in my secret judgments of others, seeing them as defective because they are not enough like me. From moment to moment, the person I am with often seems too shrill, too bland, too something-or-other to allow my own expansiveness to swing into stage center. "Feeling no need to drink, you will promptly despise a drunkard" (Kenneth Burke). So it goes with me, which is why I am not a literary critic. I have no faith that my discriminations in taste are anything but the picky awareness of what will keep me stimulated, based on the peculiar family and class circumstances that formed me. But the knowledge that my discriminations are skewed and not always universally desirable doesn't stop me in the least from making them, just as one never gives up a negative first impression, no matter how many times it is contradicted. A believer in astrology (to cite another false system), having guessed that someone is a Sagittarius, and then told he is a Scorpio, says "Scorpio—yes, of course!" without missing a beat, or relinquishing confidence in his ability to tell people's signs, or in his idea that the person is somehow secretly Sagittarian.

## 1. THE HOUSEBOAT

I remember exactly when my dislike for *joie de vivre* began to crystallize. It was 1969. We had gone to visit an old Greek painter on his houseboat in Sausalito. Old Vartas's vitality was legendary, and it was considered a spiritual honor to meet him, like getting an audience with the pope. Each Sunday he had a sort of open house, or open boat.

My "sponsor," Frank, had been many times to the houseboat, furnishing Vartas with record albums, since the old painter had a passion for San Francisco rock bands. Frank told me that Vartas had been a pal of Henry Miller's, and I, being a writer of Russian descent, would love him. I failed to grasp the syllogism, but, putting aside my instinct to dislike anybody I have been assured I will adore, I prepared myself to give the man a chance.

Greeting us on the gangplank was an old man with thick, lush, white hair and snowy eyebrows, his face reddened from the sun. As he took us into the houseboat cabin he told me proudly that he was seventy-seven years old, and gestured toward the paintings that were spaced a few feet apart on the floor, leaning against the wall. They were celebrations of the blue Aegean, boats moored in ports, whitewashed houses on a hill, painted in primary colors and decorated with collaged materials: mirrors, burlap, Life Saver candies. These sunny little canvases with their talented innocence, third-generation spirit of Montmartre, bore testimony to a love of life so unbending as to leave an impression of rigid narrow-mindedness as extreme as any Savonarola's. Their rejection of sorrow was total. They were the sort of festive paintings that sell at high-rent Madison Avenue galleries specializing in European *schlock*.

Then I became aware of three young, beautiful women, bare-shouldered, wearing white pajama pants, each with long blond hair falling onto a sky-blue halter—unmistakably suggesting the Three Graces. They lived with him on the houseboat, I was told, giving no one knew what compensation for their lodgings. Perhaps their only payment was to feed his vanity in front of outsiders. The Greek painter smiled with the air of an old fox around the trio. For their part, the women obligingly contributed their praises of Vartas's youthful zip, which of course was taken by some guests as double entendre for undiminished sexual prowess. The Three Graces also gathered the food offerings of the visitors to make a midday meal.

Then the boat, equipped with a sail, was launched to sea. I must admit it gave me a spoilsport's pleasure when the winds turned becalmed. We could not move. Aboard were several members of the Bay Area's French colony, who dangled their feet over the sides, passed around bunches of grapes, and sang what I imagined were Gallic camping songs. The French know boredom, so they would understand how to behave in such a situation. It has been my observation that many French men and women stationed in America have the attitude of taking it easy, slumming at a health resort, and nowhere more so than in California. The *émigré* crew included a securities analyst, an academic sociologist, a museum administrator and his wife, a modiste: on Vartas's boat, they all got drunk and carried on like redskins, noble savages off Tahiti.

*Joie de vivre* requires a *soupçon* of the primitive. But since the illusion of the primitive soon palls and has nowhere to go, it becomes necessary to make new initiates. A good part of the day, in fact, was taken up with regulars interpreting to first-timers like myself certain mores pertaining to the houseboat, as well as offering tidbits about Vartas's Rabelaisian views of life. Here everyone was encouraged to do what he willed. (How much could you do on a becalmed boat surrounded by strangers?) No one had much solid information about their host's past, which only increased the privileged status of those who knew at least one fact. Useless to ask the object of this venerating speculation, since

Vartas said next to nothing (adding to his impressiveness) when he was around, and disappeared below for long stretches of time.

In the evening, after a communal dinner, the new Grateful Dead record Frank had brought was put on the phonograph, and Vartas danced, first by himself, then with all three Graces, bending his arms in broad, hooking sweeps. He stomped his foot and looked around scampishly at the guests for appreciation, not unlike an organ-grinder and his monkey. Imagine, if you will, a being whose generous bestowal of self-satisfaction invites and is willing to receive nothing but flattery in return, a person who has managed to make others buy his somewhat senile projection of indestructibility as a Hymn to Life. In no sense could he be called a charlatan; he delivered what he promised, an incarnation of *joie de vivre*, and if it was shallow, it was also effective, managing even to attract an enviable "harem" (which was what really burned me).

A few years passed.

Some Dutch TV crew, ever on the lookout for exotic bits of Americana that would make good short subjects, planned to do a documentary about Vartas as a sort of paean to eternal youth. I later learned from Frank that Vartas died before the shooting could be completed. A pity, in a way. The home movie I've run off in my head of the old man is getting a little tattered, the colors splotchy, and the scenario goes nowhere, lacks point. All I have for sure is the title: *The Man Who Gave* Joie de Vivre *a Bad Name.*

"Ah, what a twinkle in the eye the old man has! He'll outlive us all." So we speak of old people who bore us, when we wish to honor them. We often see projected onto old people this worship of the life force. It is not the fault of the old if they then turn around and try to exploit our misguided amazement at their longevity as though it were a personal tour de force. The elderly, when they are honest with themselves, realize they have done nothing particularly to be proud of in lasting to a ripe old age, and then carrying themselves through a thousand more days. Yet you still hear an old woman or man telling a bus driver with a chuckle, "Would you believe that I am eighty-four years old!" As though they should be patted on the back for still knowing how to talk, or as though they had pulled a practical joke on the other riders by staying so spry and mobile. Such insecure, wheedling behavior always embarrasses me. I will look away rather than meet the speaker's eyes and be forced to lie with a smile, "Yes, you are remarkable," which seems condescending on my part and humiliating to us both.

Like children forced to play the cute part adults expect of them, some old people must get confused trying to adapt to a social role of indeterminate standards, which is why they seem to whine: "I'm doing all right, aren't I—for my age?" It is interesting that society's two most powerless groups, children and the elderly, have both been made into sentimental symbols. In the child's little hungry hands grasping for life, joined to the old person's frail slipping fingers hanging on to it, you have one of the commonest advertising metaphors for intense appreciation. It is enough to show a young child sleeping in his or her grandparent's lap to procure *joie de vivre* overload.

## 2 . THE DINNER PARTY

I am invited periodically to dinner parties and brunches—and I go, because I like to be with people and oblige them, even if I secretly cannot share their optimism about these events. I go, not believing that I will have fun, but with the intent of observing people who think a *dinner party* a good time. I eat their fancy food, drink the wine, make my share of entertaining conversation, and often leave having had a pleasant evening, which does not prevent me from anticipating the next invitation with the same bleak lack of hope. To put it in a nutshell, I am an ingrate.

Although I have traveled a long way from my proletarian origins and talk, dress, act, and spend money like a perfect little bourgeois, I hold on to my poor-boy's outrage at the "decadence" (meaning dull entertainment style) of the middle and upper-middle classes; or, like a model Soviet moviegoer watching scenes of prerevolutionary capitalists gorging themselves on caviar, I am appalled, but I dig in with the rest.

Perhaps my uneasiness with dinner parties comes from the simple fact that not a single dinner party was given by my solitudinous parents the whole time I was growing up, and I had to wait until my late twenties before learning the ritual. A spy in the enemy camp, I have made myself a patient observer of strange customs. For the benefit of other late-starting social climbers, this is what I have observed.

As everyone should know, the ritual of the dinner party begins away from the table. Usually in the living room, cheeses and walnuts are set out, to start the digestive juices flowing. Here introductions between strangers are also made. Most dinner parties contain at least a few guests who have been unknown to each other before that evening, but who the host and/or hostess envision would enjoy meeting. These novel pairings and their interactions add spice to the postmortem: Who got along with whom? The lack of prior acquaintanceship also ensures that the guests will have to rely on and go through the only people known to everyone, the host and hostess, whose absorption of this helplessly dependent attention is one of the main reasons for throwing dinner parties.

Although an after-work "leisure activity," the dinner party is in fact a celebration of professional identity. Each of the guests has been preselected as in a floral bouquet; and in certain developed forms of this ritual there is usually a cunning mix of professions. Yet the point is finally not so much diversity as commonality; what remarkably shared attitudes and interests these people from different vocations demonstrate by conversing intelligently, or at least glibly, on the topics that arise. Naturally, a person cannot discourse too technically about one's line of work, so he or she picks precisely those themes that invite overlap. The psychiatrist laments the new breed of egoless, narcissistic patient who keeps turning up in his office (a beach bum who lacks the work ethic); the college professor bemoans the shoddy intellectual backgrounds and self-centered ignorance of his students; and the bookseller parodies the customer who pronounced Sophocles to rhyme with "bifocals." The dinner party is thus an exercise in locating ignorance—elsewhere. Whoever is present is *ipso facto* part of that beleaguered remnant of civilized folk fast disappearing from earth.

Or think of a dinner party as a club of revolutionaries, a technocratic elite whose social interactions that night are a dry run for some future takeover of the state. These are the future cabinet members (now only a shadow cabinet, alas) meeting to practice for the first time. How well they get on! "The time will soon be ripe, my friends. . . ." If this is too fanciful for you, then compare the dinner party to a utopian community, a Brook Farm supper club, in which only the best and most useful community members are chosen to participate. The smugness begins as soon as one enters the door, since one is already part of the chosen few. And from then on, every mechanical step in dinner-party process is designed to augment the atmosphere of group *amour-propre*. This is not to say that there won't be one or two people in an absolute torment of exclusion, too shy to speak up, or suspecting that when they do their contributions fail to carry the same weight as those of the others. The group's all-purpose drone of self-contentment ignores these drowning people—cruelly inattentive in one sense but benign in another: it invites them to join the shared ethos of success any time they are ready.

The group is asked to repair to the table. Once again they find themselves marveling at a shared perception of life. How delicious the fish soup! How cute the stuffed tomatoes! What did you use in this green sauce? Now comes much talk of ingredients, and credit is given where credit is due. It is Jacques who made the salad. It was Mamie who brought the homemade bread. Everyone pleads with the hostess to sit down, not to work so hard—an empty formula whose hypocrisy bothers no one. Who else is going to put the butter dish on the table? For a moment all become quiet, except for the sounds of eating. This corresponds to the part in a church service that calls for silent prayer.

I am saved from such culinary paganism by the fact that food is largely an indifferent matter to me. I rarely think much about what I am putting in my mouth. Though my savage, illiterate palate has inevitably been educated to some degree by the many meals I have shared with people who care enormously about such things, I resist going any further. I am superstitious that the day I send back a dish at a restaurant, or make a complicated journey somewhere just for a meal, that day I will have sacrificed my freedom and traded in my soul for a lesser god.

I don't expect the reader to agree with me. That's not the point. Unlike the behavior called for at a dinner party, I am not obliged, sitting at my typewriter, to help procure consensus every moment. So I am at liberty to declare, to the friend who once told me that dinner parties were one of the only opportunities for intelligently convivial conversations to take place in this cold, fragmented city, that she is crazy. The conversation at dinner parties is of a mind-numbing caliber. No discussion of any clarifying rigor—be it political, spiritual, artistic, or financial—can take place in a context where fervent conviction of any kind is frowned upon, and the desire to follow through a sequence of ideas must give way every time to the impressionistic, breezy flitting from topic to topic. Talk must be bubbly but not penetrating. Illumination would only slow the flow. Some hit-and-run remark may accidentally jog an idea loose, but in such cases it is better to scribble a few words down on the napkin for later than attempt to "think" at a dinner party.

What do people talk about at such gatherings? The latest movies, the priciness of things, word processors, restaurants, muggings and burglaries, private versus public schools, the fool in the White House (there have been so many fools in a row that this subject is getting tired), the undeserved reputations of certain better-known professionals in one's field, the fashions in investments, the investments in fashion. What is traded at the dinner-party table is, of course, class information. You will learn whether you are in the avant-garde or rear guard of your social class, or, preferably, right in step.

As for Serious Subjects, dinner-party guests have the latest *New Yorker* in-depth piece to bring up. People who ordinarily would not spare a moment worrying about the treatment of schizophrenics in mental hospitals, the fate of Great Britain in the Common Market, or the disposal of nuclear wastes suddenly find their consciences orchestrated in unison about these problems, thanks to their favorite periodical—though a month later they have forgotten all about it and are on to something new.

The dinner party is a suburban form of entertainment. Its spread in our big cities represents an insidious Fifth Column suburbanization of the metropolis. In the suburbs it becomes necessary to be able to discourse knowledgeably about the heart of the city, but from the viewpoint of a day-shopper. Dinner-party chatter is the communicative equivalent of roaming around shopping malls.

Much thought has gone into the ideal size for a dinner party —usually with the hostess arriving at the figure eight. Six would give each personality too much weight; ten would lead to splintering side discussions; eight is the largest number still able to force everyone into the same compulsively congenial conversation. My own strength as a conversationalist comes out less in groups of eight than one-to-one, which may explain my resistance to dinner parties. At the table, unfortunately, any engrossing *tête-à-tête* is frowned upon as antisocial. I often find myself in the frustrating situation of being drawn to several engaging people in among the bores, and wishing I could have a private conversation with each, without being able to do more than signal across the table a wry recognition of that fact. "Some other time, perhaps," we seem to be saying with our eyes, all evening long.

Later, however—to give the devil his due—when guests and hosts retire from the table back to the living room, the strict demands of group participation may be relaxed, and individuals allowed to pair off in some form of conversational intimacy. But one must be ever on the lookout for the group's need to swoop everybody together again for one last demonstration of collective fealty.

The first to leave breaks the communal spell. There is a sudden rush to the coat closet, the bathroom, the bedroom, as others, under the protection of the first defector's original sin, quit the Party apologetically. The utopian dream has collapsed: left behind are a few loyalists and insomniacs, swillers of a last cognac. "Don't leave yet," begs the host, knowing what a sense of letdown, pain, and self-recrimination awaits. Dirty dishes are, if anything, a comfort: the faucet's warm gush serves to stave off the moment of anesthetized stock-taking—Was that really necessary?—in the sobering silence that follows a dinner party.

### 3.   *JOIE'S DOPPELGÄNGER*

I have no desire to rail against the Me Generation. We all know that the current epicurean style of the Good Life, from light foods to running shoes, is a result of market research techniques developed to sell "spot" markets, and, as such, a natural outgrowth of consumer capitalism. I may not like it, but I can't pretend that my objections are the result of a high-minded Laschian political analysis. Moreover, my own record of activism is not so noticeably impressive that I can lecture the Sunday brunchers to roll up their sleeves and start fighting social injustices instead of indulging themselves.

No, if I try to understand the reasons for my antihedonistic biases I must admit that they come from somewhere other than idealism. It's odd, because there seems to be a contradiction between the curmudgeonly feeling inside me and my periodically strong appetite for life. I am reminded of my hero, William Hazlitt, with his sarcastic, grumpy disposition on the one hand, and his capacity for "gusto" (his word, not Schlitz's) on the other. With Hazlitt, one senses a fanatically tenacious defense of individuality and independence against some unnamed bully stalking him. He had trained himself to be a connoisseur of vitality, and got irritated when life was not filled to the brim. I am far less irritable—before others; I will laugh if there is the merest *anything* to laugh at. But it is a tense, pouncing pleasure, not one that will allow me to sink into undifferentiated relaxation. The prospect of a long day at the beach makes me panic. There is no harder work I can think of than taking myself off to somewhere pleasant, where I am forced to stay for hours and "have fun." Taking it easy, watching my personality's borders loosen and dissolve, arouse an unpleasantly floating giddiness. I don't even like water beds. Fear of Freud's "oceanic feeling," I suppose—I distrust anything that will make me pause long enough to be put in touch with my helplessness.

The other repugnance I experience around *joie de vivrism* is that I associate its rituals with depression. All these people sitting around a pool, drinking margaritas—they're not really happy, they're depressed. Perhaps I am generalizing too much from my own despair in such situations. Drunk, sunbaked, stretched out in a beach chair, I am unable to ward off the sensation of being utterly alone, unconnected, cut off from the others.

An article in the Science section of the *Times* about depression (they seem to run one every few months) described the illness as a pattern of "learned helplessness." Dr. Martin Seligman of the University of Pennsylvania described his series of experiments: "At first mild electrical shocks were given to dogs, from which they were unable to escape. In a second set of experiments, dogs were given shocks from which they could escape—but they didn't try. They just lay there, passively accepting the pain. It seemed that the animals' inability to control their experiences had brought them to a state resembling clinical depression in humans."

Keep busy, I always say. At all costs avoid the trough of passivity, which leads to the Slough of Despond. Someone (a girlfriend, who else?) once accused me of being intolerant of the depressed way of looking at the world, which had its own intelligence and moral integrity, both obviously unavailable to me. It's true. I don't like the smell of depression (it has a smell, a very distinct one, something fetid like morning odors), and I stay away from depressed characters whenever possible. Except when they happen to be my closest friends or family members. It goes without saying that I am also, for all my squeamishness, attracted to depressed people, since they seem to know something I don't. I wouldn't rule out the possibility that the brown-gray logic of depression *is* the truth. In another experiment (also reported in the *Times*'s Science section), pitting "optimists" against clinically diagnosed "depressives" on their self-perceived abilities to effect outcomes according to their wills, researchers tentatively concluded that depressed people may have a more realistic, clear-sighted view of the world.

Nevertheless, what I don't like about depressives sometimes is their chummy I-told-you-so smugness, like Woody Allen fans who treat anhedonia as a vanguard position.

And for all that, depressives make the most rabid converts to *joie de vivre*. The reason for this is that *joie de vivre* and depression are not opposites but relatives of the same family, practically twins. When I see *joie de vivre* rituals, I always notice, like a TV ghost, depression right alongside it. I knew a man, dominated by a powerful father, who thought he had come out of a long depression occasioned, in his mind, by his divorce. Whenever I met him he would say that his life was getting better and better. Now he could run long distances, he was putting healthy food into his system, he was more physically fit at forty than he had been at twenty-five; now he had dates, he was going out with three different women, he had a good therapist, he was looking forward to renting a bungalow in better woods than the previous summer. . . . I don't know whether it was his tone of voice when he said this, his sagging shoulders, or what, but I always had an urge to burst into tears. If only he had admitted he was miserable I could have consoled him outright instead of being embarrassed to notice the deep hurt in him, like a swallowed razor cutting him from inside. And his pain still stunk up the room like in the old days, that sour cabbage smell was in his running suit, yet he wouldn't let on, he thought the smell was gone. The therapist had told him to forgive himself, and he had gone ahead and done it, the poor *schnook*. But tell me: Why would anyone need such a stylized, disciplined regimen of enjoyment if he were not depressed?


## 4. IN THE HERE AND NOW

The argument of both the hedonist and the guru is that if we were but to open ourselves to the richness of the moment, to concentrate on the feast before us, we would be filled with bliss. I have lived in the present from time to time, and I can tell you that it is much overrated. Occasionally, as a holiday from stroking one's memories or brooding about future worries, I grant you, it can be a nice change of pace. But to "be here now," hour after hour, would never work. I don't even approve of stories written in the present tense. As for poets who never use a past participle, they deserve the eternity they are striving for.

Besides, the present has a way of intruding whether you like it or not. Why should I go out of my way to meet it? Let it splash on me from time to time, like a car going through a puddle, and I, on the sidewalk of my solitude, will salute it grimly like any other modern inconvenience.

If I attend a concert, obviously not to listen to the music but to find a brief breathing space in which to meditate on the past and future, I realize that there may be moments when the music invades my ears and I am forced to pay attention to it, note after note. I believe I take such intrusions gracefully. The present is not always an unwelcome guest, so long as it doesn't stay too long and cut into my remembering or brooding time.

Even for survival, it's not necessary to focus one's full attention on the present. The instincts of a pedestrian crossing the street in a reverie will usually suffice. Alertness is all right as long as it is not treated as a promissory note on happiness. Anyone who recommends attention to the moment as a prescription for grateful wonder is telling only half the truth. To be happy one must pay attention, but to be unhappy one must also have paid attention.

Attention, at best, is a form of prayer. Conversely, as Simone Weil said, prayer is a way of focusing attention. All religions recognize this when they ask their worshipers to repeat the name of their God, a devotional practice that draws the practitioner into a trancelike awareness of the present, and the objects around oneself. With one part of the soul one praises God, and with the other part one expresses a hunger, a dissatisfaction, a desire for more spiritual contact. Praise must never stray too far from longing, that longing which takes us implicitly beyond the present.

I was about to say that the very act of attention implies longing, but this is not necessarily true. Attention is not always infused with desire; it can settle on us most placidly once desire has been momentarily satisfied, like after the sex act. There are also periods following overwork, when the exhausted slave-body is freed and the eyes dilate to register with awe the lights of the city; one is too tired to desire anything else.

Such moments are rare. They form the basis for a poetic appreciation of the beauty of the world. However, there seems no reliable way to invoke or prolong them. The rest of the time, when we are not being edgy or impatient, we are often simply *disappointed*, which amounts to a confession that the present is not good enough. People often try to hide their disappointment— just as Berryman's mother told him not to let people see that he was bored, because it suggested that he had no "inner resources." But there is something to be said for disappointment.

This least respected form of suffering, downgraded to a kind of petulance, at least accurately measures the distance between hope and reality. And it has its own peculiar satisfactions: Why else do we return years later to places where we had been happy, if not to savor the bittersweet pleasures of disappointment? "For as you well know: while a single disappointment may elicit tears, a repeated disappointment will evoke a smile" (Musil).

Moreover, disappointment is the flip side of a strong, predictive feeling for beauty or appropriate civility or decency: only those with a sense of order and harmony can be disappointed.

We are told that to be disappointed is immature, in that it presupposes unrealistic expectations, whereas the wise man meets each moment head-on without preconceptions, with freshness and detachment, grateful for anything it offers. However, this pernicious teaching ignores everything we know of the world. If we continue to expect what turns out to be not forthcoming, it is not because we are unworldly in our expectations, but because our very worldliness has taught us to demand of an unjust world that it behave a little more fairly. The least we can do, for instance, is to register the expectation that people in a stronger position be kind and not cruel to those in a weaker one, knowing all the while that we will probably be disappointed.

The truth is, most wisdom is embittering. The task of the wise person cannot be to pretend with false naïveté that every moment is new and unprecedented, but to bear the burden of bitterness that experience forces on us with as much uncomplaining dignity as strength will allow. Beyond that, all we can ask of ourselves is that bitterness not cancel out our capacity still to be surprised.

## 5. MAKING LOVE

If it is true that I have the tendency to withhold sympathy from those pleasures or experiences that fall outside my capabilities, the opposite is also true: I admire immoderately those things I cannot do. I've always gone out with women who swam better than I did. It's as if I were asking them to teach me how to make love. Though I know how to make love (more or less), I have never fully shaken that adolescent boy's insecurity that there was more to it than I could ever imagine, and that I needed a full-time instructress. For my first sexual experiences, in fact, I chose older women. Later, when I slept with women my own age and younger, I still tended to take the stylistic lead from them, adapting myself to each one's rhythm and ardor, not only because I wanted to be "responsive," but because I secretly thought that women—any woman—understood lovemaking in a way that I did not. In bed I came to them as a student, and I have made them pay later, in other ways, for letting them see me thus. Sex has always been so impromptu, so out of my control, so different each time, that even when I became the confident bull in bed I was dismayed by this sudden power, itself a form of powerlessness because so unpredictable.

Something Michel Leiris wrote in his book *Manhood*, has always stuck with me: "It has been some time, in any case, since I have ceased to consider the sexual act as a simple matter, but rather as a relatively exceptional act, necessitating certain inner accommodations that are either particularly tragic or particularly exalted, but very different, in either case, from what I regard as my usual disposition."

The transformation from a preoccupied urban intellectual to a sexual animal involves, at times, an almost superhuman strain. To find in one's bed a living, undulating woman of God knows what capacities and secret desires may seem too high, too formal, too ridiculous or blissful an occasion—even without the shock to an undernourished heart like mine of an injection of undiluted affection, if the woman proves loving as well.

Most often, I simply do what the flood allows me to, improvising here or there like a man tying a white flag to a raft that is being swiftly swept along, a plea for love or forgiveness. But as for artistry, control, enslavement through my penis, that's someone else. Which is not to say that there weren't women who were perfectly happy with me as a lover. In those cases, there was some love between us outside of bed: the intimacy was much more intense because we had something big to say to each other before we ever took off our clothes, but which could now be said only with our bodies.

With other women, whom I cared less about, I was sometimes a dud. I am not one of those men who can force themselves to make love passionately or athletically when their affections are not engaged. From the perplexity of wide variations in my experiences I have been able to tell myself that I am neither a good nor a bad lover, but one who responds differently according to the emotions present. A banal conclusion; maybe a true one.

It does not do away, however, with some need to have my remaining insecurities about sexual ability laid to rest. I begin to suspect that all my fancy distrust of hedonism comes down to a fear of being judged in this one category: Do I make love well? Every brie and wine picnic, every tanned body relaxing on the beach, every celebration of *joie de vivre* carries a sly wink of some missed sexual enlightenment that may be too threatening to me. I am like the prudish old maid who blushes behind her packages when she sees sexy young people kissing.

When I was twenty I married. My wife was the second

woman I had ever slept with. Our marriage was the recognition that we suited one another remarkably well as company—could walk and talk and share insights all day, work side by side like Chinese peasants, read silently together like graduate students, tease each other like brother and sister, and when at night we found our bodies tired, pull the covers over ourselves and become lovers. She was two years older than I, but I was good at faking maturity; and I found her so companionable and trustworthy and able to take care of me that I could not let such a gold mine go by.

Our love life was mild and regular. There was a sweetness to sex, as befitted domesticity. Out of the surplus energy of late afternoons I would find myself coming up behind her sometimes as she worked in the kitchen, taking her away from her involvements, leading her by the hand into the bedroom. I would unbutton her blouse. I would stroke her breasts, and she would get a look in her eyes of quiet intermittent hunger, like a German shepherd being petted; she would seem to listen far off; absentmindedly daydreaming, she would return my petting, stroke my arm with distracted patience like a mother who has something on the stove, trying to calm her weeping child. I would listen, too, to guess what she might be hearing, bird calls or steam heat. The enlargement of her nipples under my fingers fascinated me. Goose bumps either rose on her skin where I touched or didn't, I noted with scientific interest, a moment before getting carried away by my own eagerness. Then we were undressing, she was doing something in the bathroom, and I was waiting on the bed, with all the consciousness of a sun-mote. I was large and ready, the proud husband, waiting to receive my treasure. . . .

I remember our favorite position was with her on top, me on the bottom, upthrusting and receiving. Distraction, absentmindedness, return, calm exploration marked our sensual life. To be forgetful seemed the highest grace. We often achieved perfection.

Then I became haunted with images of seductive, heartless cunts. It was the era of the miniskirt, girl-women, Rudi Gernreich bikinis and Tiger Morse underwear, see-through blouses, flashes of flesh that invited the hand to go creeping under and into costumes. I wanted my wife to be more glamorous. We would go shopping for dresses together; she would complain that her legs were wrong for the new fashions. Or she would come home proudly with a bargain pink and blue felt minidress, bought for three dollars at a discount store, which my aching heart would tell me missed the point completely.

She, too, became dissatisfied with the absence of furtive excitement in our marriage. She wanted to seduce me, like a stranger on a plane. But I was too easy, so we ended up seducing others. Then we turned back to each other and with one last desperate attempt, before the marriage fell to pieces, each sought in the other a plasticity of sensual forms, like the statuary in an Indian temple. In our lovemaking I tried to believe that the body of one woman was the body of all women; all I achieved was a groping to distance lovingly familiar forms into those of anonymous erotic succubi. The height of this insanity, I remember, was one evening in the park when I pounded my wife's lips with kisses in an effort to provoke something between us like "hot passion." My eyes closed, I practiced a repertoire of French tongue-kisses on her. I shall never forget her frightened silent appeal that I stop, because I had turned into someone she no longer recognized.

But we were young, and so, dependent on each other, like orphans. By the time I left, at twenty-five, I knew I had been a fool, and had ruined everything, but I had to continue being a fool because it had been my odd misfortune to have stumbled onto kindness and tranquillity too quickly.

I moved to California in search of an earthly sexual paradise, and that year I tried hardest to make my peace with *joie de vivre*. I was sick but didn't know it—a diseased animal, Nietzsche would say. I hung around Berkeley's campus, stared up at the Campanile tower; I sat on the grass watching coeds younger than I and, pretending that I was still going to university (no deeper sense of being a fraud obtainable), I tried to grasp the rhythms of carefree youth; I blended in at rallies, I stood at the fringes of be-ins, watching new rituals of communal love, someone being passed through the air hand to hand. But I never "trusted the group" enough to let myself be the guinea pig; or if I did, it was only with the proud stubborn conviction that nothing could change me—though I also wanted to change. Swearing I would never learn transcendence, I hitchhiked and climbed mountains. I went to wine-tasting festivals and accepted the wine jug from hippie gypsies in a circle around a beach campfire without first wiping off the lip. I registered for a Free School course in human sexual response just to get laid, and when that worked, I was shocked, and took up with someone else. There were many women in those years who got naked with me. I smoked grass with them, and as a sign of faith I took psychedelic drugs; we made love in bushes and beach houses, as though hacking through jungles with machetes to stay in touch with our ecstatic genitals while our minds soared off into natural marvels. Such experiences taught me, I will admit, how much romantic feeling can transform the body whose nerve tendrils are receptive to it. Technicolor fantasies of one girlfriend as a senorita with flowers in her impossibly wavy hair would suddenly pitch and roll beneath me, and the bliss of touching her naked suntanned breast and the damp black pubic hairs was too unthinkably perfect to elicit anything but abject gratitude. At such moments I have held the world in my hands and known it. I was coming home to the body of Woman, those globes and grasses that had launched me. In the childish fantasy accompanying one sexual climax, under LSD, I was hitting a home run and the Stars and Stripes flying in the background of my mind's eye as I "slid into home" acclaimed the patriotic rightness of my seminal release. For once I had no guilt about how or when I ejaculated.

If afterward, when we came down, there was often a sour air of disenchantment and mutual prostitution, that does not take away from the legacy, the rapture of those moments. If I no longer use drugs—in fact, have become somewhat antidrug—I think I still owe them something for showing me how to recognize the all-embracing reflex. At first I needed drugs to teach me about the stupendousness of sex. Later, without them, there would be situations—after a lovely talk or coming home from a party in a taxi—when I would be overcome by amorous tropism toward the woman with me. The appetite for flesh that comes over me at such moments, and the pleasure there is in finally satisfying it, seems so just that I always think I have stumbled into a state of blessed grace. That it can never last, that it is a trick of the mind and the blood, are rumors I push out of sight.

To know rapture is to have one's whole life poisoned. If you will forgive a ridiculous analogy, a tincture of rapture is like a red bandana in the laundry that runs and turns all the white wash pink. We should just as soon stay away from any future ecstatic experiences that spoil everyday living by comparison. Not that I have any intention of stopping. Still, if I will have nothing to do with religious mysticism, it is probably because I sense a susceptibility in that direction. Poetry is also dangerous; all quickening awakenings to Being extract a price later.

Are there people who live under such spells all the time? Was this the secret of the idiotic smile on the half-moon face of the painter Vartas? The lovers of life, the robust Cellinis, the Casanovas? Is there a technique to hedonism that will allow the term of rapture to be indefinitely extended? I don't believe it. The hedonist's despair is still that he is forced to make do with the present. Who knows about the success rate of religious mystics? In any case, I could not bring myself to state that what I am waiting for is God. Such a statement would sound too grandiose and presumptuous, and make too great a rupture in my customary thinking. But I can identify with the pre- if not the post-stage of what Simone Weil describes:

"The soul knows for certain only that it is hungry. The important thing is that it announces its hunger by crying. A child does not stop crying if we suggest to it that perhaps there is no bread. It goes on crying just the same. The danger is not lest the soul should doubt whether there is any bread, but lest, by a lie, it should persuade itself that it is not hungry."

So much for *joie de vivre*. It's too compensatory. I don't really know what I'm waiting for. I know only that until I have gained what I want from this life, my expressions of gratitude and joy will be restricted to variations of a hunter's alertness. I give thanks to a nip in the air that clarifies the scent. But I think it hypocritical to pretend satisfaction while I am still hungry.

# ART

# OF

# THE

# CREEP

When I was in junior high school, during that stage when popularity becomes an obsession, there was a classmate of mine named Harold Levine who had very large ears and was cruelly if inevitably nicknamed Dumbo. The other students jeered at him and even waited for him on his way home from school; they never actually beat him up, but they tossed him around a little. It did not help his cause that Dumbo —I mean, Harold—had a rather goofy-looking stare, similar to that of *Mad* magazine's Alfred E. Newman. A scholar of medium abilities, not brilliant but certainly not dumb, Harold seemed bewildered by this victimization and came to wear a whimpering, defensive expression, which only invited more sadistic abuse.

I felt sorry for Harold and I finally told the others to leave him alone. They were being unfair; he was not responsible for the size of his ears. I even went so far as to lecture them on the idea of the scapegoat in history, and told them they were projecting their own insecurities onto Harold Levine. I was not entirely sure what "projection"—a word my Freudian parents used in arguments—meant, and I probably deserved a kick in the shins for making such a sermon. Nevertheless, the other kids heard me out. Though probably equally a misfit in the inner tabernacle of my consciousness, I was in a very different position from Harold; I had the highest grades and had somehow managed to get myself elected vice-president of the student organization, an honorific position that my classmates mistakenly thought held some power. Maybe that was why they listened to me, or maybe the Dumbo joke had simply worn thin with them by this time and they were looking for some excuse to drop it.

In any case, the campaign against Harold Levine tapered off, and somehow he got wind of his defender's name. A grateful Harold was all over me like a cocker spaniel. He insisted on walking me everywhere; he told me about his grandmother at home who never left him alone; the kid talked my ear off. This wasn't what I'd had in mind at all. At thirteen, one had an interest in pure, *abstract* justice. Like Solomon deciding between the two women fighting over the baby, I meant to settle a dispute with a swift stroke of reasoning. It hadn't dawned on me that Harold Levine would interpret my disinterested defense as an overture to friendship. Now I was in the sticky position of not wanting to inflict added cruelty on Harold, which would go against my earlier campaign, while praying he would somehow fall into a hole. I began to sympathize with his persecutors, having discovered that Harold Levine *was* obnoxious. His whiny, spineless, dependent manner barely concealed the hostility of testing one's patience to the limit. The other kids undoubtedly had detected his "creep" nature before me, although, not yet able to diagnose it as such, they had fastened on the cruder handle of his ears.

Now, you will ask, what do I mean by a creep? (You, of course, know full well what a creep is, but are waiting to see if our definitions differ.) To me, a creep is someone who walks around as if with a load in his pants. He doesn't necessarily know he has soiled his pants, and yet his nose reacts instinctively, recoiling at his own bad odor, and he walks with a step at once mincing and blocklike. The creep would like to forget that he has a body, which only draws your attention all the more to his ungainly posture as he departs. Then again, we know the creep mainly in the way he is loath to depart; he stands up, as if to say, I know you want to get rid of me, then circles back again and lingers with the stubbornness of a buzzing fly. It is part of the creep's business to make you feel soiled as well; in fact, he means to smear everything in the vicinity with his stench.

Now, creeps have a peculiar parasitic fascination for healthy, dynamic people; they will flatter the achiever with a flunky's attentions while playing on the other's success-guilt. Also, to the degree that the creep has mastered the knack of Dostoevskyan buffoonery, his public display of clownish self-humiliation can add an entertaining spice to a blandly wholesome gathering of fortune.

Nowhere is this dynamic more apparent than in seductions executed by creeps. The approach of the male creep to the opposite sex is a complicated story. His patience, his passive persistence—his very unattractiveness—are used to try to wear down a woman's resistance. Adolescent boys who have trouble making a straightforward pass often hope that if they hang around girls long enough the opportunity for sex will magically arise. The creep remains an adolescent in always standing nearby, waiting for the guard to drop.

Most women have had an experience with such a man who lingers around her, exploiting the most tenuous links—perhaps he is the friend of a man she had once, or recently, been seeing. Now he appears in her life at a time when she is most lonely and vulnerable. He offers himself around dinnertime, to share a bowl of bean soup she has made for herself; it becomes a habit for him to drop in and suggest a little walk, a cup of coffee, a chat—always something modest. The creep does not lavish money on flashy restaurants or theater tickets; if he proposes a "date," it is to something in the neighborhood or close by. This is both in order to veil his sexual intent and to add to the mystique of gray drabness. The creep announces a period not of glamour but of emotional recession, retrenchment, exhaustion. He is the harbinger of diminished expectations. If he has the luck to fit in with the mood of the moment, he may be rewarded with the highest prize, and it is up to him not to notice with what despair it has been surrendered.

The creep often preys on attractive women for several reasons. He lacks the imagination and the self-confidence to find a treasure in a seemingly plain wrapper. His own damaged self-image insists that he be recompensed with the caress of a woman desired by other men. Also, attractive women are used to the nuisance of romantic importuning, more tolerant of the spectacle of male dogginess and less apt to grant it undue importance; they may exaggerate their strength to keep saying no. Perhaps it was a handsome, confident man who hurt them; they may pity the creep, who awakens some maternal chord. For his part, the creep (though deep down the vainest of creatures) makes no effort to improve his dress or to present himself in any but the homeliest light, as though issuing a challenge to the womanly powers of imagination. It is a commonplace that some of the prettiest women can be drawn to ugly, froglike men, whose very lack of handsomeness, if the moon is right, exerts a perverse appeal. So much of what we are attracted to has an element of repulsion mixed in anyway that our advance toward it can be like daring ourselves to overcome our fear. The creep waits for just such moments of recklessness.

Meanwhile, he will have weakened the woman's resistance by playing on her own doubts about being beautiful. This is standard procedure: for every man who seduces a woman with honeyed compliments to her beauty, an equal number get just as far by withholding such statements until the woman in question feels insecure. The creep will certainly let the object of his affection know *at some point* that he finds her attractive, but after that he will scrupulously avoid flattering her looks until the woman herself begins to falter, begins to think that perhaps she has not been looking very pretty of late. In this way he tries to bring her down to his own level.

All of these strategies work, up to a point. The only problem is that once the woman has yielded, she will usually come to her senses immediately afterward and call it a mistake, a one-night stand. If she is in a particularly weakened, numbed condition, the affair may drag on for as long as two months. Eventually, however, the moment arrives when our heroine rebels and decides that kindness and curiosity have their limits. It is then that the creep will batter her with legalistic arguments and proofs, throw back at her her once murmured words of endearment, so that favors offered in an excess of generosity are made to seem, when curtailed, like defaults on contractual obligations. "At least you have to stay with me one more night," he will insist. But suddenly these procedures of wheedling and intimidation fail to work. The woman sees quite well that a kiss is not a down payment on another kiss; she has only to wait until a suitable moment, and then she can leave.

Unfortunately, she is not to escape so lightly. The creep will pester the one who has rejected him by calling her late at night, insisting that she "straighten out some confusing things" in what she has said, asking that she try to understand him at a time when he is "going out of his mind with pain." Or he will wait two weeks and ask her for a date, as though the break were a hallucination on her part; he will force her to go through it all over again. Or, if he is a wise, clever creep, he will wait six months and start rebuilding the "friendship," patiently working on the butt-ends of nostalgia, presuming no physical tie, but keeping an eye out for the moment when the woman* is again feeling distraught, abandoned, alone.

How do I know this? We are all creeps when it comes to love.

We are *not* all capable, thank God, of an even nastier behavior of which all too many women have been victims, after breaking off what had seemed an inconsequential if misguided affair. Here the ex-lover literally shadows the woman, leaving daily notes in her mailbox, calling at two in the morning and, without

---

* I have no doubt that there are women creeps as well; gender training may make their approach take somewhat different forms, but I feel neither knowledgeable nor emboldened enough to describe them.

identifying himself, hanging up, having ruined her sleep. He embarrasses her at the office; when she comes home from work she finds his car parked across the street, as if on a stakeout. He stares at her closed window blinds for hours. This is rape in all but the final act.

But such behavior crosses the line into the pathological, and I am not sure whether it is a connected if extreme extension of creepdom, or whether it belongs in a category by itself. I am tempted to argue that the art of the creep consists, by definition, of staying within the bounds of the merely aggravating.

In any case, I fear I have done an injustice to Harold Levine, who was dragged in by the ears just to get this essay going, and who is probably now a successful airplane pilot living comfortably with his wife and five kids somewhere in a big house on Long Island.

# A
# NONSMOKER
# WITH
# A
# SMOKER

Last Saturday night my girl-
friend, Helen, and I went to a dinner party in the Houston
suburbs. We did not know our hosts, but were invited on account
of Helen's chum Barry, whose birthday party it was. We had
barely stepped into the house and met the other guests, seated
on a U-shaped couch under an A-framed ceiling, when Helen lit
a cigarette. The hostess froze. "Uh, could you please not smoke
in here? If you have to, we'd appreciate your using the terrace.
We're both sort of allergic."

Helen smiled understandingly and moved toward the glass
doors leading to the backyard in a typically ladylike way, as
though merely wanting to get a better look at the garden. But I
knew from that gracious "Southern" smile of hers that she was
miffed.

As soon as Helen had stepped outside, the hostess explained
that they had just moved into this house, and that it had taken

weeks to air out because of the previous owner's tenacious cigar smoke. A paradigmatically awkward conversation about tobacco ensued: like testifying sinners, two people came forward with confessions about kicking the nasty weed; our scientist-host cited a recent study of indoor air pollution levels; a woman lawyer brought up the latest California legislation protecting non-smokers; a roly-poly real estate agent admitted that, though he had given up smokes, he still sat in the smoking section of airplanes because "you meet a more interesting type of person there" —a remark his wife did not find amusing. Helen's friend Barry gallantly joined her outside. I did not, as I should have; I felt paralyzed.

For one thing, I wasn't sure which side I was on. I have never been a smoker. My parents both chain-smoked, so I grew up accustomed to cloudy interiors and ever since have been tolerant of other people's nicotine urges. To be perfectly honest, I'm not crazy about inhaling smoke, particularly when I've got a cold, but that irritating inconvenience pales beside the damage that would be done to my pluralistic worldview if I did not defend smokers' rights.

On the other hand, a part of me wished Helen *would* stop smoking. That part seemed to get a satisfaction out of the group's "banishing" her: they were doing the dirty work of expressing my disapproval.

As soon as I realized this, I joined her in the garden. Presently a second guest strolled out to share a forbidden toke, then a third. Our hostess ultimately had to collect the mutineers with an announcement that dinner was served.

At the table, Helen appeared to be having such a good time, joking with our hosts and everyone else, that I was unprepared for the change that came over her as soon as we were alone in the car afterward. "I will never go back to that house!" she declared. "Those people have no concept of manners or hospitality, humiliating me the moment I stepped in the door. And that phony line about 'sort of allergic'!"

Normally, Helen is forbearance personified. Say anything that touches her about smoking, however, and you touch the rawest of nerves. I remembered the last time I foolishly suggested that she "think seriously" about stopping. I had just read one of those newspaper articles about the increased possibility of heart attacks, lung cancer, and birth deformities among women smokers, and I was worried for her. My concern must have been maladroitly expressed, because she burst into tears.

"Can't we even talk about this without your getting so sensitive?" I had asked.

"You don't understand. Nonsmokers never understand that it's a real addiction. I've tried quitting, and it was hell. Do you want me to go around for months mean and cranky outside and angry inside? You're right, I'm sensitive, because I'm threatened with having taken away from me the thing that gives me the most pleasure in life, day in, day out," she said. I shot her a look: careful, now. "Well, practically the most pleasure. You know what I mean." I didn't. But I knew enough to drop it.

I love Helen, and if she wants to smoke, knowing the risks involved, that remains her choice. Besides, she wouldn't quit just because I wanted her to; she's not that docile, and that's part of what I love about her. Sometimes I wonder why I even keep thinking about her quitting. What's it to me personally? Certainly I feel protective of her health, but I also have selfish motives. I don't like the way her lips taste when she's smoked a lot. I associate her smoking with nervousness, and when she lights up several cigarettes in a row, I get jittery watching her. Crazy as this may sound, I also find myself becoming jealous of her cigarettes. Occasionally, when I go to her house and we're sitting on the couch together, if I see Helen eyeing the pack I make her kiss me first, so that my lips can engage hers (still fresh) before the competition's. It's almost as though there were another lover in the room—a lover who was around long before I entered the picture, and who pleases her in mysterious ways I cannot.

A lit cigarette puts a distance between us: it's like a weapon in her hand, awakening in me a primitive fear of being burnt. The memory is not so primitive, actually. My father used to smoke absentmindedly, letting the ash grow like a caterpillar eating every leaf in its path, until gravity finally toppled it. Once, when I was about nine, my father and I were standing in line at a bakery, and he accidentally dropped a lit ash down my back. Ever since, I've inwardly winced and been on guard around these little waving torches, which epitomize to me the dangers of intimacy.

I've worked hard to understand from the outside the satisfaction of smoking. I've even smoked "sympathetic" cigarettes, just to see what the other person was experiencing. But it's not the same as being hooked. How can I really empathize with the frightened but stubborn look Helen gets in her eyes when, despite the fact we're a little late going somewhere, she turns to me in the car and says, "I need to buy a pack of cigarettes first"? I feel a wave of pity for her. We are both embarrassed by this forced recognition of her frailty—the "indignity," as she herself puts it, of being controlled by something outside her will.

I try to imagine myself in that position, but a certain smugness keeps getting in the way (I don't have that problem and *am I glad*). We pay a price for our smugness. So often it flip-flops into envy: the outsiders wish to be included in the sufferings and highs of others, as if to say that only by relinquishing control and surrendering to some dangerous habit, some vice or dependency, would one be able to experience "real life."

Over the years I have become a sucker for cigarette romanticism. Few Hollywood gestures move me as much as the one in *Now Voyager*, when Paul Henreid lights two cigarettes, one for himself, the other for Bette Davis: these form a beautiful fatalistic bridge between them, a complicitous understanding like the realization that their love is based on the inevitability of separation. I am all the more admiring of this worldly cigarette gallantry because its experiential basis escapes me.

The same sort of fascination occurs when I come across a literary description of nicotine addiction, like this passage in Mailer's *Tough Guys Don't Dance*: "Over and over again I gave them up, a hundred times over the years, but I always went back. For in my dreams, sooner or later, I struck a match, brought flame to the tip, then took in all my hunger for existence with the first puff. I felt impaled on desire itself—those fiends trapped in my chest and screaming for one drag."

"Impaled on desire itself"! Such writing evokes a longing in me for the centering of self that tobacco seems to bestow on its faithful. Clearly, there is something attractive about having this umbilical relation to the universe—this curling pillar, this spiral staircase, this prayer of smoke that mediates between the smoker's inner substance and the alien ether. Inwardness of the nicotine trance, sad wisdom ("every pleasure has its price"), beauty of ritual, squandered health—all those romantic meanings we read into the famous photographic icons of fifties saints, Albert Camus or James Agee or James Dean or Carson McCullers puffing away, in a sense they're true. Like all people who return from a brush with death, smokers have gained a certain power. They know their "coffin nails." With Helen, each cigarette is a measuring of the perishable, an enactment of her mortality, from filter to end-tip in fewer than five minutes. I could not stand to be reminded of my own death so often.

# WHAT HAPPENED TO THE PERSONAL ESSAY?

The personal or familiar essay is a wonderfully tolerant form, able to accommodate rumination, memoir, anecdote, diatribe, scholarship, fantasy, and moral philosophy. It can follow a rigorously elegant design, or—held together by little more than the author's voice—assume an amoebic shapelessness. Working in it liberates a writer from the structure of the well-made, epiphanous short story and allows one to ramble in a way that more truly reflects the mind at work. At this historical moment the essayist has an added freedom: no one is looking over his or her shoulder. No one much cares. Commercially, essay volumes rank even lower than poetry.

I know; when my first essay collection, *Bachelorhood*, came out, booksellers had trouble figuring out where to stock it. Autobiography? Self-help? Short stories? I felt like saying, "Hey, this category has been around for a long time; what's the big deal?" Yet, realistically, they were right: what had once been a thriving popular tradition had ceased being so. Readers who enjoyed the book often told me so with some surprise, because they hadn't thought they would like "essays." For them, the word conjured up those dreaded weekly compositions they were forced to write on the gasoline tax or the draft.

Essays are usually taught all wrong: they are harnessed to rhetoric and composition, in a two-birds-with-one-stone approach designed to sharpen freshman students' skills at argumentation. While it is true that historically the essay is related to rhetoric, it in fact seeks to persuade more by the delights of literary style than anything else. Elizabeth Hardwick, one of our best essayists, makes this point tellingly when she says: "The mastery of expository prose, the rhythm of sentences, the pacing, the sudden flash of unexpected vocabulary, redeem polemic. . . . The essay . . . is a great meadow of style and personal manner, freed from the need for defense except that provided by an individual intelligence and sparkle. We consent to watch a mind at work, without agreement often, but only for pleasure."

Equally questionable in teaching essays is the anthology approach, which assigns an essay apiece by a dozen writers according to our latest notions of a demographically representative and content-relevant sampling. It would be more instructive to read six pieces each by two writers, since the essay (particularly the familiar essay) is so rich a vehicle for displaying personality in all its willfully changing aspects.

Essays go back at least to classical Greece and Rome, but it was Michel de Montaigne, generally considered the "father of the essay," who first matched the word to the form around 1580. Reading this contemporary of Shakespeare (thought to have influenced the Bard himself), we are reminded of the original, pristine meaning of the word, from the French verb *essayer*: to attempt, to try, to leap experimentally into the unknown. Montaigne understood that, in an essay, the track of a person's thoughts struggling to achieve some understanding of a problem *is* the plot. The essayist must be willing to contradict himself (for which reason an essay is not a legal brief), to digress, even to risk ending up in a terrain very different from the one he embarked on. Particularly in Montaigne's magnificent late essays, free-falls that sometimes go on for a hundred pages or more, it is possible for the reader to lose all contact with the ostensible subject, bearings, top, bottom, until there is nothing to do but surrender to this companionable voice, thinking alone in the dark. Eventually, one begins to share Montaigne's confidence that "all subjects are linked to one another," which makes any topic, however small or far from the center, equally fertile.

It was Montaigne's peculiar project, which he claimed rightly or wrongly was original, to write about the one subject he knew best: himself. As with all succeeding literary self-portraits—or all succeeding stream-of-consciousness, for that matter—success depended on having an interesting consciousness, and Montaigne was blessed with an undulatingly supple, learned, skeptical, deep, sane, and candid one. In point of fact, he frequently strayed to worldly subjects, giving his opinion on everything from cannibals to coaches, but we do learn a large number of intimate and odd details about the man, down to his bowels and kidney stones. "Sometimes there comes to me a feeling that I should not betray the story of my life," he writes. On the other hand: "No pleasure has any meaning for me without communication."

A modern reader may come away thinking that the old fox still kept a good deal of himself to himself. This is partly because we have upped the ante on autobiographical revelation, but also because Montaigne was writing essays, not confessional memoirs, and in an essay it is as permissible, as honest, to chase down a reflection to its source as to admit some past shame. In any case, having decided that "the most barbarous of our maladies is to despise our being," Montaigne did succeed, via the proto-psychoanalytic method of the *Essais*, in making friends with his mind.

Having taken the essay form to its very limits at the outset, Montaigne's dauntingly generous example was followed by an inevitable specialization, which included the un-Montaignean split between formal and informal essays. The formal essay derived from Francis Bacon; it is said to be "dogmatic, impersonal, systematic, and expository," written in a "stately" language, while the informal essay is "personal, intimate, relaxed, conversational, and frequently humorous" (*New Columbia Encyclopedia*). Never mind that most of the great essayists were adept at both modes, including Bacon (see, for example, his wonderful "Of Friendship"); it remains a helpful distinction.

Informal, familiar essays tend to seize on the parade and minutiae of daily life: vanities, fashions, oddballs, seasonal rituals, love and disappointment, the pleasures of solitude, reading, going to plays, walking in the street. It is a very urban form, enjoying a spectacular vogue in eighteenth- and early nineteenth-century London, when it enlisted the talents of such stylists as Swift, Dr. Johnson, Addison and Steele, Charles Lamb, William Hazlitt, and a visiting American, Washington Irving. The familiar essay was given a boost by the phenomenal growth of newspapers and magazines, all of which needed smart copy (such as that found in the *Spectator*) to help instruct their largely middle-class, *parvenu* readership on the manners of the class to which it aspired.

Although most of the *feuilletonistes* of this period were cynical hacks, the journalistic situation was still fluid enough to allow original thinkers a platform. The British tolerance for eccentricity seemed to encourage commentators to develop idiosyncratic voices. No one was as cantankerously marginal in his way, or as willing to write against the grain of community feeling, as William Hazlitt. His energetic prose style registered a temperament that passionately, moodily swung between sympathy and scorn. Anyone capable of writing so bracingly frank an essay as "The Pleasures of Hating" could not—as W. C. Fields would say—be all bad. At the same time, Hazlitt's enthusiasms could transform the humblest topic, such as going on a country walk or seeing a prizefight, into a description of visionary wholeness.

What many of the best essayists have had—what Hazlitt had in abundance—was quick access to their blood reactions, so that the merest flash of a prejudice or opinion might be dragged into the open and defended. Hazlitt's readiness to entertain opinions, coupled with his openness to new impressions, made him a fine critic of painting and the theater, but in his contrariness he ended by antagonizing all of his friends, even the benign, forgiving Charles Lamb. Not that Lamb did not have *his* contrary side. He, too, was singled out for a "perverse habit of contradiction," which helped give his "Elia" essays, among the quirkiest and most charming in the English language, their peculiar bite.

How I envy readers of *London* magazine, who might have picked up an issue in 1820 and encountered a new, high-spirited essay by Hazlitt, Lamb, or both! After their deaths, the familiar essay continued to attract brilliant practitioners such as Stevenson, DeQuincey, and Emerson. But subsequently, a little of the vitality seeped out of it. "Though we are mighty fine fellows nowadays, we cannot write like Hazlitt," Stevenson confessed. And by the turn of the century, it seemed rather played out and toothless.

The modernist aesthetic was also not particularly kind to this type of writing, relegating it to a genteel, antiquated nook, *belles lettres*—a phrase increasingly spoken with a sneer, as though implying a sauce without the meat. If "meat" is taken to mean the atrocities of life, it is true that the familiar essay has something obstinately nonapocalyptic about it. The very act of composing such an essay seems to implicate the writer in humanist-individualist assumptions that have come to appear suspect under the modernist critique.

Still, it would be unfair to pin the rap on modernism, which Lord knows gets blamed for everything else. One might as well "blame" the decline of the conversational style of writing. Familiar essays were fundamentally, even self-consciously, conversational: it is no surprise that Swift wrote one of his best short pieces on "Hints Toward an Essay on Conversation"; that Montaigne tackled "Of the Art of Discussion"; that Addison and Steele extensively analyzed true and false wit; that Hazlitt titled his books *Table Talk, Plain Speaker,* and *The Round Table;* or that Oliver Wendell Holmes actually cast his familiar essays in the form of mealtime dialogues. Why would a book like Holmes's *The Autocrat of the Breakfast Table,* a celebration of good talk that was so popular in its time, be so unlikely today? I cannot go along with those who say "The art of conversation has died, television killed it," since conversation grows and changes as inevitably as language. No, what has departed is not conversation but conversation-flavored writing, which implies a speaking relationship between writer and reader. How many readers today would sit still for a direct address by the author? To be called "gentle reader" or "*hypocrite lecteur*," to have one's arm pinched while dozing off, to be called to attention, flattered, kidded like a real person instead of a privileged fly on the wall—wouldn't most readers today find such devices archaic, intrusive, even impudent? Oh, you wouldn't? Good, we can go back to the old style, which I much prefer.

Maybe what has collapsed is the very fiction of "the educated reader," whom the old essayists seemed to be addressing in their conversational remarks. From Montaigne onward, essayists until this century have invoked a shared literary culture: the Greek and Latin authors and the best of their national poetry. The whole modern essay tradition sprang from quotation. Montaigne's *Essais* and Burton's *Anatomy of Melancholy* were essentially outgrowths of the "commonplace book," a personal journal in which quotable passages, literary excerpts, and comments were written. Though the early essayists' habit of quotation may seem excessive to a modern taste, it was this display of learning that linked them to their educated reading public and ultimately gave them the authority to speak so personally about themselves. Such a universal literary culture no longer exists; we have only popular culture to fall back on. While it is true that the old high culture was never really "universal"—excluding as it did a good deal of humanity—it is also true that without it, personal discourse has become more hard-pressed. What many modern essayists have tried to do is to replace that shared literary culture with more and more personal experience. It is a brave effort and an intriguing supposition, this notion that individual experience alone can constitute the universal text that all may dip into with enlightenment. But there are pitfalls: on the one hand, it may lead to cannibalizing oneself and one's privacy; on the other hand, much more common (and to my mind, worse) is the assertion of an earnestly honest or "vulnerable" manner without really candid chunks of experience to back it up.

As for popular culture, the essayist's chronic invocation of its latest bandwagon fads, however satirically framed, comes off frequently as a pandering to the audience's short attention span —a kind of literary ambulance chasing. Take the "life-style" pages in today's periodicals, which carry commentaries that are a distant nephew of the familiar essay: there is something so depressing about this desperate mining of things in the air, such a fevered search for a generational *Zeitgeist*, such an unctuously smarmy tone of "we," which assumes that everyone shares the same consumerist-boutique sensibility, that one longs for a Hazlittean shadow of misanthropic mistrust to fall between reader and writer. One longs for any evidence of a distinct human voice —anything but this ubiquitous Everyman/woman pizzazzy drone, listing tips for how to get the most from your dry cleaner's, take care of your butcher block, or bounce back from an unhappy love affair.

The familiar essay has naturally suffered from its parasitic economic dependency on magazines and newspapers. The streamlined telegraphic syntax and homogenized-perky prose that contemporary periodicals have evolved make it all the more difficult for thoughtful, thorny voices to be tolerated within the house style. The average reader of periodicals becomes conditioned to digest pure information, up-to-date, with its ideological viewpoint disguised as objectivity, and is thus ill-equipped to follow the rambling, cat-and-mouse game of perverse contrariety played by the great essayists of the past.

In any event, very few American periodicals today support house essayists to the tune of letting them write regularly and at comfortable length on the topics of their choice. The nearest thing we have are talented columnists like Russell Baker, Ellen Goodman, Leon Hale, and Mike Royko, who are in a sense carrying on the Addison and Steele tradition; they are so good at their professional task of hit-and-run wisdom that I only wish they were sometimes given the space to try out their essayistic wings. The problem with the column format is that it becomes too tight and pat: one idea per piece. Fran Lebowitz, for instance, is a very clever writer, and not afraid of adopting a cranky persona; but her one-liners have a cumulative sameness of affect that inhibits a true essayistic movement. What most column writing does not seem to allow for is self-surprise, the sudden deepening or darkening of tone, so that the writer might say, with Lamb: "I do not know how, upon a subject which I began treating half-seriously, I should have fallen upon a recital so eminently painful. . . ."

From time to time I see hopeful panel discussions offered on "The Resurgence of the Essay," Yes, it would be very nice, and it may come about yet. The fact is, however, that very few American writers today are essayists primarily. Many of the essay collections issued each year are essentially random compilations of book reviews, speeches, journalism, and prefaces by authors who have made a name for themselves in other genres. The existence of these collections attests more to the celebrated authors' desires to see all their words between hardcovers than it does to any real devotion to the essay form. A tired air of grudgingly gracious civic duty hovers over many of these performances.

One recent American writer who did devote himself passionately to the essay was E. B. White. No one has written more consistently graceful, thoughtful essays in twentieth-century American language than White; on the other hand, I can't quite forgive his sedating influence on the form. White's Yankee gentleman-farmer persona is a complex balancing act between Whitmanian democratic and patrician values, best suited for the expression of mildness and tenderness with a resolute tug of elegiac depression underneath. Perhaps this is an unfair comparison, but there is not a single E. B. White essay that compares with the gamy, pungent, dangerous Orwell of "Such, Such Were the Joys . . ." or "Shooting an Elephant." When White does speak out on major issues of the day, his man-in-the-street, folksy humility and studiously plain-Joe air ring false, at least to me. And you would never know that the cute little wife he describes listening to baseball games on the radio was the powerful *New Yorker* editor Katharine White. The suppression or muting of ego as something ungentlemanly has left its mark on *The New Yorker* since, with the result that this magazine, which rightly prides itself on its freedom to publish extended prose, has not been a particularly supportive milieu for the gravelly voice of the personal essayist. The preferred model seems to be the scrupulously fair, sporting, impersonal, fact-gathering style of a John McPhee, which reminds me of nothing so much as a colony of industrious termites capable of patiently reducing any subject matter to a sawdust of detail.

The personal, familiar essay lives on in America today in an interestingly fragmented proliferation of specialized subgenres. The form is very much with us, particularly if you count the many popular nonfiction books that are in fact nothing but groups of personal essays strung together, and whose compelling subject matter makes the reading public overlook its ordinary indifference to this type of writing. Personal essays have also appeared for years under the protective umbrella of New Journalism (Joan Didion being the most substantial and quirky practitioner to emerge from that subsidized training ground, now largely defunct); of autobiographical-political meditations (Richard Rodriguez, Adrienne Rich, Vivian Gornick, Marcelle Clements, Wilfrid Sheed, Alice Walker, Nancy Mairs, Norman Mailer); nature and ecological-regional writing (Wendell Berry, Noel Perrin, John Graves, Edward Hoagland, Gretel Ehrlich, Edward Abbey, Carol Bly, Barry Lopez, Annie Dillard); literary criticism (Susan Sontag, Elizabeth Hardwick, Seymour Krim, Cynthia Ozick, Leslie Fiedler, Joyce Carol Oates); travel writing and mores (Mary McCarthy, V. S. Naipaul, Joseph Epstein, Eleanor Clark, Paul Theroux); humorous pieces (Max Apple, Roy Blount, Jr., Calvin Trillin); food (M. F. K. Fisher). I include this random and unfairly incomplete list merely to indicate the diversity and persistence of the form in American letters today. Against all odds, it continues to attract newcomers.

In Europe, the essay stayed alive largely by taking a turn toward the speculative and philosophical, as practiced by writers like Walter Benjamin, Theodor Adorno, Simone Weil, E. M. Cioran, Albert Camus, Roland Barthes, Czeslaw Milosz, and

Nicola Chiaromonte. All, in a sense, are offspring of the epi-grammatic style of Nietzsche. This fragmented, aphoristic, crit-ical type of essay-writing became used as a subversive tool of skeptical probing, a critique of ideology in a time when large, synthesizing theories and systems of philosophy are no longer trusted. Adorno saw the essay, in fact, as a valuable counter-method: "The essay does not strive for closed, deductive or in-ductive construction. It revolts above all against the doctrine—deeply rooted since Plato—that the changing and ephemeral is unworthy of philosophy; against that ancient injustice toward the transitory, by which it is once more anathematized, concep-tually. The essay shies away from the violence of dogma. . . . The essay gently defies the ideals of [Descartes'] *clara et distincta perceptio* and of absolute certainty. . . . Discontinuity is essential to the essay . . . as characteristic of the form's groping intention. . . . The slightly yielding quality of the essayist's thought forces him to greater intensity than discursive thought can offer; for the essay, unlike discursive thought, does not proceed blindly, au-tomatically, but at every moment it must reflect on itself. . . . Therefore the law of the innermost form of the essay is heresy. By transgressing the orthodoxy of thought, something becomes visible in the object which it is orthodoxy's secret purpose to keep invisible."

This continental tradition of the self-reflexive, aphoristically subversive essay is only now beginning to have an influence on contemporary American writers. One saw it first, curiously, crop-ping up in ironic experimental fiction—in Renata Adler, William Gass, Donald Barthelme, John Barth. Their fictive discourse, like Kundera's, often resembles a broken essay, a personal/philosoph-ical essay intermixed with narrative elements. The tendency of many postmodernist storytellers to parody the pedantry of the essay voice speaks both to their intellectual reliance on it and to their uneasiness about adopting the patriarchal stance of the Knower. That difficulty with assumption of authority is one rea-son why the essay remains "broken" for the time being.

In a penetrating discussion of the essay form, Georg Lukács put it this way: "The essay is a judgment, but the essential, the value-determining thing about it is not the verdict (as is the case with the system), but the process of judging." Uncomfortable words for an age when "judgmental" is a pejorative term. The familiar essayists of the past may have been nonspecialists—indeed, this was part of their attraction—but they knew how to speak with a generalist's easy authority. That is precisely what contemporary essayists have a hard time doing: in our technical age we are too aware of the advantage specialists hold over us. (This may explain the current confidence the public has in the physician-scientist school of essayists like Lewis Thomas, Richard Selzer, Stephen Jay Gould, F. Gonzalez-Crussi, Oliver Sacks: their meditations are embedded in a body of technical information, so that readers are reassured they are "learning" something, not just wasting their time on *belles lettres*.) The last of the old-fashioned generalists, men of letters who seemed able to write comfortably, knowledgeably, opinionatedly on everything under the sun, were Edmund Wilson and Paul Goodman; we may not soon see their like again.

In *The Last Intellectuals*, Russell Jacoby has pointed out the reticence of writers of the so-called generation of the sixties—my generation—to play the role of the public intellectual, as did Lionel Trilling, Harold Rosenberg, C. Wright Mills, Irving Howe, Alfred Kazin, Daniel Bell, Dwight Macdonald, Lionel Abel, etc., who judged cultural and political matters for a large general readership, often diving into the melee with both arms swinging. While Jacoby blames academia for absorbing the energies of my contemporaries, and while others have cited the drying up of print outlets for formal polemical essays, my own feeling is that it is not such a terrible thing to want to be excused from the job of pontificating to the public. Ours was not so much a failure to become our elders as it was a conscious swerving to a different path. The Vietnam War, the central experience of my generation, had a great deal to do with that deflection. As a veteran of the sixties, fooled many times about world politics because I had no firsthand knowledge of circumstances thousands of miles away (the most shameful example that comes to mind was defending, at first, the Khmer Rouge regime in Cambodia),

I have grown skeptical of taking righteous public positions based on nothing but simpatico media reports and party feeling. As for matters that I've definitely made up my mind about, it would embarrass me, frankly, to pen an opinion piece deploring the clearly deplorable, like apartheid or invading Central America, without being able to add any new insights to the discussion. One does not want to be reduced to scolding, or to abstract progressive platitudes, well founded as these may be. It isn't that my generation doesn't think politics are important, but our earlier experiences in that storm may have made us a little hesitant about mouthing off in print. We—or I should say I—have not yet been able to develop the proper voice to deal with these large social and political issues, which will at the same time remain true to personal experience and hard-earned doubt.

All this is a way of saying that the present moment offers a remarkable opportunity for emerging essayists who can somehow locate the moral authority, within or outside themselves, to speak to these issues in the grand manner. But there is also room, as ever, for the informal essayist to wrestle with intellectual confusion, to offer feelings, to set down ideas in a particularly direct and exposed format—more so than in fiction, say, where the author's opinions can always be disguised as belonging to characters. The increasing willingness of contemporary writers to try the form, if not necessarily commit themselves to it, augurs well for the survival of the personal essay. And if we do offend, we can always fall back on Papa Montaigne's *"Que sçay-je?"*: What do I know?

II

# NEVER LIVE ABOVE YOUR LANDLORD

Last week, the writing workshop I give for teachers at P.S. 90 met at my apartment. (We rotate houses, and my turn had finally come up.) Just after the class began—everyone seated in a semicircle, discussing one of their poems—there was a banging on the door, followed by the gruff voice of my landlady, Mrs. Rourke, who unfortunately lives right beneath me: "What's going on in there?"

I apologized to the group for the interruption and went to see what was on her mind. "Did you want to speak to me?" I asked, shutting the door behind me.

"What's going on? How many people you got visiting you?"

"Just about ten. They're quiet."

"Well, you can't have that many. This place isn't zoned for a school! It's against the law."

"There's no school, these people have never been here before."

"I don't care, you can't be going back and forth like this opening the door."

"No one else is coming. Don't worry."

"My husband wants to talk to you," she concluded, with the irritated snarl of W. C. Fields. They both talk that way, like Fields on a tear.

After the class I go downstairs and knock on their door. They're watching television; he's in his yellow terry-cloth robe and sandals. I make the mistake of thinking he will be more rational and calm than his wife. Addressing my comments mostly to him, I explain that I run a workshop of eleven people who meet in each other's homes, and that every three or four months it may fall on me to invite the group over. Is that all right? In fact, I know I have the legal right to visitors in my apartment, but I start by framing the request as a favor. She, suddenly well disposed, interrupts: "Jimmy, what do you think? He wants to know if it's okay."

Her husband moves his head stiffly like a G-man and looks at her intently, without answering.

"I'm bringing it up now," I explain, "so that the next time—"

"I understand, you don't want to be embarrassed," she sympathizes. If she understands this much, why did she run upstairs snapping at us like a cocker spaniel earlier?

"Right, I don't want to be embarrassed, or humiliated, in front of my guests."

"Well, it's nice of you to come and talk about it with us," she says. "What do you think, Jimmy?"

Mr. Rourke looks congenial, up to a point. Then, suddenly, his thick eyebrows knit, his voice fills with anger: "When we ask for a few extra dollars in rent you complain."

"The guy next door to you is paying fifty dollars more!" she jumps in excitedly. "And he doesn't get no separate bedroom like you. You got the Presidential Suite."

"We don't want them coming here. What we're afraid is, you got a school of some kind up there. You're running a professional office upstairs!" Rourke yells.

"The government doesn't think so. I can't even take it off my income tax."

"I don't care what the government thinks. I'm telling you, you are using it as an office. You're typing day and night. The ceiling's starting to come down. I may have to put in a whole new ceiling!" he says. (I smile at the idea that my pecking away can be causing such structural damage.) "You fill all our garbage cans with your papers—"

"Now wait a minute, that's an exaggeration."

"—And then you slam the door and the whole house shakes. I told you, mister, to fix that door, but nooooo, you don't want to. You don't want to do a lot of things!"

"Would you like to fix the door?" I ask. "It's your building."

"No, you fix it. You're a professional man."

"But let's return to the question I asked—"

"Jimmy, you're wasting his time. He wants to know about the visitors."

"We don't want 'em. They're strangers, they can't come in here."

"Mr. Rourke! I've been living here for four years, and I've had one party in all that time and a few small meetings. The group I had over tonight is very quiet. They just read and write."

"They're weird. They're bohemians, who knows? We don't want their crazy kind—"

"Have you seen them?"

"I've seen 'em all."

"You must have a periscope."

"I've seen them, and I don't want 'em around!"

"First of all, they're not bohemians. You know what they are?" I pause, and answer triumphantly: "They're *schoolteachers*."

"Schoolteachers!" Now he's really angry. "They're the stupidest of the lot. I only had two years of college myself, don't get me wrong, I'm no intellectual. But schoolteachers are the most ignorant goddamn bunch of all. They can't even speak the king's English! All a New York City schoolteacher can say is 'Be that as it may.'"

"Be that as it may! Be that as it may! That's all they know," she chimes in.

"Let me tell you something: I used to run an antique shop," he says. "And the worst people who ever came in were school-teachers and doctors. They're the kinds that give us the most trouble. We used to sell fine art sometimes, if it was included in the estate. Watercolors by John Singer Sargent, and Bierstadt. You ever heard of Bierstadt?"

"Yes. Albert Bierstadt, nineteenth-century American land-scape painter."

"Well, these—schoolteachers would ask to see everything in the store." His left eyelid with the mole started twitching just at the memory. "And then they wouldn't buy a thing. And they never even heard of John Singer Sargent!"

"But"—I almost said, *be that as it may*, and caught myself—"my understanding is that I have a legal right to invite people into my home any time I want, as long as they're not rowdy."

"I'm tellin' ya, we don't want 'em! You squawk about a few extra lousy dollars in rent. If you don't like it, why don't you move out? That's all. Buy your own building."

"I think you're overestimating my income—"

"You got plenty of money. You're a professional man. Buy your own building upstate somewhere, one of those old one-room schoolhouses. That'll solve your problem."

"All right, I won't have them over again."

He doesn't want to hear this now, he's too incensed. "Go buy your own building!" he repeats.

"I said I won't ask them over. I'm agreeing with you."

"When that door slams, the whole house shakes."

"And go easy on the toilet, Mr. Lopat," she inserts. I give her an odd look: Does she want me to flush less, or shit less? "Some-times you let the seat drop and we can hear it down here. It makes an awful racket!"

Meanwhile, their dog, a poodle, has come up and begun licking my shoe. All I can do is watch him and smile, as Mr. Rourke continues to rant. "Aries, get away from there," Mrs. Rourke cries.

"You understand, I'm not trying to be unfriendly," concludes my landlord.

"I think you *are* trying to be unfriendly," I reply, as I start to leave.

"Well, get the hell out of here!" he yells. When I reach my landing, he is still yelling. He'll cool off by tomorrow.


Although I consider myself a good tenant, clean and quiet and unobtrusive, my landlord and landlady, because of our close proximity, hear every sound I make, and cannot bring themselves to stop resenting the fact that I come in the door, that I take off my shoes, that I open the refrigerator—in short, that I live and breathe. The ideal tenant is, to them, someone who sends in the monthly rent check punctually but does not occupy the premises. I discovered this when they began fondly reminiscing about the previous tenant, a Hungarian architect who spent half the year building prefab condos in Barbados. Certainly their property must take much less wear and tear when no one is in it; alas, I can never live up to the standard set by my "invisible" predecessor, my Rebecca, as it were. When I finally complained that the tiny kitchenette in the corner of my main room had no sink and that I had to go into the bathroom to wash the dishes, they were quick to inform me that the architect never used the cooking facilities; he took all his meals in restaurants.

On the one hand, although the Rourkes rent self-contained units to a fairly transient population in the middle of Manhattan, my landlords have the almost charmingly old-fashioned, busy-body mentality of the owners of a "respectable" boardinghouse, entitled to pry into the degree of wholesomeness of their tenants. On the other hand, they seem never to have quite accepted that the entire house is not their dwelling. A thin, four-story brownstone, its scale is such that it could be a one-family home—and indeed, it began that way. When my landlady mops the stairs (she's a tireless housekeeper, I'll give her that), I hear her muttering to herself about this tenant or that, as though they were her poor relations who had overstayed their welcome.

Sometimes I watch my landlord tending the garden outside their basement apartment. From my window, I have a good over-view of him, padding around, usually in his yellow robe, squat and bowlegged as an old Japanese retiree, perfectly at peace with his roses or tomato plants. At such moments I find him admirable. When I want to get in his good graces, I ask him what he's planting this year. Rourke gives me a half-hour botanical lecture: he has shrewd eyes, and certainly realizes I don't understand or care about all this gardening lore. But such are the ways we find to get along, when we are getting along.

Once, during the winter, I came upon him in front of the house; he had just cleared a path in the snow and was admiring his shovel work. We stood around talking, and he told me he had been a semipro baseball player down in Florida before World War II. I assumed, since he is only a few inches taller than five feet, that he had played shortstop; but no, he was a first-base-man. I admired and liked him this time, too.

Sometimes I listen to his fights with his wife. (They must listen to mine as well.) Their fights are usually about money: one accuses the other of being too softhearted and letting an electri-cian or merchant gyp them. I've never heard them making love. Maybe they don't anymore, or maybe they do it very quietly.

The wife is both shriller and easier to get around. It's a tired literary device to characterize someone with an animal metaphor, but what can I do when I have such a mutt of a landlady? After scratching on my door, she bolts into the living room, her dirty-blond-gray hair plastered at odd angles from her head. "Mr. Lopat!" she barks. She has a harsh way of saying my name that stops me in my tracks, like a flashlight pointed at a burglar.

I am resigned to her letting herself in with her keys whenever she wants. One time, however, it made for some embarrassment; I was entertaining a pretty woman visitor, on my lap. Mrs. Rourke took her in immediately—sniffed her out, I should say—and proceeded to ignore her. "Mr. Lopat! Were you watering your plants too much?"

"No."

" 'Cause it's leaking over our heads. Something's leaking. Did you just water your plants?"

"No!" I said, starting to get annoyed. "I wish I had; they needed it."

"Let me take a look." She bounded over to the window on her thick little ankle-socked legs and stuck her snout under the radiator. "The board's warped! It's leaking all over. I'll go get Jimmy."

Moments later, Mr. Rourke entered with his tools, grinning from ear to ear, enjoying, it would seem, the comedy of their interrupting a romantic scene. "Will you look at that?" he declared, kneeling by the radiator cap.

"Jimmy, it's leakin' all over! I thought it was the plants but he says he didn't water the plants."

"I know that! What are you telling me that for? Don't talk nonsense, Kate. . . . How do you like that! It's been turned a full turn since the last time. Maybe you got ghosts here. I hope you're not afraid of ghosts, mister."

"No."

"Nor am I. Well, but how do you explain who did it?" he asked roguishly, the implication being that I had monkeyed with the valve. He tinkered a minute more. "I'll have to come by tomorrow and look at it." They exited as suddenly as they had appeared; back to their kennel, I suppose.


Whenever anything goes wrong with the plumbing (the pipes in the brownstone are very old), the Rourkes always try to make me feel defensive, as if it were my fault. An anally shaming connotation is given to clogged drains. One day this note was slipped under my door:

> Please do not use the wash Basin to empty the dirt and
> cat litter in. Use a Pail and throw it *in your toilet.*
>     This Past week the Basin was Packed full of junk.
> and we used $9.95 *worth* of Drain Power. Then I had to

get my Plumber to dislodge the dirt. Let the water run
to clear the drain in that sink. Please throw the stuff in
the toilet and flush. Next thing the Pipes will get
leaking.

Mrs. Rourke

My answer:

Dear Mrs. Rourke:
    What makes you think I am emptying cat litter and
dirt in the wash basin!! This is an absurd contention.
Please make sure you know whereof you speak before
you start making baseless and, frankly, fantastic
accusations.

Sincerely,<br>Phillip Lopate

I held my breath for the next few days, thinking that perhaps
I had gone too far this time. Yet when I ran into my landlady in
the hallway, she was almost respectful. Not that our epistolary
relationship ended there. I keep all the notes she slips under my
door, among which is this quaintly worded favorite:

Please stop that
jungle drum music.

———

or whatever it is.

———

I'm going out of my mind.
    Bang    Bang    Bang.
        Mrs. Rourke

Since I don't often listen to music I was a bit insulted at the time,
but I turned off the jazz station I had on.
    All these skirmishes are part of the "class struggle" that we are
obliged to wage as tenant and landlord. The trouble is, underneath everything, we like each other, which complicates the

purity of the antagonism. That murkiness began the very first day, when I answered the Rourkes' ad. I had come dressed in suit and tie, to radiate respectability; I instantly fell in love with the apartment, with its high ceilings, garden window, floor-length mirror, and genteel-seedy Edwardian furnishings. I noted the ornate molding with rhythmical slits, which Rourke proudly told me was called "dentile" work. He seemed delighted to have impressed me, a seemingly educated person, with his knowledge. Perhaps it was nothing more than that which softened him. Or perhaps they saw me, for one split second, as a sort of son. Whatever the reason, when I told them it was twenty dollars a month more than I could afford, they let me have the apartment anyway, at the lower figure.

Since then they have been playing "catch-up," trying to undo that first mistake of generosity. They grumble as though I had swindled them, refusing to acknowledge that their real bafflement is at their own initial charity. My rent has been raised many times, but it is still a bargain compared to the other rents in the building, and in light of how expensive the neighborhood has gotten. Nevertheless, I bellow like a gored bull whenever they confront me with a new increase, because I believe that it is my role to make them feel guilty for bringing up such demands, just as it is theirs to make me feel reluctant about suggesting repairs.

Once, after giving me a song and dance about rising oil fuel costs, Mrs. Rourke admitted (or I got her to admit) that this was a good time for landlords. "But we got to take in all the money we can. Supposing they put another freeze on us. Like in forty-four. So you have to charge now whatever you can get away with, 'cause it could end any minute."

"It's going to last for the indefinite future, in Manhattan at least."

"Come on, forty dollars more ain't gonna hurt ya. It's a business—you understand. If you moved out I could raise it thirteen percent extra. Everyone wants to live on this block. I got these guys living upstairs in single rooms, they pay more than you. They work for the UN and they only make twenty-three thousand."

"But I don't even make *twenty* thousand."

"But you got the possibility to make a lot more, 'cause you're on your own. These guys that work for the government or a corporation, what do they have to look forward to? They get together and drink beer at—P. J. Clarke's or someplace, and they talk about who's gonna get a raise. But you're on your own, you got all kinds of ways to make money. You could make a million. All you got to do is write garbage, trash. That's what the public wants."

"Okay, I'll try."

"Try, Mr. Lopat. You can do it."

"You could, too, probably."

"What am I going to write about? My 'misspent youth'? All the things I didn't do and should've?" she said, laughing and, much to my surprise, giving me a wink.

She does have her kindly side. Sometimes I come home and find that the bathroom floor has been scrubbed, or the dishes washed. She also fed my cat one weekend when I went away; apparently Milena resisted the dry food I had left out and was yowling in a sulk. Mrs. Rourke went out and bought her some canned liver, in spite of the fact that she hates my having a pet in the apartment.

Yesterday, Mrs. Rourke came in to investigate something and stayed to chat for over an hour. I was feeling tired and relaxed, and I encouraged her to talk. She practically told me her life story. Afterward I wrote down everything I could remember, as close to verbatim as possible. Herein, then, is

## THE LANDLADY'S TALE

*I don't like to rent to women. Because they're always picky, picky, they start finding fault with this and that. They want tiles in the bathroom. Men are more easily satisfied. You can tell a man something and he'll agree or disagree, but that's that. He says to himself, she probably had a headache today. But a woman, she's vindictive, she remembers.*

*I had one woman in here, she was a nice-looking girl, blond and slim, she said to me, "If I get this place I'll never give you a moment's trouble." So, fine,* she took the place and the next thing I know she's complaining, there's no heat. I says, Okay, I'll come up and fix it. "Oh," she says, "you can't just come into my house, you have to tell me first. You have to notify me. And you can't come today, you have to come Friday." So all right, I figured forget it. The next thing I know she's all upset. She's seen a cockroach. I said why don't you get an exterminator? She said, "I know my rights, you have to supply me with an exterminator." Oh, she was screaming like she'd never seen a cockroach before. I said, "What are you scared of a little cockroach for when you got that big gorilla sleeping in your bed?" Ha! She was so surprised when I said that. But I'd seen him coming in and out, a guy like a gorilla with a big beard. He belonged to that Puerto Rican Independence party. He had these tapes going on loud, Viva-this and Down with Anaconda-that. One day I knock on the door and I says to him, "Listen, I didn't rent my rooms for this. If you want to play your anti-American speeches why don't you put down a few bucks and hire a meeting hall?" He said to me, all red in the face, "Don't you bother me, get out of here!" I was a little scared. He could be a bomber! Could blow the whole building up! He had all these guys with Castro beards coming in and out, sitting on the stoop. Agitators. I says to him, "Listen, I'm not afraid of you. If you keep this up I'll call the FBI and have you investigated."

So the next thing I know the girl comes to me and says, "Mrs. Rourke, you got the wrong idea! He doesn't sleep with me." So I went in with my Instamatic when she wasn't there and I took pictures. He had his shoes lying on the floor and his pants and underpants! I wasn't planning to do anything with the pictures, but just if she started something. So she moves out real fast. Left me a nice note. She was a sweet-looking girl, you know. I went in there to clean up and it turned out she had shut the radiator off! That's why it was always so cold. But she wouldn't let me in to check. That's why I don't like women tenants. A friend of mine owns a building down the block, number forty-four. She rented it to a girl and the girl has her gurus coming up and down. Two o'clock in the morning they start meditatin'. Making noise, like O-maa-aa-wuuu. When everybody's sleeping. My friend says, "Oh, I want to kill that woman!" But what can she do? Nothing.

This friend of mine's daughter went to Vegas. To my way of thinking she was very plain-looking. No hips, no bust, no face, no legs, nothing. She met this insurance man who was a millionaire and she married him! I don't know what he saw in her, the daughter. Maybe it was one of those things—an attraction. Maybe he liked the way she threw the dice. He died. He had a heart attack, all of a sudden a sharp pain! The artery bursted. Now she's got a million. See, maybe if I went to Reno and been at the right spot I could've been rich by now. But instead I came to New York and I'm still struggling. I didn't plan to stay in New York. I just came here to make something of myself and get out. I came from Pennsylvania. I wanted to get into show business. But I was too short. Too short for a Roxyette. Nowadays they take 'em small. Then it was a certain look they wanted: tall, baby face, a little plump, you know. Now they like that starved look. I had a friend back then who was a big model, Babe Casey. She was a gorgeous girl. You must have seen that Unguentine ad, you know, with the girl bending over. That's her. Edna. They called her Babe though. She went into the Ziegfeld Follies. Then she married somebody rich from down South. She's probably passed on by now. Anyway, she got me a few jobs posing for ski ads. Twenty-five bucks an hour. Good money. In those days, though, you had to bring your own clothes on the job. If it was a ski shot you had to go out and buy a pair of skis.

Meanwhile I was working at the Downtown Athletic Club, waiting on tables for their luncheon meal. They only paid you a dollar an hour, but the tips were what made it. I could come home sometimes with thirty, forty dollars in change. They were always after me. One old guy says to me, "What kind of lipstick you like?" I says, "Any kind I can get!" He left me a five-dollar tip. Another guy had a big Packard, rode around with the hood down. He says to me, "How'd you like to be living in the Essex House?" "Fine," I says, "but what do I have to do for it?" Besides, I noticed that this guy had a different girl with him every time I saw him. So if you did what he said, you'd be living at the Essex House, and the next thing you knew he'd be sending up his friends to entertain. Sure! Before you knew it you'd be living the life of a real hustler. I wasn't interested in sleeping with men. Oh, I'd go on dates. When I was hungry! My girlfriend and I were living in the same residence hotel, and she was a beautiful thing, looked like Jean Harlow. The men would invite her out to dinner and she'd say, "But you have to take my girlfriend, too." We'd go to the Roxy together and then have a big meal on them and never see 'em again. Hello and good-bye, that sort of routine.

I had one fella who was after me, Ripley's secretary. You know Ripley's Believe It or Not? He was the guy who used to research it. A brilliant man, everybody said. He came to the Athletic Club, he would write me poems. All about my hair. A lovely guy. The other girls said, "Gee, you're lucky.

*That's the man for you, Kate, he'll make a great husband." But I didn't love him. He had gray hair. And I was eighteen.*

*I would always tell the men what they wanted to hear. To get a tip, you know? One customer would say, "What are you doing tomorrow?" I'd say, "Oh, it's my mother's birthday and I've got to take her out. If only I could take her somewhere special!" He'd leave me five dollars. You have to make up something interesting, that's what men like. They don't want to hear the same old story. One man says to me, "Will you be here next week?" I says, "Not only next week, I'll be here forever." That kind of thing.*

*Then I met my husband. I was living in this residence hotel on the same floor as my girlfriend, and there was a man in the middle between our two rooms. Rosenzweig. We used to share the wash basin. He'd say, "Girls, are you going to be in there for long?" And my girlfriend would say, "Yes we're going to be in there for very long. You don't like it?" He says, "I can't stand it anymore!" She was always trying to get a rise out of him. So one day he was trying to be friendly, and he invited both of us into his room. I saw he had a caricature on the wall of himself. This Mr. Rosenzweig had an unusually large—nose. And it was all there in the cartoon. I says, "That's very good, it's a good likeness." He says, "Oh, that's by my friend Jimmy Rourke, he's an artist. He's from Florida. He's coming into town next week, and if you girls are nice I'll introduce you to him." My girlfriend says, "Ah, we don't want to meet any friend of yours." She was always trying to get him riled up.*

*So the next weekend he left his door open next to the wash basin, a signal that he was inviting us to join them. They were going to a baseball game. So we all went to the game, and that's how I met Jimmy. I knew right away. I told my friend, "I found somebody I want to marry." We went together for a year. We were like two puppies. Oh, we had a lot of fun. What I liked about him was that he was so easy. If we were walking along and I saw a Max Factor makeup kit in the window that I liked, he went right inside and bought it for me. Never asked for a thing in return. Not even a kiss. Most men, they would say, "How about a kiss first?" I said to myself, Here's a man.*

*When we got married we both had jobs, so we took an eight-room apartment on West 105th Street. The rent was only fifty-four dollars a month then! I fixed up one part and rented it out to an Irish couple as a one-bedroom apartment. They were paying eleven dollars a week, which was a lot of money for the time. Then I heard about this building we're in now. A friend told me* about it. It was owned by a Jewish woman with big legs. It was getting too much for her, she was getting too old to run the place. So we bought it. Then we went into antiques. We ran antique stores for thirty years. All the dealers knew me, they used to call me Kiss-Me-Kate.

I had a friend who was an interior decorator named Gladys, she used to bring her clients around. What she would charge 'em! She'd bring in this judge's wife, Mrs. Gold. And tell her: "You have to have this Biedermeier in your home." The woman would say: "Vat I gotta haf dat ugly ting in my house?" Gladys would tell her, "But it won't look like this when I get through with it. I have the finest Italian artist who's going to transform it into the most beautiful thing you ever saw. Just write out a check for six hundred dollars, that's what I paid Mrs. Rourke for it." She'd bought it from me for two hundred! I says to her when we're alone, "Gladys, don't you have no shame at all?" She laughs and says, "Why should I? I have to take that dumb woman to lunch and all around town in cabs and I keep picking up the bill. My husband and I play cards with the judge and her. And we lose. We lose all the time, on purpose. Nah, I got no time for pitying her." "Well, that's a different story," I says. So we both had a good laugh.

When Jimmy and I sold our business we had some money to invest. But we missed our opportunities. I could have had that office building on 72nd Street for ninety-eight thousand dollars. The one with the beautiful iron doors. But Jimmy said it was too expensive. To him everything was always too expensive. You know what it's worth now? A million! The point of it is: invest. And there's nothin' like real estate. Oh, what we could have picked up after the war. But you're young and you don't want responsibilities. Invest while you're young, that's the point I'm making. I used to have this friend, Mr. Hermann, he was a stockbroker. And a real gentleman. Oh, Jimmy didn't like him! Thought he was paying too much attention to me. One time we were at a dancing party and I asked Mr. Hermann if he had any good tips for investments. He took me into his arms and started whirling me around the room, and all the while he was whispering in my ear, "Gold! Gold! Gold!"

The next thing I know, gold is going up through the ceiling. I should've listened to him. He gave me another good tip: there was a place just across the street, a penthouse. It used to be where servants hung the wash. I could have picked it up for twenty-five thousand, put in another thirty-five thousand and we'd have had a beautiful roof apartment. The sun would be shining in on us every day. I told my husband, "Jimmy, I want to move there." He says, "Go *ahead. I'll even sign the papers. But I'm staying here. I'm not going to move into no roof apartment. We'd get mugged." I says, "What do I want to go live there by myself for?" You know what I think? Jimmy was jealous! Anything to do with Mr. Hermann, he didn't trust.*

*Besides, he doesn't want to change. I heard about other places to fix up. Now I can't be bothered. I'm close to seventy, I don't want to start a whole new enterprise. We talk about who we're going to leave this house to. There's my niece, but she's still like a hippy. She's over thirty and she's taking art lessons! That's not so bad, but she's been married and divorced and got two kids and now she's getting the government to pay for her art lessons. I sort of feel she's missed the boat. Know what I mean? It's too late for that, you get past a certain point in life. . . .*

*I says, Jimmy, let's leave it to the dog!*

*There was an old guy who lived in the Dakota, left a fortune that way. The will saw that so much every month would be spent on feeding and care of the animal. So this fella who was taking care of it, he drew a good salary, he was living high, all he had to do was walk the dog and feed it. And the dog died. So the fella was devastated. He went to the lawyer and said, "What am I going to do?" The lawyer thought and thought, and finally he said, "I'll tell you what to do. Get another dog that's almost like the one who died and take care of him."*

I'll stop here, because my hand is tired. In any case, you get the idea. Twenty-four hours later, her chatter still flows on and on in my head; she's so real, Mrs. Rourke, with her innocence and her Unguentine ads, her obsession with making money and her inability to go in for the kill. Why aren't I real the way she is? She's a character, all right, and she has certainty, however narrow its intellectual base. *Ils sont dans le vrai,* said Flaubert, the visionary artist envying the bourgeoisie out for a Sunday walk in the park. How tiresome. No, I don't envy the Rourkes exactly, but I'm fond of their postwar-America outlook. I envy their past; the very word "postwar" in fact gives me a jolt of warmth, with its promise of young married couples starting off on a new life. My parents were still hopeful in 1945; I was two years old, barely able to toddle, certainly unable to appreciate the tonal brilliance of forties *film noir* or bebop that mean so much to me now. I suppose we often have a nostalgic affinity for the cultural era when we were still in the womb or barely out. A Freudian would say it was the Oedipal desire to crawl in between one's parents' lovemaking, to be in on one's conception. But the Rourkes—to think of them as a young couple, a union of baseball and the Ziegfeld Follies, with all the world ahead of them, only to end up finally, by imperceptible declensions and fateful turns, that most morally suspect of creatures, New York landlords. Well, they're honest ones, at least. Still, what happened to Jimmy's artistic ambitions? Or the children—why are there no children? Don't leave it to the poodle, for God's sake! Think of your poor, put-upon tenant, your long-lost son!

# REVISIONIST

# NUPTIALS

$N$othing arouses my ire more than the practice of brides and grooms rewriting the traditional wedding ceremony and making speeches of their vows. There is something unseemly about this intervention by the supposed recipient of grace, like Napoleon seizing the coronet and crowning himself.

Marriage I take to be a submission to the social and religious laws of the community, and the charm of the traditional ceremony was that the participants were properly submissive. Often you could not even hear the responses, they were delivered in such a murmur. The silence of the listening couple, broken only at one point by shy monosyllabic avowals, made a nice contrast to the confident, expounding voice of the clergyman or officiating party. And the familiarity of the words had a lulling effect, allowing the audience's attention to stray to physical details of dress and architecture. Traditionally, the couple were seen either in quarter-profile or with their backs fully turned. Now, as "backs to the audience" is considered a cardinal sin for stage performers, such a posture emphasized that *this* man and woman were not before us as entertainers; they were engaged in their own special drama, the importance of which permitted them the breaking of this old stage rule. Their backs provided also, I think, a screen of delicacy, to protect the feelings of those in the crowd who were less amorously blessed. It is bad enough to have to witness people in love vowing devotion forever, but to have them turn around and face us and boast is really too much.

The non-traditional newlyweds become orators instead of or-ants, and, in doing so, encourage us to judge them by the stricter critical standards of rhetoric. "I liked your speech," one says afterward to the groom, as to a politician—rather than "I'm so happy for you!"

I went to a revisionist wedding recently. First the clergy-woman, dressed as an Indian princess, disdaining any prepared texts, improvised a poem on the spot, chanting phrases about love and work and accompanying them with mime gestures of a Hopi-like nature, such as the pounding of maize and the tum-bling of a waterfall. This took place in a crowded loft in Manhat-tan. Then friends and relatives delivered testimonials to the fine characters of the lovers. A young man, stocky and bearded, who —rumor circulated—still carried a torch for the bride, read one of Whitman's short sensual poems. It seemed an odd choice, in light of the fact that the clasped bosoms Whitman was referring to belonged to two hairy men. Was this a jinx on the newlyweds? Then the mother of the bride, a notoriously critical parent, ex-pressed pride and pleasure in her daughter's recent professional successes and praised the gentleness of the groom. A sigh of relief went through the room that she had not been more patronizing. She was followed by the groom's nine-year-old daughter, who made a little speech about how much she was expecting to like her new mommy.

All these remarks were capped by the bride's and groom's prepared statements. Each several pages long, the speeches were models of nonsexist sentiment, with pledges to share the domestic work and respect the other's space. True, they were not all jargon: they had certain moments of attractive candor. The bride, for instance, stated that she was glad she would be gaining a daughter along with a husband, since she was forty and had no intention of bearing children now. The groom said he expected to retain feelings of solitude for the rest of his life. They came across in these statements as decent, warm people; yet whenever they spoke about their love, it was uncomfortable to listen in. Their language seemed more suited for a wedding anniversary than the start of a new adventure. The fact—known to all present but never mentioned—that they had been living together for six years crept into the tone of every sentence, lending both their vows an air of weary apologia.

Perhaps it would be hypocritical nowadays to pretend the bride and groom are virgins. But to present oneself as already staidly uxorious seems a step too far in the opposite extreme, and an insult to the drama of matrimony.

Not that there aren't some good arguments for revisionist wedding ceremonies. Many modern couples come from different faiths, and, given the difficulty of finding a liturgy of such neutrality that it does not mention Christ, the Torah, Buddha, or even God, one is naturally tempted to write one's own. The understandable objections of feminists to the phrase "man and wife" and to other patriarchal insinuations also make the traditional script problematic. There is also the creative urge to surpass the old form and devise something better, more contemporary. But in trying to update liturgy, one immediately runs into the danger of sounding both trendy and anachronistic: in short, silly. The truth is that few of us have the theological gravity to pull off the revision of a religious rite.

I take exception in any case to the notion that modern life is bereft of rituals, and that we need self-consciously to re-sacralize the world. There are enough natural rites of passage of the deepest nature in any person's life span, from the discovery of sex to the death of a parent. Moreover, customs cannot be new-minted by composing personalized, disposable ceremonies for every occasion. A one-time-only tradition is no tradition at all.

For a while, there were weddings publicized because of their unusual locations: people married on home plate, or at the lettuce counter of the supermarket where they first met, or in a bowling alley. But the style of the eighties seems to be domestic. The couple is married at home, ensuring them maximum supervisory control over every detail. Perhaps because many are marrying for the second or third time, they may remember back with shame to the first youthful wedding, when they were steered about by parents and clergy. This time they will give *themselves* away.

Ah, hubris. The truth is that one way or another, the newlyweds-to-be remain sacrificial lambs led to the altar. Traditionally, this symbolism of sacrifice was expressed in the pair's cramped speech and handcuffed gestural constraint. Change that, allow them a chance to babble on, and you distort the true pathos of the situation.

If there is to be any reformation in the wedding ritual, I as an old Bachelor would propose that it be made more somber. Marriage is a serious, not to say tragic, business. Were I ever to marry again, I would like both bride and groom to be dressed in black, with sackcloth and ashes, and maybe a costumed Grim Reaper with scythe standing to the side, to remind the gathered assembly that here is the death of freedom and pleasure's variety.

# ANTICIPATION OF *LA NOTTE:* THE "HEROIC" AGE OF MOVIEGOING

One has to guard against the tendency to think of one's youth as a time when the conversations were brighter, the friends truer, and the movies better. I am quite willing to let go of the first two, but it does seem to have been my luck to have come of age during a period of phenomenal cinematic creativity. I like to think of the early sixties as the "heroic" age of moviegoing, if one can call heroic an activity that consists of sitting on one's bum and letting one's thoughts be guided by a parade of cinematic sensations.

It was in 1959, while a junior in high school, that my craving for celluloid and my avocation as a film buff began. Certainly I had always liked going to movies; my parents had sent us off, when we were children, to the neighborhood double feature every Saturday morning. But the notion of motion pictures as an art form only struck me when I was about fifteen. I bought Arthur Knight's survey, *The Liveliest Art,* and went about in my thorough, solemn way trying to see every movie listed in the index. One thing that attracted me to film history was that it was relatively short, conquerable, compared to other artistic fields. The Thalia Theater's repertory schedule became my summer school catalogue that year, and I checked off nearly everything as a must-see, still happily unable to distinguish beforehand between the worth of an M and a *Captain from Koepenick*.

I went so far as to subscribe to a series of Russian silent films at the Kaufman–92nd Street Y, defiantly attending *Earth* the night before an important exam. But Dovshenko's poetic style put me to sleep; even now I have only to picture waving wheat and apple-cheeked, laughing peasants for my eyes to start to close.

In my last two years of high school I was restless and used film showings as a pretext to get out of Brooklyn, away from my family, and explore the city. The 92nd Street Y, the Sutton, and the Beekman introduced me to the posh East Side; the Art and the 8th Street Theater were my ports of entry to Greenwich Village; I learned the Upper West Side from the Thalia and the New Yorker. It was a Flaherty revival at Columbia University that first gave me the idea, walking through the campus afterward, to apply there for admission.

Sometimes a film club ad would lead me to some church basement in Chelsea, to watch an old Murnau or Preston Sturges, projected by a noisy Bell & Howell set up on a chair in the back of a rec room. Often I was the youngest member of that film addict crowd, whose collective appearance made me wonder what I was getting myself into. They were predominately male, lower middle class, with the burdened look of having come straight from work with their rolled-up *New York Posts* and ink-stained trousers; they had indoor faces with pendulous eye bags, sharp noses ready to sniff out the shoddy, and physiques that seemed at once undernourished in some parts and plump in others, the result of hasty delicatessen meals snatched before screenings. They looked like widowers or young men who had never known love—this was the fraternity I was about to join. Some seemed abnormally shy; they would arrive a few minutes early and sit as far away from everyone else as they could; at "The End" they would leave without a word. Occasionally, one of the old, bald-headed veterans would engage me gregariously in spasmodic conversation—an exchange of film titles, punctuated with superlatives, snorts, complaints about the projection or the sight lines —and I would come away touched by his kindness for having talked to an ignorant kid like me, and perhaps for this reason would feel sorry for him.

Whether the film had been glorious or dull barely mattered, so long as I could cross it off my list. The development of a taste of any sort requires plodding through the overrated as well as uncovering the sublime. If the movie had been genuinely great, I would leave the screening place inspired and pleasantly conscious of my isolation, and wander the streets for a while before taking the subway home. I came to love the way the gray city streets looked after a movie, the cinematic blush they seemed to wear. When the film had been a disappointment—well then, all the more was it a joy to get back the true world, with its variety and uncanny compositions.


At Columbia, I discovered the general appetite for films was much higher than it had been at my high school; even the average student was willing to experiment with difficult fare. I remember going down to the Village one Friday night with a bunch of other dateless freshmen to see Kurosawa's *Ikiru*, part of a memorable season of Japanese premieres. Before the movie, just to get in the mood, we ate cross-legged on the floor at a Japanese restaurant. I adored *Ikiru*, with its perversely slow framing scene of the wake and its heart-wrenching flashbacks; but it also meant a lot to be sitting before it in a row of studious boys who I hoped would remain moviegoing friends. My own gang, as in *I Vitelloni* —except it didn't happen with this bunch. It took a while before I found my real film companions.

From time to time, film criticism would appear in the *Columbia Daily Spectator* by an upperclassman, James Stoller. His articles were so stylistically mature and so informed that they seemed to me to be written by a professional quarterly critic rather than a college student. I developed an intellectual crush on this Stoller: if his opinion differed from mine, I would secretly revise my own. I had been, for example, avoiding Satyajit Ray's films because their packaging suggested what Andrew Sarris called "dull UNESCO cinema." But Stoller wrote that the *Apu* trilogy was great, so I went, and he was right.

Finally I decided I had to meet James Stoller. Palms sweating, I summoned the courage to call his room from the phone downstairs in his dormitory. I explained that I was a fellow film lover. Could I stop by sometime and talk with him? Sure, come on up, he said.

It shocked me to see the great critic living in so tiny and shabby a room: a double-decker bed; a narrow desk, which he shared with his roommate; a single chair; and books. We had no place to sit but the lower bunk bed. It always surprised me— having come from a ghetto—that parts of Columbia should look so seedy and run-down. I suppose I was expecting the Ivy League to be a step upward.

Stoller himself gave an impression of fastidious hesitation and social awkwardness. I had come prepared to play the role of the freshman ignoramus and so was puzzled when he reacted incredulously to my praise of his articles, retreating into a modest shrug. When I asked if he had been yet to Michelangelo Antonioni's *L'Avventura*, the *cause célèbre* that had just opened and which I was dying to see, he said he had, and fell silent. "Well, what did you think of it?" I prodded, expecting him to erupt with the equivalent of one of his articles. "It's—terrific, I guess, I'm not sure, I need to watch it a few more times. . . . Go see for yourself." He was uncomfortable being put on the spot.

I rushed to see *L'Avventura*. It was the movie I had been preparing for, and it came at the right time in my development. As a child, I had wanted only action movies. Dialogues and story setups bored me; I waited for that moment when the knife was hurled through the air. My awakening in adolescence to the art of film consisted precisely in overcoming this impatience. Overcompensating, perhaps; I now loved a cinema that dawdled, that

Antonioni had a way of following characters with a pan shot, letting them exit and keeping the camera on the depopulated landscape. With his detachment from the human drama and his tactful spying on objects and backgrounds, he forced me to disengage as well, and to concentrate on the purity of his technique. Of course the story held me, too, with its bitter, world-weary, disillusioned tone. The adolescent wants to touch bottom, to know the worst. His soul craves sardonic disenchantment.

I rushed back to Stoller, now ready to discuss the film. He listened patiently and with quiet amusement to my enthusiasm. Indeed, this turned out to be our pattern: I, more ignorant but more voluble, would babble on, while he would offer an occasional objection or refinement. It was only by offering up chatter that I could get him to correct my misconceptions and to educate me cinematically.

This was not yet the era of film appreciation courses. Nor would we have dreamed of taking any offered; it was a point of pride to gather on our own the knowledge of our beloved, semi-underground subject, like the teenage garage-band aficionados of today.

Stoller introduced me to his friend Nicholas Zill, a film-obsessed sophomore, and we soon became a trio. Zill was a mischievous, intelligent boy of Russian Orthodox background who was given to sudden animated inspirations. The three of us took long walks together in the Columbia neighborhood, leap-frogging in our conversation from one film to another. Once, coming to a dead stop on the sidewalk, Zill asked me in horror, "You mean you haven't seen *Diary of a Country Priest?*" At such moments I felt like the baby of the group.

Zill and I both shared a zest for the grotesque, or what has been somewhat ponderously called "convulsive cinema," "the cinema of cruelty." I must say, these predilections were kept to the level of aesthetic appreciation; in our daily lives we were squeamishly decent, even if Zill, a psychology major, seemed to like cutting up rats. Nothing pleased us more than to talk about the beggars' orgy in *Viridiana*, or the maiming finale in *Freaks*, or choice bits in *Psycho*. We would go on in this perverse vein until Stoller was forced to remonstrate (which was probably why we did it). Stoller always championed the humane, the tender, the generous, and domestically observant moviemakers: Renoir, Ophuls, Truffaut, Satyajit Ray, Cukor, Borzage. It was typical for a powerless student like me to be drawn to Buñuelian fantasies of surrealist immorality and Raskolnikovian license. Much rarer was it to find balanced humanity in a nineteen-year-old, like Stoller. If I have come around over the years to his point of view, at the time I was looking for antisocial shivers, sliced eyeballs.

Nick Zill wanted to make movies—as I suppose we all did—but he went further in imagining bizarre film scenarios. He had already shot a film in high school; I remember it only as a disorganized romp of him chasing pretty girls, or was it pretty girls chasing him? In any case, he had registered an organization called Filmmakers of Columbia with the Campus Activities Office, so as to be able to borrow equipment and accept university funds should one of his projects ever get going. Filmmakers of Columbia existed only on paper; there were no meetings, even the title was pure wish fulfillment. As it happened, there *were* a number of "isolated" Columbia filmmakers (i.e., not in our circle) around, the most notable being young Brian DePalma. We did not know whether to consider DePalma's hammy experimental shorts like *Wotan's Wake* intentional or unintentional jokes, but we agreed that he had no future as a film director and that he was not a seriously knowledgeable, rigorous *cinéaste* like ourselves.

Sometimes I would go over to my friends' rooms and pass the time looking through their film magazine collections. Stills on glossy periodical stock particularly fascinated me. To stare at a shot from *Gilda*, say, with Rita Hayworth in her sheath dress before a palm-treed nightclub stand, was to enter a fantasy as satisfyingly complete, in its own way, as having seen the movie. A single frame, snatched from twenty-three others per second, is not intended to possess the self-complete wholeness of an art photograph, but for that very reason it evokes more the dream

of continuing motion. Stills from the silent era, with their gestural intensity and powder-white ingenues' faces; soft-lit glamour
shots from the thirties; the harsh key lighting and seamy locales
of the forties—all were infinitely suggestive of the way the reigning fashions, film stock, decor, directorial style, and technology
blended to produce a characteristic period image.

The desultory quality of these browsing sessions showed we
were perhaps not so far removed from that age when we'd col-
lected comic books and baseball cards. The point was not to read
the articles straight through (one could always go back for that),
but to be splashed by a sea of information: film festival roundups,
news of film productions, historical rediscoveries. By leafing
through these magazines together we shared a mood of sweet
latency, imagining the films we had in store, like provincials
dreaming of life in the capital. Cinema was a wave originating
elsewhere, which we waited to break over us. This waiting had
something to do with the nature of adolescence itself; it also
reflected the resurgence of European films at the time.

To be young and in love with films in the early 1960s was to
participate in what felt like an international youth movement.
We in New York were following and, in a sense, mimicking the
cafe arguments in Paris, London, and Rome, where the cinema
had moved, for a brief historical movement, to the center of
intellectual discourse, in the twilight of existentialism and before
the onslaught of structuralism.

In retrospect, I may have undervalued the American studio
films of the early sixties. At the time, having just lived through
the Eisenhower fifties, I was impatient with what seemed to me
the bland industrial style of most Hollywood movies (then sym-
bolized by the much-maligned Doris Day); I could spot Art much
more easily in foreign films, with their stylized codes of realism
(sex, boredom, class conflict, unhappy endings) and their arty
disjunctive texture. It took a certain sophistication, which I did
not yet have, to appreciate the ironies behind the smooth-crafted
surfaces of the best Hollywood genre movies. Our heroes in the
French New Wave explicitly credited Hollywood films with the
inspiration for their own personal styles, of course, but I accepted

this taste partly as a whimsical paradox on their part without really sharing it, except in the case of rebels like Samuel Fuller or Frank Tashlin, whose shock tactics made them "almost" European.

Sometimes, instead of studying, I would end up in the film section of the college library poring over books on movies by writers like Béla Balasz, Raymond Spottiswoode, Siegfried Kracauer, Hortense Powdermaker—even their names were irresistible. Or I would struggle through the latest *Cahiers du Cinéma* in the periodicals section. As if my French were not imperfect enough, the *Cahiers* critics confounded me further with their profundity-mongering style, rarely passing a simple judgment without at the same time alluding to Hegel. I was never sure that I fully understood anything in *Cahiers*, except for the interviews with salty old Hollywood directors, and the rating system, with stars like a Michelin guide: ** *à voir*, *** *à voir absolument*, and a black dot • for *abominable*.

*Sight and Sound* was a breeze in comparison, although I was ashamed to admit to my friends how much I got from the English journal. It was considered stodgy and rearguard, perhaps because it was the official organ of the British Film Institute, but probably more because it took issue with *Cahiers du Cinéma's auteur* line— and we were deeply devoted auteurists. (I am using this term as shorthand for a critical approach recognizing the director as the main artist of a film, and looking at the body of a director's work for stylistic consistencies.)

I hesitate to raise a last-ditch defense of the *auteur* theory, so tattered has its flag become in recent years. Suffice to say that I remain loyal to the ideals of my youth. Say what you may against the *auteur* theory, it was good for adolescents: it gave us a system, and—more important—it gave us marching directions; it encouraged hero worship; it argued for the triumphant signature of selfhood in the face of conformist threats; it made clear distinctions between good and bad; and it blew the raspberry at pious sentiment.

Andrew Sarris's auteurist breakdown of American directors, which first appeared as a special issue of *Film Culture*, spring 1963, influenced us deeply partly because of its ruthlessly hierarchical ranking system: Pantheon Directors, Second Line, Likable But Elusive, Esoterica, Less Than Meets the Eye, and that most sinisterly fascinating of categories, Fallen Idols. It was here we learned to curl our lips at respected names like Fred Zinnemann, David Lean, and Stanley Kramer—liberal directors whose hearts and themes may have been in the right place but whose earnestly conventional handling of *mise-en-scène* seemed unforgivable.

Ah, *mise-en-scène!* That camera style that favored flowing tracking shots and pans, wide angles and continuous takes; that followed characters up staircases and from room to room, capturing with rich detail their surroundings: the unfolding-scroll aesthetic of Mizoguchi, Ophuls, Murnau, Dreyer, Welles, Renoir, and Rossellini. Not only did this style seem deeper and more beautiful because it allowed more of a spiritual, contemplative feeling to accumulate than the rapid montage style, it was, if you bought all the arguments (and I did), more ethical. Why? Because it was less "manipulative." It offered the viewer the "freedom" to choose what to pay attention to in a long shot, like a theater spectator, rather than forcing the point with a close-up detail. The deep-focus style could also be seen as sympathetic to a progressive, left-wing political view, because it linked the characters inextricably to their social contexts. In retrospect, some of these claims seem contradictory, a result, perhaps, of the admirable critic André Bazin's need to reconcile his own Catholicism and Marxism and film tastes, however farfetched the synthesis. There also seems something curiously puritanical about the austere aesthetic of refraining from making cuts—something finally self-defeating, as well, since movies will always be assembled from pieces of spliced film.*

Nevertheless, I was so impressed by the style of slow cutting that each time a shot, having started to build up a pleasurable suspense in me, was broken by what seemed to me a "premature"

---

* This antagonism toward montage was carried to extremes by the *auteur*-ist *New York Film Bulletin,* which swore that it would trade all of Eisenstein for any one sequence in a Stanley Donen musical.

cut to change the angle, I would wince, as if personally nicked. Watching television at home with my parents, during a filmed series like "Maverick," I would call out the cuts, just to prove my thesis that the editing followed a predictable metronomic pattern of one shot every four seconds or so. Threatened with bodily harm if I kept up this obnoxious routine, I maintained the practice silently in my head.

It would infuriate me when the *Times's* critic, Bosley Crowther (our favorite arch-Philistine), based his argument solely on content without saying a word about a film's visual style. How could he reject a film because he found the characters unsympathetic, or because of its "controversial" treatment of violence, organized religion, sexuality? Clearly, the real ethical questions were things like: Why did the director cheat with so many reaction shots? Why that gloopy slow-motion sequence?

For a certain kind of youth, the accumulation of taste becomes the crucible of self, the battleground on which character is formed. I must mention how much we hated Ingmar Bergman. Although his films had done more than anyone else's to build an audience for art films, his own popularity condemned him in our eyes: he was the darling of the suburbs and the solemn bourgeoisie who ate up the academic symbolism of *Wild Strawberries*. I once debated a fellow student for six hours because he called *The Seventh Seal* a great movie. Now I have come to love certain Bergman films (especially the early ones, like *Monika* and *Illicit Interlude*), but then, no, impossible. It was precisely because Bergman was so much an *auteur*, but not "our kind," that he posed such a threat. Like political radicals who reserve their greatest passion for denouncing liberals, we had to differentiate ourselves from the Bergmanites.

Our man was Godard. His disruptive jump cuts and anarchoclassical sensibility spoke directly to our impatient youth. Belmondo in *Breathless* was our heroic mouthpiece, whether talking to the camera or lying on the pavement: underneath that fierce hoodlum's exterior we recognized a precocious, wounded film addict. With their cinematic self-referentiality, Godard's films showed me my brothers, those equally unhappy captives of shadows. I confess I also found solace in Godard's portraits of women as either fickle betrayers or masochistic victims, which dovetailed nicely with my own adolescent fears of the opposite sex.

Even when Godard seemed momentarily to flirt with the Right, this didn't bother me. At the time I was fairly apolitical: one should not confuse the early sixties with the late. By 1968, the students at Columbia would have more important things to argue about than the merits of Gerd Oswald's *Screaming Mimi*. But in 1960–64, our politics *were* the *politiques des auteurs*. We looked for our morality in form: "The angles are the director's thoughts; the lighting is his philosophy" (Douglas Sirk).

It may seem arrogant to identify more with the directorial/ camera viewpoint than with the protagonists', but that was precisely what the *auteur* theory encouraged us to do. Besides, if I could take the position of "I am a camera," this identification had less to do with superiority and more with fear and shyness, that shyness which in adolescence cooks up to pure alienation. If I went to a party, I would pretend to be filming it because I was too timid to approach the girls I liked. In classrooms where the professor droned on, I would escape by thinking, Where would I place the camera if I were making a documentary of this? Always my camera would start well back from the action, not only because of a preference for the long-shot aesthetic, but also because I felt so far apart from the vital center of life. Around this time I even had a dream in which I was directing a movie sequence inside a greenhouse: I was sitting behind the camera on a mechanical dolly, and I kept calling for the camera to be pulled farther and farther back, against the technicians' murmured warnings, until finally I crashed through the glass. Had I been perceptive, the dream might have warned me that I was on the edge of losing control; instead, I accepted it as a satisfying omen that I was going to become a film director.

It is a truism that moviegoing can become a substitute for living. Not that I regret one hour spent watching movies, then or now, since the habit persists to this day, but I would not argue either if someone wanted to maintain that chronic moviegoing often promotes a passivity before life, a detached tendency to aestheticize reality, and, I suppose, a narcissistic absorption that makes it harder to contact others. "Only connect," people were fond of quoting Forster at the time. For me, "connect" meant synchronizing my watch with the film schedules around town.

Often I would cut classes to catch an afternoon matinee at one of the little art houses in the Carnegie Hall area. Putting my feet up in the half-empty theater during intermission, I would listen in on the conversation of the blue-haired matinee dowagers: "I couldn't make head or tails of that movie the other day!" "I'm glad you said that. And they don't need to show such explicit stuff on-screen." Many an afternoon I shared with those old ladies, wondering what they were making of the capricious, Hitchcockian 360-degree tracking shots in, say, Chabrol's *Leda*. Or I would roam around Times Square, up and down 42nd Street (then a mecca of cinema gold, both foreign and domestic), enjoying the reverse chic of seeing a sacred Melville, Franju, Walsh, Losey, or Preminger film in such sordid surroundings.

In retrospect, the mystery to me is, how did I pay for all those movies? Even taking into consideration student discounts, early-bird specials, and the fact that movies were so much cheaper then, I must have spent a good part of my food money on tickets. But at least I could keep up with Stoller and Zill.

Nick Zill had been living in a railroad flat on West 106th Street, along with three other roommates. Since one of Nick's roommates worked in an art film distribution company, he was able to bring sixteen-millimeter prints home to screen. The first time Nick invited me over for a screening in their living room, I stumbled over bodies and wine bottles to find a space on the floor. The idea of being part of a small, "invited" group watching a bona fide rare movie, Renoir's *La Marseillaise*, was heaven. I had been infected early on by the mystique of the lost, the rare, the archival film; one had only to advertise a movie as "forgotten" and I could barely stay away. Like an epicure dreaming of delicacies he has never tasted, I would fantasize being elected presi-

dent just so I could order a screening in the White House den of
Visconti's *Ossessione* (then tied up in litigation) or Eisenstein's
*Bezhin Meadow*, or all of Louise Brooks's films, or that Holy Grail
of *cinéastes*, the eight-hour *Greed*. And here I was, ensconced in
a similar lucky place, the very hardness of Nick's wooden floor a
mark of privilege. Most of the West 106th Street audience had a
less reverential attitude, drawn simply by the lure of a free movie.

When Nick told me he was moving, and that I could take
over his room if I wanted, I jumped at the chance to become a
resident member of the West 106th Street film club. Perhaps I
should have thought twice about it. In this dilapidated tenement
building, which the city has since torn down, the rooms were so
dark and closetlike that Zill once used one for a sensory depri-
vation experiment, locking his younger brother in and covering
the windows. My own room looked out on a brick wall, and its
only light source was a naked bulb that hung from the ceiling
like a noose.

I mention the squalor of our living conditions because it
seems somehow connected to the movie hunger. Not only did
the silver screen offer a glamorous escape, it sometimes did just
the opposite, held up a black-and-white mirror to our grainy,
bleakly uncolorful lives. One found romantic confirmation in the
impoverished locations of Italian neorealist and French New
Wave pictures. If the hero in *Diary of a Country Priest* (which I had
since seen) could die in a humble room like mine, the shadows
forming a cross on the cracked walls above his pallet, then my
own barren walls were somehow blessed, poeticized.

Do what I might, however, I was unable to find more than a
few moments a week of daily life charged with that poetic transcendence I had come to expect from the movies. I wanted life
to have the economy and double meaning of art. But more often
I simply felt torn by a harsh, banal pain that had no cinematic
equivalent. As the unhappiness increased, I began, almost in
mechanical response, to think of killing myself.

If I reflect back to what brought on this crisis, I have to admit
that it all feels very remote by now; I am no longer the teenager

I once was; every cell in my body has since changed, biologically if not cognitively. Still, I can try to piece together the reasons. Some of my pain, I suspect, came from the fact that I had been a "star" in high school, while my first year at Columbia, surrounded by other high school stars, plunged me into such anonymity as to make me misplace all sense of self-worth. Too, I was living on my own for the first time. Though I had run away from home, I think I felt "abandoned" by the ease with which my parents had let me go. They were too financially strapped to help me, and I was wearing myself out at odd jobs while studying full time. In the process I managed to lose forty pounds: a six-footer, I had gone from 165 pounds to a gaunt 125, as though trying to prove, against my own assertions of independence, that I was unable to take care of myself properly. Malnutrition may have affected my mental outlook more than I realized; in any event, I began to feel utterly hopeless and tired with life. I saw patterns of despair everywhere: in the street, in the sky. The arguing and drug taking of my roommates filled me with distress, contempt, and self-contempt for failing to forgive them. The urge to destroy myself took on an autonomous momentum and ironclad logic of its own. In retrospect, I was suffering from a kind of disease of logic, predicated on an overestimation of my reasoning powers; another way of putting it is that I was living entirely in my head.

Some of my unhappiness had to do with virginity. I was unable to break through to women—not only sexually but on all levels—to ask them for the least human companionship. Going to Columbia (an all-male school at the time), and immersed in this milieu of latent homosexuality, which was threatening my identity in its own way, I was frightened of women yet filled with yearning for them. It pained me even to see lovers taking liberties on the screen. Movies, saturated with the sensual, mocked me by their constant reminder that I was only a spectator.

At the same time, movies helped push me deeper into a monastic avoidance of the body. In the cinematic postulant, there is an ascetic element that exists, paradoxically, side by side with the worship of beauty: a tendency to equate the act of

watching a film with praying.* One day I was at my job at the
library, cataloguing book slips, when, light-headed with overwork and lack of sleep, I heard someone address me from behind.
"Are you a Benedictine?" I turned around and no one was there.
It seemed I had had an auditory hallucination, but even if I had
merely overheard a scrap of conversation, I was spooked by the
sense that someone was mocking me, unmasking my shameful
monkish nature.

In Godard's *Masculin-Féminin* there is a scene with the hero,
Paul (Jean-Pierre Léaud), sitting in a movie theater watching a
Swedish film. On the sound track are his thoughts: "This wasn't
the film we'd dreamed of. This wasn't the total film that each of
us carried within himself . . . the film that we wanted to make
or, more secretly, no doubt, that we wanted to live." Paul's confusion between movies and reality, his yearning for an alternate
existence, his absorption of all the social distress and pain around
him, and his inability to connect with women, driving his chic
girlfriend away with his gloomy overseriousness, add up to the
fate of many Godard heroes: suicide. Unless I am mistaken,
suicide was in the air, in the cinematic culture of the early sixties;
perhaps it was no more than a facile narrative solution for movies
made by young men who were fond of indulging their existential
self-pity. In any event, I fell right in with the mood.

Between screenings of Vigo's *L'Atalante* and *Zéro de Conduite* at
West 106th Street, I told my older brother that I was thinking of
killing myself. Distressed, he counseled patience, but it was too
late to listen. Vigo's dream of a man and a woman drifting down
the Seine in a houseboat, touching each other, seemed insult-
ingly unreachable.

A few nights later I swallowed twenty sleeping pills with the
aid of a quart of Tropicana orange juice. I had already written a

* Years ago, the Anthology Film Archives even constructed a Temple of Cinema in which each seat was separated from its neighbors by a black partition,
not unlike a stiffened monk's cowl, which made contact with one's companion
nigh impossible and forced the viewer into solitary contemplation of the mysteries.

suicide note with quotes from Paul Goodman and Freud—I can laugh at it now—and I lay down to die in my sleep. But stomach pains kept me awake: the beef stew I had eaten earlier at Columbia's dining hall (it is that wretched institutional food I have to thank for being alive today) and the acidic orange juice refused to digest. After an hour's uncomfortable attempt to ignore the stomach and think easeful, morbid thoughts, I leaned over the side of my bed and vomited—whole chunks of beef stew and carrots in a pool of orange juice. Then I called out to my roommates and told them what I had done. They rushed me to St. Luke's Hospital, where my stomach was pumped—so unpleasant but revivifying an experience that when the resident asked me in the middle of it why I had tried to do myself in, I was unable to think of a single reply. I stayed in the hospital's psychiatric ward for two weeks.

The afternoon I was released, my brother met me at the hospital and we went straight downtown to see a double bill at the Bleecker Street Cinema: *Grand Illusion* and *Paths of Glory*. Still movie-hungry after a two-week drought—or else piggishly overindulgent, like a tonsillitis patient demanding all the ice cream he can eat—I insisted we race uptown to see *Zazie dans le Métro*, the Malle film that Stoller had praised in a recent review. What an orgy! I had gotten suicide out of my system, but not cinema.

I must backtrack a little. Before the suicide attempt, at the beginning of my sophomore year, Stoller, Zill, and I had agreed that Filmmakers of Columbia should run its own film series at the college, both to show movies we wanted to see and to raise money for future productions. Zill had surprised me by proposing that I be made president of the organization. Granted, his fear of being held fiscally responsible for our new venture may have had something to do with offering me this honor, but I accepted it with pride.

We began sending away for film rental catalogues and, when they arrived, poring over them like kids let loose in a candy store. We were free to order any movie we wanted to see, provided it was available in sixteen millimeter—and provided we occasionally considered commercial factors. It might be interesting, for instance, to rent all of the Brandon catalogue's Eastern European arcana, but if nobody came to *Ghetto Terezin* or *Border Street*, we would still have to shell out the seventy-five dollars' rental. The decision was made to balance our schedule with obscurities like Griffith's *Abraham Lincoln* and *Border Street* on the one hand, and moneymakers like Hitchcock's *Notorious* and *Rock Around the Clock* on the other. We booked the films, wrote the blurbs, ground out a flyer, and held our breaths.

Nick called me at the hospital, unable to believe, among other things, that I had attempted suicide two weeks before the opening of our Filmmakers of Columbia series. Shouldn't that have been enough to live for? No, I insisted stubbornly. Nevertheless, I got swept up immediately and fortunately into the venture, making business phone calls from the psychiatric ward while Zill and Stoller ran around town distributing flyers.

The first night of the film series drew a sellout crowd for Kurosawa's *Drunken Angel* and Kenneth Anger's *Fireworks* (a homo-erotic short that had not been seen in New York for many years). I was so excited counting the money we made that I couldn't watch the movies. The next day, the dean called me into his office and told me he had heard about *Fireworks*, and to "keep it clean from now on."

A happier period began for me. Stoller introduced me to a woman named Abby, and we started going out together. Though the affair lasted only three months, it served its purpose. I also began writing film reviews for the *Columbia Daily Spectator* and stories for *Columbia Review*, the literary magazine, and no longer felt so neglected on campus. Moreover, the film series was a big hit, and was to continue successfully for years—helping to put me through college, in fact. Susan Sontag, who was then a religion professor at Columbia and already a force in the New York cultural life—especially to us *cinéastes*—gave her blessing to the series by periodically attending. Stoller and Zill gradually withdrew from the activity, although they continued to offer programming suggestions. And Jim Stoller provided one of our most memorable evenings by agreeing, after lengthy persuasion, to play piano behind Pabst's *The Love of Jeanne Ney*; it was a treat to see him overcome his compulsive modesty and perform in public.


We were all waiting impatiently for the sequel to *L'Avventura. La Notte* was said to feature a dream cast of Jeanne Moreau, Marcello Mastroianni, and Monica Vitti. Meanwhile, the art theaters kept our excitement at a boil by showing some of Antonioni's early films, like *Il Grido* and *Le Amiche*, which only deepened our admiration for our own "Michelangelo."

By the time the first ads appeared announcing the premiere of *La Notte*, I had worked myself into such a fit of anticipation that my unconscious mind jumped the gun: I began dreaming, for several nights in a row, preview versions of *La Notte*. When I finally saw it, the film became a normal extension of my dream life. Several of us went on opening night, waiting in line for an hour for tickets. I was with Carol Bergman, a Barnard girl whom I'd fallen in love with (and would marry a year later), and I held her throughout the film, perhaps undercutting the full impact of Antonioni's despondent message. It was great to see an Antonioni movie through the comfortable bifocals of being in love; when one is happy, one can look at both comedy and tragedy with equanimity.

Primed to adore *La Notte*, I did. Especially the ending, with the camera pulling away from Moreau and Mastroianni groping each other desperately in the lush grass at dawn. We left the theater quoting the Master's latest koan: "Sometimes beauty can lead to despair."

It was Jim Stoller, as usual, who saw problems with Antonioni's new direction before the rest of us did. After voicing objections, in his *La Notte* review, about the "sloppily paced" party sequence, the "leaden and insistent" symbolism, and the academic "discontinuous editing" in the walk sequence which was "used to develop a series of explicit, one-to-one meanings as in Eisenstein," Stoller went on to raise a more telling objection. Antonioni, he felt, had stacked the cards by denying any reference to a worthy model of behavior, any "point worth aspiring to," if only in the past, and any real engagement between the characters.

Of course I disagreed at the time, finding Stoller's demand sentimental. More to the point, this was disloyalty! I tried to argue him out of his position. But the words "card stacking" continued to roll uneasily around my brain.

My own disappointment with Antonioni came later with *Blow-Up,* though that derived partly from a misunderstanding, having wrongly elevated him to the level of philosopher in the first place. I had followed the lead of the press, which trumpeted his every quote as a weighty pronouncement: "Eroticism the Disease of the Age: Antonioni." Even his interview silences were reported as evidence of deep thought. It was partly the burden placed on Antonioni to be the oracle of modernity that forced him into ever more schematic conceptions. When his subsequent films exhibited signs of trendy jet-setting, hippie naïveté, and sheer woolly-headedness—even if the visuals remained stunning —I, like many of his fans, felt betrayed. It took me years to figure out that most film directors are not systematic thinkers but artistic opportunists. Maybe thanks to Coppola, Cimino & Company, we have reached a more realistic expectation of directors today; we are more used to the combination of great visual style with intellectual incoherence. But at the time we looked to film-makers to be our novelists, our sages.

Film enjoyed as never before (or since) the prestige of high culture. English professors with whom I had difficulty making office appointments would stumble across my legs in Cinema 16 showings; they would interrupt themselves in class to gush about a movie; they would publish essays comparing Resnais's ordering of time to Proust's.

The euphoria and prestige that surrounded films in the early sixties seem, in retrospect, deserved. The French New Wave— Godard, Truffaut, Varda, Chabrol, Rivette, Resnais, Malle, Rohmer—had all burst on the American scene at once; Antonioni, Visconti, Rossellini, Fellini, Buñuel, Bergman, Welles, Minnelli, Satyajit Ray, Wajda, Losey, Torre Nilsson, and the Brazilian

Cine Novo group were already operating in high gear; the New American Underground of Brakhage, Mekas, Warhol, Anger, etc., was in its heroic phase; and the lingering activity of such old masters as Renoir, Dreyer, Ford, Hawks, Lang, Hitchcock, and Ozu provided a sort of benign historical link to the golden age of silent cinema. A whole apparatus had sprung up to support this moviemaking renaissance; the art-house circuit, new movie journals, museum and university studies, and, like a final official seal of legitimacy, the establishment of the New York Film Festival.

I covered that first New York Film Festival in 1963 for the *Columbia Daily Spectator*. The air at Lincoln Center on opening night was alive with high hopes, with the conviction that we were entering a fat time for movies. Everyone, from dignitary to hungry film buff, seemed grateful to the ones who had given us a film festival; New York City was finally linked with Europe.

It was a banner year. The festival premieres included Buñuel's *Exterminating Angel*; Olmi's *The Fiancés*; Polanski's *Knife in the Water*; Ozu's *An Autumn Afternoon*; Bresson's *Trial of Joan of Arc*; Resnais's *Muriel*; Losey's *The Servant*; Rocha's *Barravento*; Mekas's *Hallelujah the Hills*; Marker's *Le Joli Mai*; Kobayashi's *Harakiri*; ROGOPAG by Rossellini, Godard, Pasolini, and Gregoretti; Blue's *The Olive Trees of Justice*; De Antonio's *Point of Order*; and Melville's *Magnet of Doom*. There were also first-shown retrospectives of the uncut Ophuls's *Lola Montez*, Mizoguchi's *Sansho the Bailiff*, Kurosawa's *I Live in Fear*. At the time, I did not appreciate what an unusually fortunate confluence of circumstances was reigning in the cinematic heavens; I thought it would go on forever with the same incandescence.

At college, I was still struggling with the question of whether to become a writer or a filmmaker. While writing came easily to me, I felt I had to try to make my own movie. I could not remain always a sponge for others' celluloid visions. So I adapted one of my short stories to a screenplay, took the profits from the film series, and gathered volunteer actors and technicians.

Orson Welles once said that *Citizen Kane* succeeded because he didn't know what could or couldn't be done in motion pictures. I wish to report that my movie didn't work for the same reason. I chose an impossibly complicated scheme: three unreliable narrators in the space of a twenty-minute film. Completed in my senior year, 1964, *Saint at the Crossroads* was "over two years in the making": in addition to the usual problems with a tiny budget and a volunteer crew—camera leaks, personality clashes, absenteeism, inappropriate weather—the fancy synch-sound equipment we had rented for the dialogue scenes failed to synchronize. Sound was our undoing; in the end we had to rent a dubbing studio. The visuals, however, were very pretty, largely due to my cameraman, Mark Weiss, who alone on the set knew what he was doing. There was an obligatory Antonioniesque sequence in Riverside Park where boy and girl, walking together, grow farther apart with each shot. They reach the pier where an elaborate tracking shot surrounds them as they kiss, then shows each looking away moodily at the water. . . .

I stayed up all night with the sound man to do a final mix, rushing to complete the film for its scheduled premiere. We finally got the mix done at eight o'clock Saturday morning—just in time for me to grab a taxi to my job as a weekend guard at the Metropolitan Museum. As the cab approached the museum, I looked out, blinking my eyes in the morning light, and saw Susan Sontag and three men in tuxedos, laughing with champagne glasses in their hands as they tripped around the fountain. Right out of *Last Year at Marienbad.*

*Saint at the Crossroads* premiered at Columbia, paired with Fellini's *Il Bidone.* Many of the exiting spectators were heard to remark "The sound was a problem," then lower their voices as they saw the filmmaker standing by. Once more Stoller came to the rescue, salving the pain with a positive review of *Saint at the Crossroads* in the *Spectator.* Admitting there were some "technical infelicities and rather disorienting violations of film grammar," he went on with a friend's partisan eye to discover "some very considerable achievements. If Lopate continues making films—as he should—he will soon, or next, give us something of surprising originality and power." No thanks: I had had my fun; I would become a writer. It was easier and cheaper to control pens and paper than actors. Besides, I could not stand the prospect of again disappointing so many volunteers because of my inexperience. Making that one twenty-minute film had taught me the enormous difference between having an aesthetic understanding of film and being confronted with the demands of transferring three dimensions into two on an actual set.

Gershom Scholem once characterized youth movements by their chatter, as distinguished from true language: "Youth has no language. That is the reason for its uncertainty and unhappiness. It has no language, which is to say its life is imaginary and its knowledge without substance. Its existence is dissolved past all recognition into a complex flatness." I am not sure I agree, even looking back with memory's foreshortened lens, that this period of my youth was complexly flat; it seems in some ways to have been unusually rich. But certainly we had no real perspective, which is why we called on movies to be our language and our knowledge, our hope, our romance, our cause, our imagination and our life.

# MODERN
# FRIENDSHIPS

Is there anything left to say about friendship after so many great essayists have picked over the bones of the subject? Probably not. Aristotle and Cicero, Seneca and Montaigne, Bacon and Samuel Johnson, Hazlitt, Emerson, and Lamb have all taken their cracks at it; since the ancients, friendship has been a sort of examination subject for the personal essayist. It is partly the very existence of such wonderful prior models that lures the newcomer to follow in the others' footsteps, and partly a self-referential aspect of the genre, since the personal essay is itself an attempt to establish a friendship on the page between writer and reader.

Friendship has been called "love without wings," implying a want of lyrical afflatus. On the other hand, the Stoic definition of love ("Love is the attempt to form a friendship inspired by beauty") seems to suggest that friendship came first. Certainly a case can be made that the buildup of affection and the yearning

131

for more intimacy, without the release of sexual activity, keeps friends in a state of sweet-sorrowful itchiness that has as much romantic quality as a love affair. We know that a falling-out between two old friends can leave a deeper and more perplexing hurt than the ending of a love affair, perhaps because we are more pessimistic about the latter's endurance from the start.

Our first attempted friendships are within the family. It is here we practice the techniques of listening sympathetically and proving that we can be trusted, and learn the sort of kindness we can expect in return. I have a sister, one year younger than I, who often took care of me when I was growing up. Once, when I was about fifteen, unable to sleep and shivering uncontrollably with the start of a fever, I decided in the middle of the night to go into her room and wake her. She held me, performing the basic service of a friend—presence—and the chills went away.

There is something tainted about these family friendships, however. This same sister, in her insecure adolescent phase, told me: "You love me because I'm related to you, but if you were to meet me for the first time at a party, you'd think I was a jerk and not worth being your friend." She had me in a bind: I had no way of testing her hypothesis. I should have argued that even if our bond was not freely chosen, our decision to work on it had been. Still, we are quick to dismiss the partiality of our family members when they tell us we are talented, cute, or lovable; we must go out into the world and seduce others.

It is just a few short years from the promiscuity of the sandbox to the tormented, possessive feelings of a fifth grader who has just learned that his best and only friend is playing at another classmate's house after school. There may be worse betrayals in store, but probably none is more influential than the sudden fickleness of an elementary school friend who has dropped us for someone more popular after all our careful, patient wooing. Often we lose no time inflicting the same betrayal on someone else, just to ensure that we have got the victimization dynamic right.

What makes friendships in childhood and adolescence so poignant is that we need the chosen comrade to be everything in order to rescue us from the gothic inwardness of family life. Even if we are lucky enough to have several companions, there must be a Best Friend, knightly dubbed as though victor of an Arthurian tournament.

I clung to the romance of the Best Friend all through high school, college, and beyond, until my university circle began to disperse. At that point, in my mid-twenties, I also "acted out" the dark competitive side of friendship that can exist between two young men fighting for a place in life and love, by doing the one unforgivable thing: sleeping with my best friend's girl. I was baffled at first that there was no way to repair the damage. I lost this friendship forever, and came away from that debacle much more aware of the amount of injury that friendship can and cannot sustain. Perhaps I needed to prove to myself that friendship was not an all-permissive, resilient bond, like a mother's love, but something quite fragile. Precisely because Best Friendship promotes such a merging of identities, such seeming boundary-lessness, the first major transgression of trust can cause the injured party to feel he is fighting for his violated soul against his darkest enemy. There is not much room to maneuver in a best friendship between unlimited intimacy and unlimited mistrust.

Still, it was not until the age of thirty that I reluctantly abandoned the Best Friend expectation and took up a more pluralistic model. At present, I cherish a dozen friends for their unique personalities, without asking that any one be my soul-twin. Whether this alteration constitutes a movement toward maturity or toward cowardly pragmatism is not for me to say. It may be that, in refusing to depend so much on any one friend, I am opting for self-protection over intimacy. Or it may be that, as we advance into middle age, the life problem becomes less that of establishing a tight dyadic bond and more one of making our way in a broader world, "society." Indeed, since Americans have so indistinct a notion of society, we often try to put friendship networks in its place. If a certain intensity is lost in the pluralistic model of friendship, there is also the gain of being able to experience all of one's potential, half-buried selves, through witness-ing the spectacle of the multiple fates of our friends. Since we cannot be polygamists in our conjugal life, at least we can do so with friendship. As it happens, the harem of friends, so tantaliz-ing a notion, often translates into feeling pulled in a dozen dif-ferent directions, with the guilty sense of having disappointed everyone a little. It is also a risky, contrived enterprise to try to make one's friends behave in a friendly manner toward each other: if the effort fails one feels obliged to mediate; if it succeeds too well, one is jealous.

Whether friendship is intrinsically singular and exclusive, or plural and democratic, is a question that has vexed many com-mentators. Aristotle distinguished three types of friendship in *The Nicomachean Ethics*: "friendship based on utility," such as business-men cultivating each other for benefit; "friendship based on plea-sure," like young people interested in partying; and "perfect friendship." The first two categories Aristotle calls "qualified and superficial friendships," because they are founded on circum-stances that could easily change; the last, which is based on admiration for another's good character, is more permanent, but also rarer, because good men "are few." Cicero, who wrote per-haps the best treatise on friendship, also insisted that what brings true friends together is "a mutual belief in each other's goodness." This insistence on virtue as a precondition for true friendship may strike us as impossibly demanding: who, after all, feels him-self good nowadays? And yet, if I am honest, I must admit that the friendships of mine which have lasted longest have been with those whose integrity, or humanity, or strength to bear their troubles I continue to admire. Conversely, when I lost respect for someone, however winning he otherwise remained, the friendship petered away almost immediately. "Remove respect from friendship," said Cicero, "and you have taken away the most splendid ornament it possesses."

Montaigne distinguished between friendship, which he saw as a once-in-a-lifetime experience, and the calculating worldly alliances around him, which he thought unworthy of the name. In paying tribute to his late friend Etienne de la Boetie, Montaigne wrote: "Having so little time to last, and having begun so late, for we were both grown men, and he a few years older than I, it could not lose time and conform to the pattern of mild and regular friendships, which need so many precautions in the form of long preliminary association. Our friendship has no other model than itself, and can be compared only with itself. It is not one special consideration, nor two, nor three, nor four, nor a thousand: it is I know not what quintessence of all this mixture, which, having seized my whole will, led it to plunge and lose itself in his; which, having seized his whole will, led it to plunge and lose itself in mine, with equal hunger, equal rivalry. . . . So many coincidences are needed to build up such a friendship that it is a lot if fortune can do it once in three centuries." This seems a bit high hat: since the sixteenth century, our expectations of friendship may have grown more plebeian. Even Emerson, in his grand romantic essay on the subject, allowed as how he was not up to the Castor-and-Pollux standard: "I am not quite so strict in my terms, perhaps because I have never known so high a fellowship as others." Emerson contents himself with a circle of intelligent men and women, but warns us not to throw them together: "You shall have very useful and cheering discourse at several times with two several men, but let all three of you come together, and you shall not have one new and hearty word. Two may talk and one may hear, but three cannot take part in a conversation of the most sincere and searching sort."

Friendship is a long conversation. I suppose I could imagine a nonverbal friendship revolving around shared physical work or sport, but for me, good talk is the point of the thing. Indeed, the ability to generate conversation by the hour is the most promising indication, during its uncertain early stages, that a possible friendship will take hold. In the first few conversations there may be an exaggeration of agreement, as both parties angle for adhesive surfaces. But later on, trust builds through the courage to assert disagreement, through the tactful acceptance that differences of opinion will have to remain.

Some view like-mindedness as both the precondition and product of friendship. Myself, I distrust it. I have one friend who keeps assuming that we see the world eye-to-eye. She is intent on enrolling us in a flattering aristocracy of taste, on the short "we" list against the ignorant "they"; sometimes I do not have the strength to fight her need for consensus with my own stubborn disbelief in the existence of any such inner circle of privileged, cultivated sensibility. Perhaps I have too much invested in a view of myself as idiosyncratic to be eager to join any coterie, even a coterie of two. What attracts me to friends' conversation is the give-and-take, not necessarily that we come out at the same point.

"Our tastes and aims and views were identical—and that is where the essence of a friendship must always lie," wrote Cicero. To some extent, perhaps, but then the convergence must be natural, not, as Emerson put it, "a mush of concession. Better be a nettle in the side of your friend than his echo." And Francis Bacon observed that "the best preservative to keep the mind in health is the faithful admonition of a friend."

Friendship is a school for character, allowing us the chance to study in great detail and over time temperaments very different from our own. These charming quirks, these contradictions, these nobilities, these blind spots of our friends we track not out of disinterested curiosity: we must have this information before knowing how far we may relax our guard, how much we may rely on them in crises. The learning curve of friendship involves, to no small extent, filling out this picture of the other's limitations and making peace with the results. (With one's own limitations there may never be peace.) Each time I hit up against a friend's inflexibility I am relieved as well as disappointed: I can begin to predict, and arm myself in advance against repeated bruises. I have one friend who is always late, so I bring a book along when I am to meet her. If I give her a manuscript to read and she promises to look at it over the weekend, I start preparing myself for a month-long wait.

Not that one ever gives up trying to educate the friend to one's needs. I approach such matters experimentally: sometimes I will pride myself in tactfully circumventing the friend's predicted limitation, even if it means relinquishing all hope of getting the response I want; at other times I will confront a problem with intentional tactlessness, just to see if any change is still possible.

I have a dear old friend, Richard, who shies away from personal confidences. Years go by without my learning anything about his love life, and he does not encourage the baring of my soul either, much as I like that sort of thing. But we share so many other interests and values that that limitation seems easily borne, most of the time. Once, however, I found myself in a state of emotional despair; I told him I had exhausted my hopes of finding love or success, that I felt suicidal, and he changed the topic, patently embarrassed. I was annoyed both at his emotional rigidity and at my own stupidity—after all, I'd enough friends who ate up this kind of confessional talk, why foist on Richard what I might have predicted he couldn't, or wouldn't, handle? For a while I sulked, annoyed at him for having failed me, but I also began to see my despair through his eyes as melodramatic, childish petulance, and I began to let it go. As it happened, he found other ways during our visit to be so considerate that I ended up feeling better, even without our having had a heart-to-heart talk. I suppose the moral is that a friend can serve as a corrective to our insular miseries simply by offering up his essential otherness.

Though it is often said that with a true friend there is no need to hold anything back ("A friend is a person with whom I may be sincere. Before him I may think aloud," wrote Emerson), I have never found this to be entirely the case. Certain words may be too cruel if spoken at the wrong moment—or may fall on deaf ears, for any number of reasons. I also find with each friend, as they must with me, that some initial resistance, restlessness, psychic weather must be overcome before that tender ideal attentiveness may be called forth.

I have a good friend, Charlie, who is often very distracted whenever we first get together. If we are sitting in a cafe he will look around constantly for the waiter, or be distracted by a pretty woman or the restaurant's cat. It would be foolish for me to broach an important subject at such moments, so I resign myself to waiting the half hour or however long it takes until his jumpiness subsides. Or else I draw this pattern grumpily to his attention. Once he has settled down, however, I can tell Charlie virtually anything, and he me. But the candor cannot be rushed. It must be built up to with the verbal equivalent of limbering exercises.

The Friendship Scene—a flow of shared confidences, recognitions, humor, advice, speculation, even wisdom—is one of the key elements of modern friendships. Compared to the rest of life, this ability to lavish one's best energies on an activity utterly divorced from the profit motive and free from the routines of domination and inequality that affect most relations (including, perhaps, the selfsame friendship at other times) seems idyllic. The Friendship Scene is by its nature not an everyday occurrence. It represents the pinnacle, the fruit of the friendship, potentially ever-present but not always arrived at. Both friends' dim yet self-conscious awareness that they are wandering conversationally toward a goal that they have previously accomplished but which may elude them this time around creates a tension, an obligation to communicate as sincerely as possible, like actors in an improvisation exercise struggling to shape their baggy material into some climactic form. This very pressure to achieve "quality" communication may induce a sort of inauthentic epiphany, not unlike what happens sometimes in the last ten minutes of a psychotherapy session. But a truly achieved Friendship Scene can be among the best experiences life has to offer.

I remember one such afternoon when Michael, a close writer-friend, and I met at a cafeteria on a balmy Saturday in early spring and talked for three and a half hours. There were no outside time pressures that particular afternoon, a rare occurrence for either of us. At first we caught up with our latest business, the sort of items that might have gone into a biweekly bulletin sent to any number of acquaintances. Then gradually we settled into an area of perplexing unresolved impressions. I would tell Michael about A's chance, seemingly hostile remark toward me at a gathering, and he would report that the normally ebullient B looked secretly depressed. These were the memory equivalents of food grains stuck in our teeth, which we were now trying to free with our tongues: anecdotal fragments I was not even sure had any point, until I started fashioning them aloud for Michael's interest. Together we diagnosed our mutual acquaintances, each other's character, and, from there, the way of the world. In the course of our free associations we eventually descended into what was really bothering us. I learned he was preoccupied with the fate of an old college friend who was dying of AIDS; he, that my father was in poor health and needed two operations. We had touched bottom—mortality—and it was reassuring to settle there awhile. Gradually we rose again, drawn back to the questions of ego and career, craft and romance. It was, as I've said, a pretty day, and we ended up walking through a new mall in Houston, gawking at the window displays of that bland emporium with a reawakened curiosity about the consumer treats of America, our attentions turned happily outward now that we had dwelt long enough in the shared privacies of our psyches.

Contemporary urban life, with its tight schedules and crowded appointment books, has helped to shape modern friendship into something requiring a good deal of intentionality and pursuit. You phone a friend and make a date a week or more in advance; then you set aside an evening, like a tryst, during which to squeeze in all your news and advice, confession and opinion. Such intimate compression may add a romantic note to modern friendships, but it also places a strain on the meeting to yield a high quality of meaning and satisfaction, closer to art than life, thereby increasing the chance for disappointment. If I see certain busy or out-of-town friends only once every six months, we must not only catch up on our lives but convince ourselves within the allotted two hours together that we still share a special affinity, an inner track to each other's psyches, or the next meeting may be put off for years. Surely there must be another, saner rhythm to friendship in rural areas—or maybe not? I think about "the good old days" when friends would go on walking tours through England together, when Edith Wharton would bundle poor Henry James into her motorcar and they'd drive to the South of

France for a month. I'm not sure my friendships could sustain the strain of travel for weeks at a time, and the truth of the matter is that I've gotten used to this urban arrangement of serial friendship "dates," where the pleasure of the rendezvous is enhanced by the knowledge that it will only last, at most, six hours. If the two of us don't happen to mesh that day (always a possibility)—well, it's only a few hours; and if it should go beautifully, one needs an escape hatch from exaltation as well as disenchantment. I am capable of only so much intense, exciting communication before I start to fade; I come to these encounters equipped with a six-hour oxygen tank. Is this an evolutionary pattern of modern friendship, or only a personal limitation?

Perhaps because I conceive of the modern Friendship Scene as a somewhat theatrical enterprise, a one-act play, I tend to be very affected by the "set," so to speak. A restaurant, a museum, a walk in the park through the zoo, even accompanying a friend on shopping errands—I prefer public turf where the stimulation of the city can play a backdrop to our dialogue, feeding it with details when inspiration flags. True, some of the most cherished friendship scenes have occurred around a friend's kitchen table. The problem with restricting the date to one another's houses is that the entertaining friend may be unable to stop playing the host, or may sink too passively into his or her surroundings. Subtle struggles may also develop over which domicile should serve as the venue.

I have a number of *chez moi* friends, friends who always invite me to come to their homes while evading offers to visit mine. What they view as hospitality I see as a need to control the *mise-en-scène* of friendship. I am expected to fit in where they are most comfortable, while they play lord of the manor, distracted by the props of decor, the pool, the unexpected phone call, the swirl of children, animals, and neighbors. Indeed, *chez moi* friends often tend to keep a sort of open house, so that in going over to see them—for a *tête-à-tête*, I had assumed—I will suddenly find their other friends and neighbors, whom they have also invited, dropping in all afternoon. There are only so many Sundays I care to spend hanging out with a friend's entourage before becoming impatient for a private audience.

Married friends who own their own homes are much more apt to try to draw me into their domestic fold, whereas single people are often more sensitive about establishing a discreet space for the friendship to occur. Perhaps the married assume that a bachelor like myself is desperate for home cooking and a little family life. I have noticed that it is not an easy matter to pry a married friend away from mate and milieu. For married people, especially those with children, the home often becomes the wellspring of all their nurturing feelings, and the single friend is invited to partake in the general flow. Maybe there is also a certain tendency on their parts to kill two birds with one stone: they don't see enough of their spouse and kids, and figure they can visit with you all at the same time. And maybe they need one-on-one friendship less, hampered as they are by responsibilities that no amount of camaraderie or discussion can change. Often friendship in these circumstances is not even a pairing, but a mixing together of two sets of parents and children willy-nilly. What would the ancients say about this? In Rome, according to Bacon, "the whole senate dedicated an altar to Friendship, as to a goddess. . . ." From my standpoint, friendship is a jealous goddess. Whenever a friend of mine marries, I have to fight to overcome the feeling that I am being "replaced" by the spouse. I don't mind sharing a friend with his family milieu—in fact I like it, up to a point—but eventually I must get the friend alone, or else, as a bachelor at a distinct power disadvantage, I risk becoming a mere spectator of familial rituals instead of a key player in the drama of friendship.

A person living alone usually has more control over his or her schedule, hence more energy to give to friendship. If anything, the danger is of investing too much emotional energy in one's friends. When a single person is going through a romantic dry spell he or she often tries to extract the missing passion from a circle of friends. This works only up to a point: the frayed nerves of protracted celibacy can lead to hypersensitive imaginings of slights and rejections, during which times one's platonic friends seem to come particularly into the line of fire.

Today, with the partial decline of the nuclear family and the search for alternatives to it, we also see attempts to substitute the friendship web for intergenerational family life. Since psychoanalysis has alerted us to regard the family as a minefield of unrequited love, manipulation, and ambivalence, it is only natural that people may look to friendship as a more supportive ground for relation. But in our longing for an unequivocally positive bond, we should beware of sentimentalizing friendship, as saccharine "buddy" movies or certain feminist novels do, of neutering its problematic, destructive aspects. Besides, friendship can never substitute for the true meaning of family: if nothing else, it will never be able to duplicate the family's wild capacity for concentrating neurosis.

In short, friends can't be your family, they can't be your lovers, they can't be your psychiatrists. But they can be your friends, which is plenty. For, as Cicero tells us, "friendship is the noblest and most delightful of all the gifts the gods have given to mankind." And Bacon adds: "it is a mere and miserable solitude to want true friends, without which the world is but a wilderness. . . ."

When I think about the qualities that characterize the best friendships I've known, I can identify five: rapport, affection, need, habit, and forgiveness. Rapport and affection can only take you so far; they may leave you at the formal, outer gate of goodwill, which is still not friendship. A persistent need for the other's company, for their interest, approval, opinion, will get you inside the gates, especially when it is reciprocated. In the end, however, there are no substitutes for habit and forgiveness. A friendship may travel for years on cozy habit. But it is a melancholy fact that unless you are a saint you are bound to offend every friend deeply at least once in the course of time. The friends I have kept the longest are those who forgave me for wronging them, unintentionally, intentionally, or by the plain catastrophe of my personality, time and again. There can be no friendship without forgiveness.

# A PASSION
# FOR
# WAITING

$O$ne of the things for which I chastise myself most often is that I have never learned to sit around bars or cafes for hours, just being a regular. I envy people who can, because they seem somehow effortlessly to be able to make themselves part of a community—and in big cities, any sense of fellowship is at a premium. But even when I try to dawdle, with the assistance of a book or newspaper, my impatience forces me to get up after an hour and ten minutes at most. Apparently I lack what Walter Benjamin called "that passion for waiting, without which one cannot thoroughly appreciate the charms of a cafe." For me it's partly physiological: I feel a signal from my gluteus maximus saying, Time to go! And when the muscular impatience doesn't nudge me along, the fear of getting bored does.

The camaraderie of regulars in a bar or cafe looks very tantalizing from the outside, and yet it feels spitefully closed to an outsider like me, who has never gained the knack of sitting around making small talk. Even as a teenager I found it beyond my driven capacity to hang out at the street corner with kids my age. I have never belonged to a Boy Scout troop or gang or college fraternity or social club, so itchy does group time-marking palaver make me. And now it's clear I will never have the patience to become an alcoholic. (Certainly you need to be patient to knock back one drink after another; it also helps to have a large social tolerance and a strong posterior.) People doubt that I'm a writer when I tell them I don't drink much: writers are supposed to pass their life apprenticeships in saloons. Just think how many plays I might have written by now if I'd been able to frequent some colorful watering hole, soaking up the dialogue of unforgettable denizens with their wonderful wasted lives and pipe dreams. . . .

Sometimes I stare through the tinted windowpane at the laughing patrons of the corner Irish bar; once or twice a year I even make myself go in, nursing a beer and gazing at the ball game while trying to imbibe the atmosphere. But as soon as some stranger who has had a few begins to tell me his life story, covering me with undeserved tenderness one moment and arbitrary scorn the next, I can't help thinking about making my getaway. And, of course, the barfly can see that in your eyes, no matter how far gone he is. As an elderly tippler once elucidated with a sort of compassionate wonder for both our positions: "I understand that . . . people who don't drink . . . find people who do drink . . . drunk."

But it isn't only alcoholic establishments I can't bear to hang around long enough to become a habitué. I get fidgety in coffee-houses as well. It takes a certain philosopher type to sit there hour after hour over a chessboard, waiting for someone to come by and finish the game with him. I remember those artisans of bohemian indifference from the fifties: their craft is dying out. Well, I tell myself, such laziness was never the American way. We need to be getting about, doing something. Though the Eastern sages often counsel the wisdom of inaction, I have too much of the work ethic in me to master that discipline. Even when alone in my house, it seems next to impossible to "do nothing": I must write letters, pay bills, make phone calls, read, watch the news. . . . And yet there is something about coffeehouses that remains tempting in the abstract.

What I miss being part of is not the coffeehouse as it crops up now, with its fly-in-amber air of studied indolence, but the institution as it throve in its legendary prime, during the seventeenth and eighteenth centuries. The London coffeehouses played an immense role in the intellectual life of that time: the latest plays, satires, political pamphlets were circulated, discussed, sometimes even written there; the witty remarks of a Swift or Goldsmith were sparked there, and quickly made the rounds; Addison and Steele's newssheets, *Tatler* and *Spectator*, sprang from the concentration of coffeehouse life. Their first issues were actually subdivided according to the coffeehouse from which their intelligences were ostensibly gathered: political news from one establishment, literary talk from another, religion, fashions, and so on, from still others. In those days not only layabouts but the most vitally active, prolific members of society frequented coffeehouses. It was your social duty and pleasure to spend a portion of the day there; you knew you could expect to meet your friends at such-and-such an inn between certain given hours.

How few of us have the opportunity to see our good friends daily! You would learn a friend differently if you were to encounter him or her in casual circumstances six times a week. But why speak only of friends? Without meeting places like the old coffeehouses it becomes harder to follow in detailed continuity the lives of our enemies, rivals, and indifferent acquaintances. Phonies, poseurs, scoundrels, hacks, wasted talents, and eccentrics fill the pages of seventeenth- and eighteenth-century English literature, and they are described with the easy, semi-disdainful pluralism that can only follow from the recognition that these marginal characters played a permanent role in one's daily life. The coffeehouse, like the French *salon* (which has also all but disappeared), provided an excellent laboratory for the investigation of human typology. Not for nothing did character study come of age as a literary form in this period: Johnson's *Lives of the Poets* (particularly his biography of Savage), and Boswell's own masterpiece of portraiture, so dependent on daily contact with its subject, and Fielding's social novels, or, across the Channel, La Bruyère's *Characters* and Diderot's *Rameau's Nephew*—these works view the specimen range of human nature both as individuals and as larger social types invited to play a role in the public arena.

The coffeehouse in its prime, then, if we can believe the descriptions that have come down to us, helped promote man as a public creature, with a lively interest in the external world and an active political, partisan responsibility. The subsequent decline of this sort of civic activity—along with or in part because of the decrease in convivial public spaces and meeting places—has turned man more private and inward. In the past, institutions like the coffeehouse acted as an informal brake on each person's isolation. Even Kafka, that arch-solitary, was a familiar figure in the literary cafes of Prague, and must have taken some bleak comfort, one assumes, from the surrounding swirl of opinions and egos.

Eastern European cities have always enjoyed a particularly vivid cafe culture. S. M. Ulam gives a charming account in his memoirs, *Adventures of a Mathematician*, of the Polish school of mathematicians getting together at the "Scottish Cafe," writing equations on the white marble tabletops with pencils, engaging in theoretical sessions that lasted up to seventeen hours, interrupting themselves only for mediocre meals and plentiful drinks. Eventually one of them brought in a large notebook to preserve the processes. "A waiter would bring it out on demand and we would write down problems and comments, after which the waiter would ceremoniously take it back to its secret cache." This notebook, which miraculously survived the Nazi occupation, was later published; it became famous in mathematical circles as *The Scottish Book*.

Such intellectual camaraderie and self-forgetful cooperation represent the high-water mark in my romance of coffeehouses. But having said so many idealized things about them, I have to admit that I would probably have been just as uncomfortable hanging around them then. For one thing, I lack the *Sitzfleisch*, the sitting power. It would also be difficult for me, knowing my competitive nature, to spectate in loud brilliant groups, waiting to insert an occasional *bon mot* of my own through the fumes of conversation. Even if the Algonquin circle were to be revived tomorrow, with a chair for me, and if the talk were particularly sophisticated and bitchy, I would probably feel too threatened to stick around for long. I suspect I have more interest in regretting these roundtables of intellect as something the contemporary world has deprived me of, than in actually joining one if given the chance.

III

# CHEKHOV FOR CHILDREN

1

*"And life itself is boring, stupid, dirty . . . it strangles you, this life. You're surrounded by weird people, nothing but country bumpkins, and after living with them for two or three years, little by little you get to be weird yourself.* [Twirling his long mustache] *Look how I've grown this enormous mustache . . . it's a silly mustache. I've grown weird. Nurse . . . I haven't grown stupider; my brains are still in the right place, thank God, but my feelings have somehow gone numb. I don't want anybody, I don't need anything, I don't love anybody . . . want anybody, except maybe you.* [Kisses her head] *When I was little I had a nurse like you."*

—Dr. Astrov, to the Nanny, Uncle Vanya, Act I

The characters in Chekhov's plays are tormented by the thought that they are misspending their lives and that perhaps it is already too late. Their ambitions have led nowhere; they are stagnating; they reach for a romantic solution but fall in love with the wrong person; each thinks himself or herself the noble exception to a landscape of utterly monotonous banality. They can often be comic in their self-deluded, manic bitterness, and they are capable of great animation in their talking jags, but invariably they lapse back into a state of passivity and remorse.

As Gorky wrote of Chekhov: "In front of that dreary, gray crowd of helpless people there passed a great, wise and observant man: he looked at all these dreary inhabitants of his country, and, with a sad smile, with a tone of gentle but deep reproach, with anguish in his face and in his heart, in a beautiful and sincere voice, he said to them: 'You live badly, my friends. It is shameful to live like that.' "

To no one's surprise, Chekhov is hardly a staple in the elementary school repertoire. With Shakespeare, there is a long, honorable tradition of elementary school productions: some of the comedies, like *A Midsummer Night's Dream*, clearly have potential to charm younger children, and a good sword-clanging drama like *Macbeth*, with its witches and magic spells, can also appeal to juvenile actors if cleverly abridged. True, Shakespeare's vocabulary is difficult, but this courtly language itself can be an attraction, lending a distanced charm of dress-up and fairy tales to the enterprise. The drama of Chekhov, on the other hand, is neither distanced enough to conjure up an exotic world nor contemporary enough to attract by its familiarity. Not only do the realism, the *ennui*, the pauses, the lack of physical action and spectacle all count against attempting Chekhov at this level, many would question whether such a view of life, such tableaux, are suitable for children at all. With Chekhov, it is not a matter of risqué material—of too much sexuality or violence; since the playwright is very moderate in these respects—but of a perspective so wholly, darkly adult in its awareness of time running out that some would argue it is unfair to subject children in their innocence to such gloomy prospects.

I must say right off that I think it is a very good thing for children to see what adult futility looks like (they see it anyway, whether we want them to or not), and to get an insight into the mistakes and the paralyses that hinder many grownups, so that they will not squander their own opportunities. To phrase the issue in larger terms, I think it good for children to gain a realistic view of life no matter what, and a harm for them to be "sheltered" from learning the truth and confined in an artificial world of cuteness. I realize this is part of a very touchy debate among parents and educators, and that each person who raises children draws the line at a different place, whether it is at letting them go to a funeral or allowing them to see certain movies. In this debate I generally take the side of John Holt, who argued in *Escape from Childhood*:

> Most people who believe in the institution of childhood as we know it see it as a kind of walled garden in which children, being small and weak, are protected from the harshness of the world outside until they become strong and clever enough to cope with it. Some children experience childhood in just that way. I do not want to destroy their garden or kick them out of it. If they like it, by all means let them stay in it. But I believe that most young people, and at earlier and earlier ages, begin to experience childhood not as a garden but as a prison. What I want to do is put a gate, or gates, into the wall of the garden, so that those who find it no longer protective or helpful, can move out of it and for a while try living in a larger space.

In June 1979 a dozen ten- to twelve-year-olds put on a full-length version of Anton Chekhov's *Uncle Vanya*, which was a gate to the larger world. They put it on before an initially indulgent but skeptical audience. Many who came to support the children in what they assumed would be an impossible undertaking were rather startled to find themselves pulled into the original drama as Chekhov had written it; they were unexpectedly moved by the characters. And I was in a sense the most surprised, knowing from having directed the play how catastrophically it could have gone.

What fascinated me all along about the *Uncle Vanya* project was that it pushed to the limits certain assumptions about proper educational practice, and continually butted against larger philosophical questions: What is the nature of childhood? Are children radically different from adults, or subtly different? What is "appropriate" for children at different ages, both from a developmental-learning and from a responsibly ethical point of view? Then came certain technical questions: Could this thing even be done? What were the capacities for memorization of ten- to twelve-year-old schoolchildren with no previous theatrical training? Granted that children understand a lot: What *would* be above their heads? Was there something they could not be made to understand? Could children connect with and feel compassion for issues they had never faced? What would be the difference between working on a play in which the children were highly motivated and familiar with the material beforehand (as with *West Side Story*, the production of which I had undertaken six years previous) and attempting a play in which the teacher's lone enthusiasm might have to overcome a good deal of indifference and resistance? What part ought a teacher's private obsessions and artistic tastes play in the educational process? Where does one draw the line between experimentation and self-indulgence?

I must say that I felt myself on firmer ground in answering the anxiety that I was robbing children of their "innocence" than I did in silencing personal doubts that this was nothing but an extravagant out-of-control whim, in which I might be using these children to satisfy my own pedagogic ambitions and need for excitement and escape. One thing is certain: I could have waited a million years before a group of sixth graders approached me and proposed that we do *Uncle Vanya*. No, the suggestion had to spring from me. It came about this way.

2.

*"Autumn roses, beautiful, sad roses. . . ."*

—*Vanya, Act III*

In my creative writing classes at P.S. 90, I had been working on dialogue scenes with Monte Clausen's fifth/sixth-grade class. (P.S. 90 is a racially mixed school on the Upper West Side of Manhattan, where I had been directing an Arts Team full time for Teachers and Writers Collaborative.) Over the years I had noticed that, although the kids wrote capable stories and poetry, their dialogue scenes were no better than rudimentary, generally amounting to little more than exchanges of one-liners in which two characters drove each other to greater and greater degrees of exasperation. I was puzzled as to why even the most sophisticated of these child writers so rarely took advantage of the variations in speech length that are a natural part of conversation, instead clinging to a monotonous Ping-Pong of dialogue.

I thought I would also talk to this class about the manifest and latent levels of conversation: plant the suggestion that a person may be hiding his or her true meaning, or may even be unconscious of it. I wanted to explain how sometimes in plays the audience was conscious of a danger the character wasn't, which made for suspense; or how the audience saw one character coming to the truth while another was still in the dark (like the famous scene of the husband under the table in *Tartuffe*). The more I considered it, the more I saw that a good deal of dramatic interest in the theater derived precisely from the playwright's selective presentation and suppression of information. The audience was gradually put in the know and then was left to experience the delicious irony of each character's battle with self-delusion until the "recognition" or "discovery" scene finally occurred, which it did with twice the force because of the buildup.

All this is obvious to the average playgoer, but how to put

such structurally complex ideas across to fifth graders? (Children love suspense, but it is precisely this kind of careful foreshadowing that they as writers are weakest at.) I decided I needed a long scene—and I thought of the sequence in *Uncle Vanya* when Sonia goes to Elena and tells her that she loves Dr. Astrov. Elena offers to sound out Astrov about his true feelings for Sonia. The problem is that Astrov is secretly in love with the beautiful Elena, and Elena . . . is a little taken with Astrov herself. After reassuring the homely Sonia that she will speak to Astrov on her behalf, Elena is left alone and delivers a monologue in which she makes it clear that she herself is tempted by Astrov. Astrov enters with some ecological charts (the ostensible pretext of this interview) and proceeds to expound at great windy length on the demise of flora and fauna in their district, all of which information leaves Elena cold. She brings the subject around to Sonia's crush. Astrov admits he does not "admire" Sonia "as a woman." But then he turns the tables on Elena and accuses her of toying with him. "You know why I come here every day," he cries. "And *who* I come to see. . . . All right? I'm conquered, you knew it even without the questioning. *[Folds his arms and bows his head]* I give up, here, eat me!" Elena protests, Astrov tries to trap her in an embrace and make an assignation, he declares his love in mumbled fragments, she is a picture of conflicted behavior, one moment saying go away, the next moment sinking her head on his shoulder. Vanya—also in love with Elena—comes in while they are embracing. He has seen it all.

A dizzying sequence of emotional transition—from friendship to love to ambivalence to contempt to loyalty to betrayal—all in ten pages. When I looked for the episode in my copy of *Uncle Vanya*, I somehow got sucked into reading the whole play again. It struck me as such a wonderful piece of writing. Oh, to be able to teach such a play! But that was getting ahead of myself; I doubted that the class would sit still even for a reading of this longish scene. I stalled for two weeks, meanwhile teaching other lessons. Then, finally, I went ahead, partly because I had already spent the money photocopying the scene for the class, and partly because I had to get this damn Chekhov lesson out of my system.

Their rapt interest surprised me as I read it aloud. What I hadn't bargained for was that the dramatic situation (X intervening for Y to find out Z's romantic feelings) was one they were going through at this particular stage of their boy-girl careers. No one in class had the nerve to ask someone out straightforwardly, so these matters were handled indirectly through a best friend. After the reading I analyzed the scene to the class as a triangle of unrequited love: John loves Marsha, Marsha loves Fred, etc. I had no doubt they would understand what I was talking about because unrequited love starts very early—even second graders can relate to these bruises. In any case, we went over the complexities of the action, and I asked them how each character felt about the others. The discussion was rich. Did they think Astrov really loved Elena? (Not sure.) What does Sonia mean by "Uncertainty is best"? Why does Elena say one thing and do another? They liked the scene because it was romantic and embarrassing—perfect for ten-, eleven-, twelve-year-olds. They roared at Astrov's lovemaking ("Here, eat me!"). Meanwhile, I was able to explain a few technical points about writing dialogue scenes. Mission accomplished. I might have left it at that.

But now I was thinking: What if I took a small group of interested students and started an *Uncle Vanya* study group. Just to read the play, mind you. ("And put it on!" a maniacal inner voice suggested.) No, I had to devise the project step by step, like a three-stage rocket, at each point ready to self-destruct if one of the parts fizzled. First stage, part one, was the lesson. That had worked out well, so we could move on to the second stage: a reading group. We would approach *Uncle Vanya* as a piece of literature. Perhaps that was even a more advanced and satisfying educational idea than this vulgar notion that we had to mount our own production. But if—if—the kids were interested, if the idea came from them, we then . . . could consider . . . look into . . . see if it was even feasible. Ah, but what a coup it would be! What a march I would steal on all the other writers in the schools—forget the writers, even the theater people! Who had ever heard of an artist-in-the-schools pulling off such a thing?

Chekhov by children. We could get the local TV stations to cover it. I would be modest at interviews: Please—the children did it all, speak to them. . . .

Another restlessness was, I should admit, working inside me. After ten years of teaching children writing by using examples from one-page poems and choice prose fragments, the first few sentences of a novel, I yearned to sink my teeth into a complex, meaty, sustained piece of literature. One of the frustrations that writers face in working with children is that we always seem to be offering up slivers of literary models. But what made me fall in love with literature in the first place was fat novels, five-act plays. I loved the repetitions of themes, the rise and fall, even the doldrums, the calms, the tedium itself, and the big payoff, which could only occur when the writer had built up a meticulous architectural structure to house it. I felt like a fraud sharing lyrical bursts of expression with children and pretending that they were all there was to literature, while my own love was for the grand arch, the passage of time, the slow transformation of characters. Here at last would be a chance to dig in and demonstrate how a great literary work was like music, with patterns and refrains and variation, adagios as well as allegros. . . .

Hadn't I paid my dues already with years of meeting children on their own cultural terms—helping them make superhero comic books and vampire movies? Let them come to me this time, I thought. I was tired of scaling everything down to miniature size. On the brink of one of those periodic crises of staleness endemic to the teaching profession, I decided my only antidote might be a project of deep selfishness. *Uncle Vanya* was a play I liked and was reasonably sure I would not tire of. Therefore, we would study *Vanya*.

3 .

*"It's a long time since I've played.
I'll play and cry—cry like a fool."*

—Elena, Act II

I went to the Drama Bookshop and looked through all the *Vanya* translations. To my disappointment, none of them seemed exactly right. In some ways I liked the Stark Young version best, but it was rather stodgy and Victorian; the Tyrone Guthrie version was more modern but a bit too slangy and slick for my taste. In the end I settled for the Guthrie version because it was a cheaper paperback and because the bookstore had more copies.

Then I went to Monte Clausen, the classroom teacher, and we drew up a list of the dozen or so children who would be involved out of the pool of twenty who had already volunteered. I should say in passing that Clausen is an extraordinary elementary school teacher who has himself done science projects of immense scope and technical difficulty. At the moment he and his kids were building a model of the Brooklyn Bridge in the back of the classroom; the year before, he had lent his engineering expertise to our radio station project. Monte Clausen was one of a number of gifted, Ivy League–educated men drawn into elementary school teaching during the sixties by a combination of downwardly mobile idealism and the need to avoid the draft. With the thin, almost gaunt physique of a dedicated marathon runner, soulful eyes, a prematurely bald head, and a drooping mustache, this very popular teacher had a perfectionist streak tempered by a fatalistic sense of humor, reserved for inevitable snafus. I doubt if I would have attempted a project as farfetched as *Uncle Vanya* with any of the other teachers I was working with at the time. That he was someone like me who warmed to improbable schemes—we had once tried to build a waterfall in the Writing Room, a total fiasco, as it turned out—and that we were friends outside of school reassured me that he would be forgiving of the possible strains created by kidnapping his kids for so time-consuming a project. Monte knew already that I might want to put on the full-length play. He chuckled as he wrote in his Attendance Book: "Group for Uncle Vanya. (Uncle Vanya??!!!)"

These were the criteria for selection to the *Uncle Vanya* study group: (a) the probability that the particular child would be interested in this sort of venture; (b) my hunch that a kid would ultimately be good in a certain role—if ever it came to that; (c) racial balance; (d) intellectual capacity and maturity (there were a few exceptions to this); (e) Clausen's desire to include one or two kids who, thus far in the year, had been walking around lost in space.

Clausen's class held a goodly pool of intelligent and competent children, many of whom I regretted having to leave out. But it also had the peculiar limitation of a shortage of eligible boys. I could have cast the female parts in the play twice over, whereas it was really a struggle to find enough "mature" boys; the boys tended to be shorter and more babyish than the girls.

The core of the group I had chosen hung out together after school, frequented the same luncheonette, and came with its own pecking order. The clique included Lisa, Mylan, Slim, Jamal, and Sasha—if you went up against any of them you were accountable to the others. The rest of the eleven kids in the group were outsiders, loners; they looked to me for support and fair play whenever the clique got too pushy. The group broke down like this:

*Angus* was, already in my mind, a potential Uncle Vanya. He was a white fifth grader with large glasses and a thoughtful, deliberate way of speaking; something of a genius perhaps—in any case, very bright, with an unusual, technical mind—given to speculations; disliked by many of his classmates, considered "flaky" and "weird," he would sometimes raise his hand and then not remember by midsentence what he had started to say. His fourth-grade teacher was shocked when she learned I had given Angus the longest part in the play: "He blanks out!" she said. "He'll stare into space and forget where he is."

*Mylan* was tremendously popular, gracious, gushing with perceptions and energy. A good writer, dancer, actress, and pal. Half-black, half-white, the child of divorced parents, she seemed to have an unusual amount of insight for a sixth grader. And if a sixth grader can be said to possess glamour, Mylan had it.

*Jamal* was a mischief-maker and prankster. He wore a cat-that-ate-the-canary grin at all times. Often quite admirable and sweet, with a big Afro and handsome *café-au-lait* skin, he had the habit of slyly pushing one's patience to the brink, so as to ensure that one did not rely on him too much. He was one of my favorites, though not many shared my taste.

*Slim*, Jamal's best friend, was respected by the other children, though still a mystery to me. Even-tempered, white, nice-looking, with a shaggy dog haircut, just barely stopping at his eyes, he struck me as the strong and silent type.

*Rebecca* was a loner, bright, hypersensitive, upset by her parents' divorce; generally very cooperative; experienced. She had already trod the boards off-off-Broadway in a child role. A little plain of face, she would make an excellent Sonia.

*Lisa* was just a good kid to have around, the kind that teachers depend on to carry a new activity—capable, solidly intelligent, mature, a leader though still only a fifth grader. The rap on her was that she was coasting a little, had never been challenged to her fullest. Still, she would be good for any of the roles: she read well and with expression.

*David* was another fifth grader. I heard he had cried on the first day of school because he missed his fourth-grade teacher. But lately he was showing signs of mental growth underneath his baby fat. Who would ever have guessed at the beginning of the year that this rosy-cheeked cherub would be perfect as the Professor—an aged, sour, hypochondriacal intellectual?

*Ayesha* was highly theatrical; her mother was an actress. She had a powerful appearance, queenly, coal-black, flamboyantly baubled. She wrote beautifully, but she was also something of a bully, beating up on other children (especially boys), exploding, leading mutinies and walkouts. She would get tired suddenly, refuse to work anymore. I kept forgetting that this powerfully built girl had a fragile constitution, and had been in and out of hospitals with kidney problems.

*Kioka* was very sweet, matronly, black, and composed. A late transfer, she seemed never to have "joined" the class. She had no ambition to be seen by an audience and rather dreaded the idea. But Clausen had thought it would be a good experience for her to be part of this group.

*Sasha* wanted to be in on everything though she rarely initiated activity. Pint-sized, squeaky, she didn't have the charismatic presence of a principal lead, but I thought she would make a good extra and assistant director.

*Randi* was shy, humorous, and reliable. I pictured her as another extra and backstage organizer.

It helped that I had worked with a number of these children (Angus, Sasha, Mylan, Lisa, Jamal) on smaller plays and on films in past years. I knew their potential and their quirks, and they knew mine.

The reading of the play took up three afternoons. Lisa began, magically setting the scene in a calm, mature, respectful voice. Some of the other children, however, read so poorly that it unnerved me: I had assumed they were all reading at grade level at least. This did not bode well for putting on a full production. I stopped and explained the more difficult words, discussed some of the unfamiliar Russian details. On the whole, the reading aloud of the text offered cautious affirmation, if only because everyone was decently behaved. Maybe they simply wanted to get out of class, to be part of a privileged group. They neither liked nor hated *Uncle Vanya*: a few remarked that it was "boring" and "nothing really happens," but for the most part they took it at face value. They simply wanted the fun of putting on a play, any play, and asked when we could start holding tryouts. I grasped that the abstraction of a literary study group would have no meaning for them, and so proceeded timorously to stage three.

4 .

*"It's funny—if Uncle Vanya says something, or that old idiot,
my mother-in-law, it's all right; everybody pays attention. But if I
so much as utter a single word, everybody gets upset. The very
sound of my voice disgusts them."*

—*Professor Serebriakoff, Act II*

Tryouts were held in mid-January. I encouraged everyone to
read for as many parts as they liked. These readings were a lovely
part of the process: the kids would divide up into groups of twos,
threes, or fours and go off into the stairwell or hallway to practice
the scene of their choice without my help. Then they would all
come together and take turns performing the scenes for each
other. It was fascinating to see three different Vanyas or Sonias
in the space of an hour.

After a few weeks, the obviousness of certain choices became
clear to all. Despite the fact that all the boys wanted the starring
role and that Angus was maybe the least popular child in that
group, everyone agreed that Angus *was* Vanya. Similarly, Mylan's
flair for the part of Elena and David's surprising gift for re-
creating the invalidish, grumbling Professor were indisputable.
Ayesha accepted with good grace that she made a wonderful old
Nurse (her characterization was complete the moment she read
for the part), in spite of her preference for the part of the beautiful Elena. Kioka was pressed into being Vanya's mother. Sasha
and Randi agreed to be workmen in walk-on parts, and also to
take charge of props and scenery. There was virtually no disagreement about these decisions. Children may lie, but they have
an amazing honesty when it comes to recognizing objectively
the competence of their peers.

I still had a problem casting two key characters, Astrov and
Sonia. Neither Jamal nor Slim was particularly impressive as Dr.
Astrov, and both Rebecca and Lisa would have made convincing
Sonias. I decided to sound out the cast individually, to solicit

their private opinions while also discussing with each one the character he or she had been selected to play. My first conference was with Mylan. She confided in me that she had gone out with Jamal the year before and that under no circumstances would she play love scenes with him. "I mean, I like Jamal and all, he's nice in his way, but he's just too immature, and I would be embarrassed to death to play a love scene with him and I *know* neither Lisa or Rebecca will." With that word of advice, I cast Slim as Dr. Astrov. The whole cast breathed a sigh of relief. Jamal got the comic role of "Waffles" Telegin, the obsequious family hanger-on.

Each of the potential Sonias was excellent in a different way: Rebecca had the injured, long-suffering, neurotic sensitivity of someone who has judged herself, in Sonia's words, "not pretty," and she was wonderfully expressive and had stage experience, but Lisa (who was, regrettably for the part, extremely pretty) had a gravity and a consoling adult quality that was also thrilling. Moreover, I dared not go against the power of the clique by depriving Lisa of a major role. Finally I decided to let them both be Sonia, in separate performances. I reasoned that role-doubling happens all the time in opera repertory companies. It led to headaches, and the girls were able to rehearse only half as much as the other actors, but somehow it still seems to me to have been the only choice.

I was discontented with the Guthrie translation; we needed our own version. I asked the kids to go through the scripts and suggest any changes or cuts. Then I sat down at the typewriter with the Stark Young, Tyrone Guthrie, and Marian Fell versions open to the same scene, the kids' recommendations in my lap, and chose what seemed to me the best translation of each phrase from the standpoints of literary power and "speakability" by the children. At times I paraphrased, using my own wording. With a foreign language dramatic classic you are never sure you are dealing with the pure text; this way we had more leeway for the children to put things in their own words without the guilt of violating the author's sacrosanct syllables. Had the text been in English—Shakespeare or Shaw—I would have been more hesitant about altering the language.

As for cuts, all I trimmed in the end were some of Astrov/ Slim's longer speeches. If we were going through the trouble of putting on *Uncle Vanya*, we might as well do it whole.

In our first rehearsals we went slowly over the script, clearing up small points of meaning. I discovered that, sophisticated as these Upper West Side/Broadway kids appeared, they often did not know the meanings of ordinary words like "pompous," "uncertainty," "squabbling"—much less *samovar*. Sometimes we would rehearse a scene for weeks and the actor would develop just the right intonation and expression, then I would learn that he hadn't the foggiest notion what he was saying. Such was the case with David, who had spoken the phrase "to find yourself in this morgue!" many times over, until one day he turned to me and asked: "What *is* a 'morgue'?"


I also delivered a brief lecture on Russian history, with high points like the freeing of the serfs (contemporaneous with our Civil War), the assassination of the tsar, the flowering of Russian literature, the mood of post-heroic exhaustion and *ennui* around 1900 (the date of the play), and, looking ahead, the Russian revolution. I attempted to give a picture of the Russian social classes so the children would understand the economic position of the sort of people Chekhov was writing about, provincial landed gentry who were losing their wealth, and who, in this "hour of sunset," were torn between living in the big cities or in the country. Actually, I had visions of the play occasioning much more elaborate curriculum spinoffs: Clausen and I would co-teach a unit on Russia, we would read other writings by Chekhov and the major Russian authors, I would have the cast write analyses of their characters and rewrite the ending of *Uncle Vanya*. Most of these schemes, educationally desirable as they may have been, never came to anything for the simple reason that rehearsals took up all of our time. In fact, the kids were already panicking from having to memorize lengthy parts and complete their regular homework every night. Some members of the cast did go to the library to look up Russian costumes. Some rewrote the ending of *Vanya*, and read other Chekhov stories and plays from the books I donated to the class library. They confessed to me that *The Cherry Orchard* was "too difficult," confirming my suspicion that *Uncle Vanya* was the sunniest, clearest, and, of Chekhov's four major plays, the most "do-able" for grade school children.

So much for curriculum tie-ins. We always came back to the text, understanding and reinterpreting it. Because my background is as a writer and not as a man of the theater (I have, in fact, no theatrical background or training to speak of), I approached *Vanya* primarily as a writer's play. Rather than spending a good deal of time on stage business and blocking, I focused instead on the words of the play, the double messages, the psychology, the patterns. Sometimes the children would spot them first, as when they pointed out how each character complains at one point or another that no one is listening to him. One day they noticed all the statements about weather; I tried to get them to figure out their dramatic function. Or, we could come to a line like "I have no hope, none, none." Does Sonia really mean it? Not exactly. Why does Sonia not understand in Act II that Dr. Astrov had rejected her? "Because she doesn't want to understand." Very good. Move on. I wish I had taped these discussions to verify just how much the children understood, how startling their insights were. I am convinced that in the end they grasped all the rich undercurrents in Chekhov, that they were not merely child-puppets mouthing incomprehensible lines, but it took a while. And it took even longer before they acquired a taste for this delicacy.

5 .

*"Old people are like children, they want people to feel sorry for them. But no one feels sorry for old people."*

—*Nurse Marina, Act II*

In the rehearsals, the children often struck, quite unself-consciously, an amazingly Chekhovian note. One would wander off toward the window, another would be totally self-absorbed, a group would be atomized and looking in four different directions. It made me think that perhaps a stronger tangential connection than I had anticipated existed between Chekhov's world and the world of childhood: the lassitude, the petulance, the waiting for something to happen.

One of the theories I was testing—a theory I had concocted after a disastrous showing of *Citizen Kane* some years earlier to fifth and sixth graders—was that children had a hard time relating to the theme of life dwindling away. They could take sudden death with aplomb; catastrophe found them ever-willing spectators; but the slow dribbling away of potential, the diminution of vital powers, the compromises of integrity comprised by a sense of adult failure, irked them. Or so it seemed to me. Now this assumption was being called into doubt: there were moments when they seemed to get closer to a Chekhovian spirit than any professional production I had ever seen.

However, whole dimensions were still being missed. They played *Vanya* too darkly; it was *too* gloomy, *too* severe. The kids tended to take literally every character's "I'm so miserable" without understanding the Russian braggadocio in some of these assertions of suffering. They also seemed to miss half the irony. Slim would say "Thank you very kindly" in a friendly voice when a workman was pulling him away from his pleasant surroundings to attend a patient, without catching Astrov's acerbic side. Broad sarcasm was grasped a little better. But they had a hard time with self-irony (hard for any actor). Chekhov's characters, after all, are rather intelligent, conscious beings, for all their blind spots: they have a good sense of how they "sound" to others. Elena is both a shallow flirt and a much deeper woman criticizing the shallow flirt. If you play her only the first way you get cardboard.

There was still another level of irony to be grasped: the playwright's attitude toward his characters. Could the kids be made to appreciate that, while the characters may be complaining about their miseries, Chekhov is also inviting us to laugh at them? Would they understand the play as a *comedy*? This was hard for the children to see because there was very little comic stage business, aside from the pistol-shooting at the end of Act III. The humor in Chekhov's lines—those dry cackles of character observation that would eventually draw smiles and laughter out of our adult audience—was something the children still had to take my word for.

All this made me wonder about the developmental acquisition of the faculty of irony. Within this cast of ten- to twelve-year-olds, there was enormous variation. Angus, among the youngest in the group, led the way, as he so often did, in grasping the dynamic of self-irony (the actor standing off from his character, who is already standing off from himself—and then reintegrating the three). Slim brought up the rear. The others straggled in between. In order to lay a firmer foundation for these concepts, I devoted a lesson in Clausen's class to irony. I read from Swift's *A Modest Proposal*, got from the kids a list of things they hated, then asked them to select one and write an essay praising it. I was attempting to teach them to lie and tell the truth at the same time.

One way to lighten the tone of our production was to point out all of the text's humor and irony; another was to wean the children from a uniform tone of hopelessness. I told the cast: "You must play Chekhov for hope. Otherwise it won't work, there won't be any tension or suspense. Sonia must think she *might* get Astrov, Vanya must be at least momentarily optimistic about Elena, even though you as actors already know that in the end it doesn't work out."

To help them see some of these points, I rented a sixteen-millimeter print of Sir Laurence Olivier's *Uncle Vanya*, with Olivier as Astrov, Michael Redgrave as Vanya, Joan Plowright as Sonia, Rosemary Murphy as Elena, and Max Adrian as the Professor. I had seen this performance many years before on television and had loved it. I realized that I was taking a risk in showing them such a polished production—an actor friend warned that it might "crush them"—but it seemed to me that the kids were far enough along in their own characterizations to benefit from exposure to a superb model without necessarily being dominated by it. Ha! Not only were they not overawed by the Olivier version, but they went so far as to criticize it, and thought they could do *much* better. Everyone objected that Joan Plowright as Sonia was ridiculously "overacting" (a criticism I often hurled at them), with her quivering chin and wet eyes holding back the tears. Vanya/Redgrave was too "weak." Most thought Astrov "all right," but Slim *loathed* Olivier. He took to leaving the room whenever Sir Laurence came on-screen. And Mylan asked me afterward, "How come *you* said that I was supposed to make Elena sympathetic as well as flighty, but *she* just did the flighty business, la-de-da and all that?" "Well, you're right, Mylan; maybe we can do better. There are a lot of ways to play *Uncle Vanya*."

The funny part was that, perhaps because I was seeing it so much through the kids' eyes, I agreed with most of their objections. As I watched this production that I had been so moved by years before, it struck me now as stiff and English-repressed, at the same time hysterically forced and overtheatrical. Part of the problem may have been the transfer of a production originally designed for stage to the film medium, so that gestures like Olivier arching his brows, meant to be caught in the last row, tended to look very hammy on-screen. Also, *Vanya* is such a delicate ensemble play that a charismatic actor tends to smother it: this Olivier-directed production might have been more aptly titled *Dr. Astrov*. But the major problem was that we had already started our own *Uncle Vanya*; its seeds were growing inside us; as our inner vision conflicted with the Olivier version we had no choice but to declare it a "counterfeit."

A few practical improvements, which Ayesha, more respectful of professional acting craft, picked up from the film and urged successfully on the others, were: (a) that the characters laughed at each other's witty remarks and were not always in a dour humor; (b) that they sometimes moved around as they spoke. We did not have to *sit* quite so much.

The screening of the film reassured me, in a way; I realized how complex and mountainous a theater classic is, and how easy it is to fall short of it. If we should fail at *Uncle Vanya*, well, so had many others, among them actors of the highest caliber. Scarcely a production of Chekhov in the last twenty years had not been criticized for being forced, phony, trendy, overly neurotic, or false to the spirit of the playwright. It was finally in that sense, even more than in attempting a work rarely done by children, that we had taken on an infinite, staggering challenge.

6.

*"What still gets to me is beauty. I have an eye for beauty."*

—Astrov, Act II

The major struggle was with memorization. The children had Act I and most of Act II down, but they bogged down in Act III, for what felt like months. It seemed that their heads could not hold any more. Angus and Slim had poor memories to begin with —and they had the biggest parts. Mylan discovered a method that worked for her: writing down speeches from memory and then comparing them with the script to catch her errors. Lisa invented a pictorial mnemonic device, connecting picture-symbols with arrows so that her diagram for a speech resembled a treasure map. Sasha drilled the kids when I was not around; they went to each other's houses and practiced. But it was never enough—no matter what they did, they didn't know their parts and we could hardly focus on nuances when they were still stumbling over their lines.

Eventually I understood that this was not just a mechanical

problem, but a resistance to letting *Uncle Vanya* take over their lives. Perhaps they had never before known what it was like to be possessed by a task; there is inevitably a revulsion, a queasiness that occurs just before the moment of going under. The children were expressing in their eyes that imminent loss of independence. Ayesha raged that she had to rehearse so much. Slim would cry "Oh, no!" when I came to get him, whining that he had "no more time for math!" Scheduling tensions arose: another teacher wanted to use Mylan and Ayesha in a dance recital, the kids had to do their reports on the energy crisis. And not only was there competition from schoolwork: some of these children had a dizzying after-school agenda. Angus went to Boy Scouts, Stamp Club, Religious Instruction, Fencing, and who knows what else. No wonder he blanked out occasionally, pulled as he was in so many different directions between his parents' and his teachers' and my pressures. But still I was angry that he—they—did not give *Uncle Vanya* a higher priority. "You're the *star* of the *show*. When are you going to memorize it? *July?*" They had to understand, it seemed to me, that this was a unique experience in their lives, and that eventually they would have to put everything else behind them and everything they had into it if they wanted to get something out of it.

Clausen remarked astutely: "The trouble with doing *Uncle Vanya* is that it has to reach a very high level of success before people will even begin to take it seriously, whereas most school activities, however Mickey Mouse they may be, work on the basis of minimizing the chances of failure in order to build up self-confidence." I seemed to be moving in the opposite direction, making us all go out on a limb with a project whose risk of failure was great and whose probability of success slender.

Suddenly Kioka "quits," says she doesn't feel part of the group and is being picked on. I get down on my knees and coax her to remain. Ayesha and Jamal have a fight; she beats him up and he cries. Jamal is forever slipping out of the room with Slim to do mischief. Rebecca thinks I'm neglecting her, that I'm rehearsing Lisa more. Lisa is coasting. Moreover, she has started, in her cool way, to probe and raise doubts: "Maybe this is too difficult for us." Or, "Phillip, why did you pick *Uncle Vanya* in the first place?" "I wanted you to know how people can throw their lives away so that you won't make the same mistake," I snarl. "You mean," says Slim quietly, "like throwing your life away doing a play?"

Sasha is both efficient and officious. Half the time she is my right-hand man, an invaluable assistant; the other half she is planning months in advance for the cast party and considering whom to exclude. Angus is tense. And I myself am going through a sulk, because I have decided absurdly that the kids never show any "gratitude" to me. I am obsessed by their never saying thank you, always taking for granted the extra time and money I am putting into this. Of course, what I don't understand until much later—when the gratitude erupts almost embarrassingly from all sides—is that they are so dependent on me at this stage (I being the only one with a plausible map) that their symbiosis surpasses such petty acknowledgments. Since it is my dream to begin with, and it is I who have gotten them into this mess, I should be much more grateful to them than the other way around. Nevertheless, I am tired and miffed. When they want to get my goat they complain that the play is "boring." "It's *about* boredom, it's not the same as boring," I counter. "No, it's *boring!*"

Only David, that angel of cooperation, and Mylan are always there to support me. One day, when the rest of the cast leaves after a particularly turgid rehearsal, Mylan stays behind. She wants to talk about life with me, have a serious adult conversation. So we talk about depressions—she is in the middle of one, to my surprise—and about moods and her parents' divorce and the fact that she will have to spend the next few years with her father in Colorado. She will miss her little sister terribly, and her mother, of course. But she talks with humor and warmth: somehow, Mylan's "depression" is as sparkling as most other people's liveliness. I realize I am being—cheered up.

By now, both of us are in a good mood, and Mylan in her frisky way starts imitating all the adults at school. I ask her to do an imitation of me. She won't. I ask her what the kids think of me, why they seem to get such pleasure in provoking my anger.

She says, "Most of the kids consider you more as a friend than a
teacher and so they don't always listen, the way they don't listen
to each other, and then they get surprised when you become like
a disciplinarian." This surprises me. I doubt that they regard me
on the same level as their friends, I have never tried to be other
than an adult and a teacher, and yet I can appreciate how they
might see my stern, demanding behavior as an irrational contradiction to my looseness at other times. I guess what I want them
to know is that I am not demanding to be obeyed because I am
the Boss, the figure of adult authority, but because the task demands it. Meanwhile, I am placated.

7 .

> *"The weather is charming, the little birds sing, we all live in this
> world in harmony—what more could we have! [Accepting a
> glass of tea] Thank you, from the bottom of my heart."*
>
> —*Waffles, Act I*

Full-cast rehearsals always carried the risk of discipline problems—a dozen kids to control. Duets and solos, on the other
hand, were parts I could rehearse over and over: I'd pull a couple
of kids out of class and we'd work on tiny details in a relaxed
atmosphere. I particularly loved the beautiful two-women scenes,
like the one in which Sonia and Elena make up and pledge their
friendship. The feeling of comradeship in that scene, as Mylan
and Rebecca or Lisa did it, was very strong and touching. I found
myself having them redo it on occasion, not only to perfect some
little detail but just to see it again. Those girls could take direction. What a thrill to tell your actors to change their approach
and then actually watch them execute things according to your
instructions! These small, closed rehearsals also gave each actor
the chance to take risks, to experiment, without trying the
group's patience.

One day, Lisa started twirling around as she was saying her

lines about Astrov to Mylan. She thought her waltzing was a goof, and half expected me to get annoyed, but I was enchanted. It gave a nice lilting feeling to the scene. I encouraged them all to move whenever and wherever the spirit took them. Rather than blocking their movements in advance with chalk marks, which I thought would make them too self-conscious, I urged them to pay attention to the impulses in their bodies that told them to stand up or sit down or carry out a verbal phrase with a gesture.

This opened up a whole new play for them. They began wandering, pacing, retreating when their character was embarrassed, working off their nervous child-energy with spontaneous strolls. Angus showed genius at this, though sometimes he went too far, and one day while circling in his stockinged feet he made me seriously dizzy.

I had to tread a fine line between wanting them to be serious about rehearsing and encouraging them to "play" with the material, even if that was done in the spirit of sabotage. Some of these subversions were hilarious. There was their Robot *Uncle Vanya*, in which they surprised me by moving and talking like mechanical men. There was Horsey *Uncle Vanya*—Mylan had perfected a neigh and delivered all her lines whinnying. David and Angus had worked up a Donald Duck voice for the fight between Vanya and the Professor: "Quack quack you have quruined my life!" They had also rewritten the ending to their satisfaction: Elena is shot, Sonia marries Astrov, the Professor marries the Nurse, and all go off to Africa.

Perhaps the most satisfying rehearsals were the line readings, when I told them they didn't have to "act" but merely to recite the lines as a memory test. As they were speaking their lines, Lisa would be bouncing a rubber ball against the wall, Slim stretching out on the floor, Mylan pacing and chewing her nails, Angus reading a comic book on the radiator. This was truly the Child's *Uncle Vanya*. If only we could have put it onstage like that: I was tempted—we could have had one of the most true-to-life, natural performances of Chekhov in ages. But again, my actors had no idea how close they were to the spirit of the play. They thought they were being naughty.

Slim's *Frankenstein* portrayal of Astrov with stiff arm and leg movement was unfortunately not a parody. When he got nervous his whole body stiffened up. He seemed solemn and wooden to me; I despaired of ever seeing any of the charming, raffish, ironic side of Astrov shine through him. Perhaps it is easier to find cranky eccentrics like Vanya at sixth-grade level than jaded *roués* like Astrov. But I could not resign myself to having one of my main actors pull the whole production down. I began to think about getting a replacement from another class, like smooth-talking, debonair Robert Kowalski. As Easter approached, I even discussed with Monte Clausen the prospect of offering Slim the option of bowing out gracefully. Clausen talked it over with the boy, sounding him out tactfully as to whether the part was too much for him. Slim answered with dignity that he thought he would like to stick with it.

It occurs to me in retrospect that I had trouble appreciating Slim as much as he deserved because he was so different from the kind of child I had been. Slim was athletic, scientifically inclined, popular with girls—perhaps I was simply jealous of him. I had a much easier time identifying with Angus, whose large glasses and precocious manner reminded me more of myself as a boy. Let no one think that a teacher, even an experienced one, is immune to these types of transferences and unconscious rivalries with children.

The kids had been instructed to paraphrase if they forgot their lines. Angus was good at this, and sometimes could invent whole passages of Vanyaesque rant, so close was he to the character. Occasionally, though, he would end up completely confusing himself and everyone else; the beginnings and ends of his speeches were needed to cue the other actors. In time his co-actors, realizing that he had the largest burden of memorization and by now rather tolerant of his idiosyncrasies, adopted a jazzy flexibility in scenes with him. They would whisper key words to Angus when he forgot his lines, which usually set him on the right track again. But there was one speech that he always muddled—a speech that he would reparaphrase each time, and each time it would come out differently. Finally I told him he just had to know it cold.

"This is the only speech in the play that really gives me trouble," Angus said. "Let's take a look at it," I said. Vanya is attacking, in Act I, Elena's fidelity to her aged husband: "Because such fidelity is false from beginning to end. It has a fine sound to it but no logic. If a woman is unfaithful to an old husband whom she hates, that is considered immoral, but for a woman to silence in herself her poor youth and all her vital feelings—that is moral, I suppose." The speech is difficult first because it calls for sarcasm, second because, as Angus pointed out, Vanya is a moral man and therefore violating his principles when he advocates unfaithfulness. Angus put it this way: "He wants to do the wrong thing but he can't because he knows what wrong is. So he tries to fool himself by being clever."

Angus himself was changing through the experience of his starring role. For one thing, he had become more popular. For another he was less tightly controlled and premeditated, less likely to have to think over every word before saying it. His sense of humor had grown, too, or else he was more willing to let it show. His mother, coming by for rehearsals, was stunned to see him scampering around, playing the clown: "This is a side of Angus I have never seen!" One wisecrack of his neatly captured the paradox of our child-adult production. He was supposed to say of Elena: "Ten years ago, I used to meet her at my sister's. She was seventeen then and I was thirty-seven. Why didn't I fall in love with her and propose to her then?" Instead Angus gave the line as: "Ten years ago, I used to meet her at my sister's. I was twenty-seven and she was seven. Why didn't I fall in love and propose to her then? Goo-goo-ba-ba. Hey, wanta get married?" I realized that he was saying something about his own age, which was embarrassingly closer to infancy than to forty.

8 .

*"There was a time when I thought that every person who was odd was crazy, abnormal, and now I'm of the opinion that the normal state of man is to be odd. So you're completely normal."*

—Astrov, Act IV

One of the oddities of working with ten- to twelve-year-olds on *Uncle Vanya* was that the play began to sound more and more "childish" to me. Chekhov at times seemed to me a rather juvenile writer with a limited, repetitious mind, whose melodramatic plots had a silly side. For instance, the Professor's villainous attempt to sell the farm and boot its real owners out now seemed labored and contrived. Of course, I suspected that I had simply gotten too close to the play to see it fairly anymore, and that the children's behavior at rehearsals had infiltrated my perception of Chekhov. Still, for a week or two there I lost all feeling for *Uncle Vanya*. So did the kids, I imagine. I wonder how people put on ordinary plays for a living, if one can grow numb to such a treasure as this.

The kids had still not gotten Act III down, and with three weeks to go until our performance date, Act IV was nothing but a distant hope. I pleaded, scolded, raged. The one thing I wouldn't do was to praise them when they were merely mediocre. Visitors who came by to watch rehearsals were very impressed, and a little surprised, I think, to find me so parsimonious with my praise. But it seemed to me we had passed the point of supportive "stroking"; any enthusiastic response had to be genuine or it would undermine the truth of future compliments. We were all co-workers now, and the mark of respect I paid them was to assume they could do the job.

One afternoon, the cast—as if playing a prank on me after having driven me crazy the day before—performed an Act II and Act III that was on such a high level that no one knew what to make of it. The actors who were not in the scene watched, for once, those who were with catlike absorption. We all learned something that day: mainly, that we could do it. I had seen bits and pieces of *Uncle Vanya* come alive at different rehearsals, only to watch the cast nervously kick it away and destroy the mood with self-protective frivolity, as though unwilling to raise expectations in me or themselves that they were capable of sustained intensity. Now we knew better.

I might add that some of these magic moments in rehearsals were never equaled in performace (though no rehearsal as a whole came up to the performances in consistency). How I would have loved to splice, like a film editor, the best Act II from one rehearsal with the best Act III from another. Such an assemblage would have made up the ideal production of *Uncle Vanya* by our cast, but that version exists only in my head, and will never be seen by anybody else. In compensation for the loss of those perfect interpretative moments, the theatrical process gives us—especially in amateur productions—the kamikaze thrill of diving into pure, terrifying surprise with every live performance.

Refusing to waste the production on the school auditorium, where the horrible acoustics and odor of old cheese sandwiches (it doubled as a lunchroom) would have strained the suspension of disbelief to the breaking point, I looked around for other halls. I managed to secure the nearby Symphony Space, a grand old movie palace that had been taken over by a nonprofit organization for use by local musical, theater, and community groups. They waived their usual fee since we had no money to pay them, asking only that they be given the whole box office gate for the evening performance. And they let us have four rehearsals on their stage—a generous amount, considering the demand for it among their performing groups.

Most of the time we still rehearsed in the Writing Room (an ordinary-sized classroom) or, occasionally, in the school auditorium. It was difficult to make the transition from one space to another. A tone of intimacy had been created in the Writing Room, which did not translate easily to the school auditorium stage, or to the even larger Symphony proscenium, with its mysterious ropes and wires and backstage passageways. The Symphony Space was in fact too big for us; it seated a thousand in the orchestra and balcony combined. I would have much preferred a little jewel box of a chamber theater seating two hundred, all close enough so that the children would not have had to raise their voices, but there was no such facility in the neighborhood, and we were lucky to be getting the Symphony. The day *Uncle Vanya* went up on the Symphony's theater marquee, it made the whole production seem more real to the kids. "We're going to be on Broadway!" bragged Randi, and in truth the Symphony was located on the Great White Way, only fifty blocks north of the legitimate-theater district. But it also raised the ante: we had to do well now. As one of our stars put it, "I wouldn't be so nervous but we're going to be in a real theater."

Now each one had to concentrate on facing the audience and throwing his voice. The small, cherished, naturalistic style of acting that had developed in the Writing Room seemed lost at first on the Symphony stage. It was pathetic; nothing came across. "Louder!" I kept calling. "Exaggerate more! Make it bigger!" In fact, I hated to force them away from their quiet underplaying and into that strident incisiveness which is so irritating to me when I go to the theater. I much prefer the more muted screen acting, where the audience seems almost to be eavesdropping, but the medium had its demands, and we had to bow to them. The kids had to be made at least somewhat aware of the necessity to project forward or the audience simply would not hear them, which, in a play so dependent on dialogue, would be disastrous. For a week, I entertained the possibility of stringing a set of microphones above the stage, but in the end the technical difficulties and cost forced me to give up this idea. Besides, it would be cleaner with natural sound. But no matter how many times I told the cast to speak louder, they had a hard time accepting the fact that they needed virtually to yell every line.

They loved the feeling of the larger Symphony stage, but in the beginning their wanderings always seemed to take them back, back into the sheltering regions of the stage where their voices were lost in the side flats and against the rear wall. I knew that they were afraid of the stark confrontation with an audience (even a hypothetical audience) downstage, and I sympathized. But they would have to overcome it.

In the meantime, the rest of Clausen's class was readying the scenery. Sasha took charge of scenery and props, and, with the aid of an art teacher, supervised the painting of several large backdrops. Sasha was everywhere, making lists of props, bossing around other children, throwing fits when something was out of whack. She had developed an enormous sense of responsibility for this production, one equal to mine, and I found myself leaning on her more and more as my lieutenant. I made her the prompter as well, which touched off an argument between us. One day she was in the wings and Jamal forgot his lines; the cast waited in silence for more than a minute. "Where's the prompter?" I yelled from the pit. Sasha stuck her head out: "He knows his lines, he's just pretending not to." "Sasha, don't get psychological on me. If they don't say their lines, just prompt! *Prompt!*" She ran into the pit and started weeping several rows behind me. "I quit!" she said. "I don't want to be prompter anymore." All the children onstage looked at me with solemn, accusing faces, as if to say, "You've gone too far this time." I knew I was partly wrong; in fact, I had told Sasha once before that she shouldn't give anyone his lines too quickly, she should let everyone have a chance to figure them out; but I could not bring myself to apologize to her immediately, as I would have done with another kid. She and I were so hitched to this production that we had started acting like an old married couple. At the end of the scene, I turned to her and begged her forgiveness. She accepted, but firmly refused to return to the prompting job.

9.

*"Such goings-on—shouting and yelling, shooting. . . . Shameful, that's what it is, shameful. . . . [Sighing] It's ages since I tasted any noodle soup."*

—Nurse Marina, Act IV

By the first of June I had finished off all my other writing classes and was doing nothing but *Uncle Vanya*. I had decided to rehearse lightly in the last two weeks so as not to exhaust the kids. I was a little worried about the problem of their physical stamina, as we had never rehearsed all four acts together and the show would probably come to more than two hours. On top of that, I didn't want to push them too hard because they had to have some emotion left for the performances. So I concentrated on getting some of the other parts of the production ready. The scenery was going well; the kids had painted a large flowered wallpaper interior and then brown-washed it to make it look faded. There was also a pretty outdoor country scene, with birds and trees. We had gotten some old couches and a writing desk from Sasha's mother, and a real samovar from another parent. Three other kids from Clausen's class had worked out a pattern for the lighting; Angus's mother was helping with the costumes: babushkas, evening dresses, nightshirts, vests, and ties. We had printed up programs and flyers and sent children out to plaster the neighborhood with them. And we were starting to collect a number of volunteer kids who wanted to be in on the glamour and excitement of the final days.

I remembered this same momentum developing with *West Side Story*, some six years before. But that earlier production had had larger resonance: the whole school community had gotten excited, partly because more children were involved, partly because it was the first big theatrical at P.S. 90 (people were more jaded now); but more crucially, because *West Side Story* was a popular musical that everybody already loved, whereas *Uncle Vanya* seemed to be generating a lower order of curiosity. It was more like facing a cultural duty than an anticipated pleasure. I had to accept the fact that *Uncle Vanya* would probably go over the heads of many children and even some of the adults. Tickets for our evening show were not selling as quickly as they had with *West Side Story*. The principal, Mr. Jimenez, who had always shown an interest in our big creative projects, had already informed me that he would not be able to attend either performance, which hurt.

I also had a more private, protective feeling toward *Uncle Vanya*—as one might for an unsuccessful second novel—than I had had toward the crowd-pleasing *West Side Story*. It seemed to me (how quickly we forget) that *West Side Story* had been easier to put on; no nuanced, sophisticated acting was necessary, just twenty seconds of dialogue, then a musical number. I did not remember having been afraid so far along in the *West Side Story* process that it might not come off, but I was having real fear of failure in the pit of my stomach right up to the last day of *Uncle Vanya*. In a sense I was competing with myself and that earlier success. To complicate things, the children themselves knew all about it: several of them had read the *West Side Story* section in my book *Being with Children* (it was in the school library). They even asked, "Are you going to write about *us*, Phil?" Certainly not, I said, and meant it. To imagine such commemoration in advance would jinx us.

We had scheduled two performances, one in the morning for all the upper grades of P.S. 90, one in the evening for the parents and community. I had been noticing that Slim seemed to be getting stronger as Astrov. No matter how much directing advice you give, the actor finally has to figure it out by himself, has to go off and think long and hard about the character. And this Slim had done. I told him how much more self-assured he sounded; he blushed, and Lisa said, "That's the first time you've complimented Slim in months!" They were keeping track of my compliments. One day Slim came in triumphantly and told me that he knew his entire part: his mother had been quizzing him every night and he had it down pat. It was true. I was so glad Slim had stuck with it: he taught me more about the progress a child was capable of than any of the others.

Mylan I knew I could depend on to do a good job; she seemed consistently professional. The two Sonyas were a treat to watch. Angus was getting there. The final dress rehearsal went brilliantly through all of Acts I and II. "Uh-oh," said Sasha, conscious of the theatrical superstition. "It's going too well—and it's the dress rehearsal!" Fortunately, things fell apart in the second half: it was sloppy, slow, anarchic, dreadful.

The afternoon before the first performance, we had a low-key run-through of the still uncertain Act IV. We also had a quiet meeting, everyone sitting onstage, in which I listed the possible things that could go wrong (and the best ways to adjust to them). These ranged from stage fright and blank memory to duds in the cap pistol, falling scenery, tomatoes thrown, fights breaking out in the audience. I reminded them that during the love scene between Slim and Mylan they could expect an uproar from the kiddie audience. It was also possible that some children might be bored, and that a teacher might decide to take her class away during intermission. Significant looks were exchanged; everyone knew Mrs. Jacoby was the teacher I meant. They had already anticipated that the first performance, before their peers, would be the harder. Jamal surprised me by saying, "That's okay. They're just childish little babies. It's not our fault if this is too mature for them." He had already acquired the artist's advance defense mechanism for rejection by the public.

10.

*"I'm just as unhappy as you are, maybe, but I don't give up. I bear it and I'll go on bearing it till the end of my life. Then you bear it too, Uncle!"*

—*Sonia, Act IV*

At seven-thirty the next morning I showed up at the Symphony with my bag of groceries (cheese, crackers, strawberry soda for the drinking scenes, and fresh roses) and waited for the bleary-eyed theater manager to open the doors. The kids arrived moments later. They hung the scenery, set up props for Act I according to the list we had made, inserted the caps into the cap pistol. Angus's mother took the nervous actors into the dressing room and applied their makeup.

The kids at the light board set the lights for Act I. The classes started arriving a few minutes to nine: all the fifth- and sixth-grade classes would be attending, and a few third/fourth-grade teachers had managed to sneak their classes in at the last moment, on the pretext that someone had a brother or sister in the cast. I doubted if the youngest kids would get much out of *Vanya*, but there was nothing much I could do at this point.

When the time came to start I sat in the front row, ready to dart backstage if needed. Our two "old women," Ayesha and Kioka, looked honestly wizened and grandmotherly. Lisa would be prompter, since it was Rebecca's turn to play Sonia. Their joking rivalry had given a new twist to the theatrical cliché as each encouraged the other to "break a leg."

Ayesha took her place onstage, sighing and knitting; the audience grew hushed; I signaled the lighting booth; the lights went dark in the pit; Slim/Dr. Astrov had already made his entrance and was pacing around, ready to respond to the first line in the play: "Have some tea, my boy."

So the first performance began. It was a restrained opening, until Angus came onstage, setting the play spinning like a top.

Angus knew his lines pretty well by heart, and moreover he was giving it that extra something, improvising gestures and motions I had never seen him do before. He seemed possessed. The other actors reacted gratefully to his powerful lead, at the same time appearing a little in awe of his demonic stage presence. All except Mylan, who came on with her own energy, determined to project. Her Elena had taken on a little Mae West and Sadie Thompson in response to the live audience. There were already rumors backstage that some of the children were not speaking loudly enough, and Mylan was going to be heard. She practically directed the others while onstage by the emphatic way she placed herself and delivered her lines. I was glad for her take-charge air, even as I regretted the slight coarsening of, and remove from, her character.

When Act I ended, I ran onstage to help move furniture. The children were excited that they had gotten through the first part —"so far so good!" But they knew that they would have to speak a great deal louder to reach the classes in the back rows during the next act.

Act II began with one of my favorite scenes in the play: the reproachful duet between husband and wife, the Professor and Elena. Mylan brought her tone down (as I'd instructed) and David made the hypochondriac egoist as sympathetic as I have ever seen him played. Rebecca was very touching as Sonia. I was already beginning to wish I had cast her for the evening performance; I consoled myself with the logic of throwing the more professional actress to the tougher (children's) audience. Slim's somewhat herky-jerky interpretation of Astrov had grown on me. He did a great drunk scene, which bought waves of laughter from the kids. However, he and Mylan backpedaled away from each other like unicyclists during the love scene, disappointing the audience.

I was so hyperconscious of the audience's responses, supersensitive to the backstage whispers and the footsteps of stagehands during scenes, that the play itself, *Uncle Vanya*, passed me by. I couldn't feel it. The kids' fright had constricted their voice boxes so that the words came out correctly but without the full passion or authority I knew they were capable of delivering. Either that, or I was too numb with terror to notice how much *was* getting across.

Later, the cast was ebullient. "We did it!" they cried in the dressing room. "No one messed up his lines, Phillip. We did the whole thing perfect. Except for—" and they bubbled forth with the anecdotes of catastrophes skirted that all actors must tell to rid themselves of adrenaline: of how Sasha almost couldn't find the gun, how Angus forgot his line so Mylan made a bridge to her next speech, wasn't that clever? I congratulated them heartily, disguising the fact that I felt a little let down. Somehow, after all that work we had put in, I had expected it to be better. I was down on myself, too, for not being satisfied with the kids' best efforts. Teri Mack and Sue Willis, my Teachers and Writers colleagues, had loved it, but they were artists who had worked on plays with kids for years and could see the effort that had gone into the show. Some of the regular teachers were not sure what to make of the production. I might have allowed myself to be talked into ignoring my own inner doubts were it not for these others' puzzled responses. The performance had clearly not convinced everyone. I wanted it to be so strong that it made every spectator a believer.

A word should be said about the audience. They were remarkably attentive throughout, and as quiet as anyone can expect of five hundred children sitting for two and a half hours in the dark. Nor should it be assumed that P.S. 90 children were especially well behaved or always given to honoring the hard work of other children: I had seen pandemonium and fistfights break out during a visiting school's production of *Oklahoma*. But they watched *Vanya* with an eerie respectfulness, treating it as if it were a sober tragedy. All of the classes stayed until the end, which was itself a tribute. Some kids seemed deeply involved; others were no doubt bored and restless, but went no further showing it than a pantomime of yawns. Others leaned forward, straining to catch each actor's voice. All of the children seemed to understand that something "important" was going on before their eyes, even if they didn't quite get it. For many of them, it was probably their first experience of serious theater.

The first performance had, in short, its virtues and its partisans, but I still sensed we could do better. In the meantime, I was exhausted.

After everyone had gone, Mylan and her little sister stayed behind with me in the dressing room. Mylan wanted to get my honest impressions of how it had gone. Already so grown-up in certain ways, she had a love of postmortems that she knew I shared. But she also seemed to be checking to see if I was all right. Again, Mylan pulled me out of the doldrums by getting me to discuss everything with encouraging candor. I got the impression that she was also flirting with me—and I with her! It is a cliché in the theater that the director falls in love with his leading lady. Since adults are not supposed to fall in love with children, let us simply say that I appreciated Mylan's timely attentions.

11.

*"Second of February, vegetable oil twenty pounds. . . . Sixteenth of February, again vegetable oil twenty pounds. . . ."*

*—Vanya, doing accounts, Act IV*

I had decided to regard the first performance as a dry run. This was, in effect, our one uninterrupted dress rehearsal before the real test. We still had a day intervening before the Thursday night performance to work out the kinks.

On Wednesday, I talked to the cast as a group. The kids were in great shape, they were telling me not to be so nervous. Clausen had instructed them to calm me down. He had gotten his own case of stage fever, of course, and was by now thoroughly involved in the production. On Thursday night he would direct traffic from the wings, freeing me to watch the performance from the audience. Clausen's pride in the project and in his kids was wonderful to see.

My speech to the group went as follows: first I complimented them, then I "calmly" pointed out areas for improvement. I spoke about the need for stillness: raising the shiver down their own backs and causing it in the audience. They had to rediscover the freshness of the play's emotions, take time to feel things, not be afraid to let a moment of silence spread, that's what Chekhov's pauses were put there for in the first place. Play with the pace if you feel like it. Not everything should be so even, so mechanically equal in importance, as on Tuesday morning. Stretch out a passage, give some words the emphasis they deserve. . . .

We still needed to work on the love scene between Astrov and Elena. Romance was an integral part of the play. A kiss would have been perfect, but barring that, the semblance of one would suffice. "You tell Slim he has to do it," Mylan whispered to me. "I'll do it if he does it. He's the one who's messing up." The rumor had already spread that Mylan liked Slim in real life. Slim, on the other hand, was very attached to Lisa, which also had to be corrected for onstage. He would follow Lisa with his eyes when, as Astrov, he was supposed to be utterly indifferent to her as a woman. I had to keep reminding him to neglect Lisa/Sonia for Mylan/Elena. The discordance between art and life was throwing this scene off.

I took Mylan and Slim into the assistant principal's office and locked the door. "These are your instructions. You must have five to ten seconds' contact. Slim, you must put your arm around her waist at the words, 'You can't escape.' Mylan, you put both arms around him then. And you put your head on his shoulder" (this wasn't easy, since Mylan was taller than Slim) "after you say 'Have mercy.' Now try it." I stood back and watched their all-thumbs attempt. "One must get the sense that electric currents are pushing you toward and away from each other, and that no matter what words you say to protest, your bodies are obeying their own laws. Slim, try to turn her more toward you."

"You don't know, Phillip. Slim really is a Dr. Astrov in real life!" said Mylan. "He's fresh!" Slim turned beet red and laughed.

I demonstrated what I wanted with both partners, to reduce to a kind of dance step what had been too fraught with circumstance, but of course my intervention only led to more hysterics. Slim did not relish taking me in his arms, and Mylan cried "No kiss!" when I approached her as Astrov.

The night of the big performance, two telegrams were hanging on the dressing room mirror, one from the Parents Association and one from Mylan's father in Colorado.

Lisa was the only one who had not yet gone through the experience of acting her role before a live audience, and I was a little concerned about her, but she assured me she knew her lines. She had put her hair up in a bun and worn glasses and a dowdy blouse to make herself look less pretty. It was Lisa who started the kids "meditating" an hour before performance. I came backstage behind the side-flats and found them all kneeling or sitting alone, breathing deeply into themselves. What a sight! I tiptoed away; I could not have asked for a better way to focus them, though it would have seemed pretentious for me to ask them to meditate.

Sasha showed up late, on roller skates, with a tape recorder, a Polaroid camera, and every other imaginable gadget. It was her intention to "document" the play both by recording it in front of the stage on her rinky-dink tape recorder and by snapping flash photographs. I tried to explain to her that there was more than enough work to do backstage, getting the props ready for each act. Besides, my Teachers and Writers colleague, Teri Mack, had already set up a video camera in the aisle to tape the performance.

The audience began filing in a half hour early, while we were still putting up scenery. There was no curtain at Symphony Space, so all changes had to take place before the audience's tolerant view. I was too nervous to talk to the incoming crowd, but I recognized many reliable faces. About two hundred people, not as large a crowd as I had dreamed of (partly my fault, since I hadn't taken enough time away from the production to handle publicity or to delegate the responsibility for it properly), but certainly a decent turnout. The familiar greetings of many P.S. 90 playgoers with each other gave the theater a warm feeling of community. The director of Symphony Space made a welcoming speech and we were ready to begin.

## 1 2 .

*"We shall rest! We shall hear the angels, we shall see the whole sky full of diamonds, we shall see how all earthly evil, all our sufferings, are drowned in a mercy that will fill the whole world. And our life will grow peaceful, tender, sweet as a caress. I believe, I do believe. . . . [Wipes away his tears with a handkerchief] Poor, dear Uncle Vanya, you're crying. . . . In your life you haven't known what joy was; but wait, Uncle Vanya, wait. . . . We shall rest. . . . We shall rest. . . . We shall rest!"*

*—Sonia, final speech, Act IV*

The play was terrific. The acoustics were great; you could hear every word. The adults in the pit responded well to the ironic lines, and their laughter put the actors in a relaxed mood. They could feel a live audience enjoying every moment of them. As I watched the play in my seat, getting shivers from the drama, forgetting that these were children or even actors, receiving the full double-edged meaning of Chekhov's lines, I realized what people meant by "the miracle of the theater." That night was a miracle. I knew it was because I had seen that earlier daytime performance, which had been adequate but had not moved me at all. This time there was gooseflesh. I could see why theater folk are so superstitious and, more to the point, so often seem to have a personal relation to God. You start believing in divine intervention when all those random, unreliable elements cohere.

Lisa slowed everyone down; she was on edge, more so than the others, but her seriousness took the form of delaying and going inward, which quieted the cast. A sort of serene sadness played in her movements. There was one woman from Russia in the audience; she had nothing to do with P.S. 90 but had merely wandered in off the street to see *Uncle Vanya*. She told me later that all the children were good, but that Angus and Lisa had the real "Chekhov acting style."

It was Angus's evening. No one could stop talking about him afterward. And rightly so—this was an *Uncle Vanya* with Vanya at the heart of it. I watched him in total belief. So far as I was concerned, his was the definitive Uncle Vanya; as long as I live I will think of Vanya as a boy with a scowling, scrunched-up face and forlorn posture and imperious arm gestures. He and some of the other kids were 20 percent better than I had directed them to be. The truth is that they had peaked at just the right time, in the evening performance. Mylan, having gotten her role down long before the others, had added exuberant *femme fatale* flourishes. She was having a great time onstage. They were all learning enormous amounts about acting each time they performed before a live audience.

One of the curiosities of this production was that the children still seemed to be acting for themselves, rather than to the audience. As often as I had urged them not to show their backs, in the end I stopped nagging about it, because I preferred them to react naturally to each other even if it meant momentarily turning away. The audience became, in effect, eavesdroppers on a world that was not staged for them. Such a solution, coming as it did out of the children's instinctive preferences as well as their amateur limitations, enhanced the purity of the Chekhovian mood.

I kept moving from seat to seat in the large hall, to make sure that the voices were carrying everywhere, but also to be part of different sections of the audience. The play so absorbed me that it was as though I were hearing *Uncle Vanya* for the first time, wondering how it would turn out. Only one funny moment jarred the illusion of life: in the middle of Mylan and Lisa's poignant duet, which was going perfectly, Sasha appeared at the apron of the stage and snapped what must have been two of the longest and loudest Polaroid flash exposures in the history of tactlessness. Mylan froze. The whole audience waited for Sasha to get out of the way, but she stood her ground. It occurred to me that she had never quite accepted not getting one of the major roles and that this was her unconscious revenge.

During intermission the audience seemed collectively to pinch themselves in happy surprise at how well it was going. They were happy, too, I thought as they jammed the lobby, to be escaping momentarily that morbid world of provincial Russia. Angus's name was on everyone's lips. And suddenly, the star himself appeared in the lobby, as did the other actors—racing down the aisles to hear their praises sung. They were forgetting my orders about staying in character! But the audience loved this touch of unprofessionalism. They could return to clucking over the kids as cute.

People were shaking my hand as though it were already over. I worried that the tension might seep out of the second half but was too elated to stay away from congratulations. One parent, who had supported our activities over the years, said to me: "Phil, I have to admit that when I heard you were doing *Uncle Vanya* with the kids, I thought, 'This time he's really flipped his lid.' Forgive me, I owe you an apology." His comment gave me an uneasy, sickening feeling, as I realized how close I had come to destroying their confidence in me. All it would have taken— would still take—was one panicky actor.

The second half maintained the high quality of the first. The love scene between Mylan and Slim was neither the backpedaling race of the first performance nor a real clinch, but some compromise in between. The last act, when Elena, the Professor, and Astrov leave the farm one by one and Sonia and Vanya are left alone, turning to "work" as a momentary anodyne for their abandonment, had a nice hushed floatiness. I had wanted Lisa to take Sonia's magnificent "We shall rest" speech slowly, so that the audience would know the end had come. The ending had been too sudden on Tuesday morning, partly because Rebecca had rushed her lines, partly because the lighting crew had forgotten to fade out slowly. This time we had worked out a new staging where both Angus and Lisa would stand at the edge of the stage for her long speech, and the lights would begin their slow fade in the middle of it. Lisa pulled a blank, a few lines into the speech, but then her groping through it, her pauses, her difficulty in trying to remember made the speech sound even more sincere and moving. It was as though she were struggling to find the right words with which to console Vanya and herself.

The lights went out and Lisa's father stood up with tears in his eyes. Then everyone applauded. We had rehearsed the bows and they were fairly neat. Mylan called me onstage (as I had asked her to, not trusting to spontaneous acclamation) and I thanked everyone behind the scenes and ended by proposing, tongue in cheek, "Next year, *The Cherry Orchard*." Inwardly I thanked God for saving my skin: I promised myself this was the limit, that I would never try anything so difficult with children again.

"We did it! We did the Impossible!" cried Angus to anyone backstage who would listen.

1 3 .

*"They're gone!"*

—*Mme. Voitskaya (Vanya's mother), Act IV*

The next day I had arranged to take the cast as a treat to the Russian Tea Room, after three o'clock. This sounds more generous than it was: I had asked them to bring their own money, about five dollars each, but promised that I would escort them and treat anyone who couldn't swing the finances. (Somehow, certain adults still got the idea that I was paying for everyone; their eyes misted over, so great is the need for people to find "Mr. Chips" figures in everyday life.)

An essential part of the cast by now, Monte Clausen came with us. On the subway the kids were making uneasy jokes about not being let in, and when they entered through the Russian Tea Room's revolving doors and gazed up at the swank interior I could see them go stiff with fright. True to their nightmare, the hostess took one look at the gang of children and refused to seat us. "But I made a reservation for thirteen yesterday," I said, retreating toward the back of the restaurant. "You stay there!" she added. "I'll go ask the manager." I saw them conferring and the manager frowning. I advanced toward them and started to explain that this group had just put on *Uncle Vanya* and wasn't it appropriate that they have tea at the Russian Tea Room—but apparently I had already committed a great sin by passing beyond the *maître d*'s red sash, since they both looked up in horror and motioned me back, caring not at all to hear my sentimental explanation.

They finally decided to seat us. So the great menus were brought and the waitress put on her children-serving smile. I had expected the kids to be full of talk about their triumph the night before. But for the first half hour they were so intimidated by the fancy surroundings that they compensated by playing a game of Rich People. Ayesha said, "I almost drowned in my bathtub yesterday. Gracious! A hundred feet is really too big for a bathtub." David cracked, "I only sold two yachts yesterday." These were mostly middle-class kids, but they had evidently never been in a joint like the Russian Tea Room before. One more educational experience. I drew their attention to the polished samovars and the paintings and the waiters' red peasant smocks: "If only we could have had some of those for the play!" Gradually, they settled comfortably into the surroundings, and stuffed éclairs and swan-shaped cakes into their mouths, and drank tea in a glass, *à la Russe*. I ordered an "Uncle Vanya," a sweet cocktail which happened to be listed under that name on the menu, and let them each take a sip. "My mother's going to kill you when she finds out, Phil!" Mylan said.

"It's finished!" cried David. "I feel so sad about it. We worked for so long, and now there's no more *Uncle Vanya.* . . ."

Jamal, meanwhile, was stealing every sugar cube and matchbook in sight. The kids stocked up on free postcards on the way out. They had promised they would take me out once or twice during rehearsals, and I had made the same promise to them, but in the end we went Dutch, as was fitting. They were still handing me crumpled dollar bills as we headed up 57th Street past Carnegie Hall, happy to be in the warm sun again. Some were running ahead, mixing with the five o'clock crowd, while others continued to feed me bills from their pockets.

The dollar bills that children give you are different from other people's currency. They are bunched up and folded six times over and very, very sweaty. They don't know how to lie flat. They made my wallet bulge for days afterward.

I could go on to justify *Uncle Vanya* in traditional educational terms by saying that it increased the children's vocabulary, reading, and memorization skills; taught them a good deal about acting, literature, and Russia; and helped instill the values of patience, endurance, and team cooperation. I also recognize that it represented a kind of luxurious excess: it was educationally inefficient and labor-intensive, took too many hours away from other endeavors, involved only a third of the class, and was never organically integrated into the rest of the curriculum. It did not resolve, one way or the other, those large philosophical questions about the nature of childhood I posed in the beginning, however tantalizingly it brushed against them. Nor, given the typical constraints of the American school day and the myriad pressures put on teachers, would I expect such an effort to be easily replicated. I had a uniquely advantageous set of circumstances, and I feel intensely grateful to the P.S. 90 community for having given me the latitude to take such a risk of failure with their children. I wish there were more room allowed in the educating of our young for attempting such follies, such adventures that challenged children to the limits of their (surprisingly expandable) capacities.

That summer I went away to the country for vacation. I was sharing a house in Wellfleet with several people, and we would often meet in the course of the day for a few moments on the sun deck, exchanging pleasantries about the weather or non sequiturs accented with glints of confession in a manner that reminded me uncannily of *Uncle Vanya*. Snatches of *Vanya* would come back to me as my housemates and I sat facing the pond, looking not at each other but outward toward that external point, where the audience would have been. In the architecture of the summer cottage, with visitors coming and going, each of us entering and exiting group scenes from his or her world of privacy, the wisdom of Chekhov's observations struck me time and again. I would mumble Vanya's irritable lines to myself as I retreated to my room, annoyed at some social snub or aroused by some amorous triangulation. And I could have sworn that, miles away, on their own vacations, the kids were also remembering the lines of the play, and connecting them with the life they were seeing all about them.

# ON
# SHAVING
# A BEARD

I have just made a change that feels as dramatic, for the moment, as switching from Democrat to Republican. I have shaved off my beard. Actually I clipped it away with a scissors first, then I went in for the kill with a safety razor. The first snip is the most tentative: you can still allow yourself the fantasy that you are only shaping and trimming, perhaps a raffish Vandyke will emerge. Then comes the moment when you make a serious gash in the carpet. You rub the neighboring whiskers over the patch to see if it can still be covered, but the die is cast, and with a certain glee the energy turns demolitionary.

As I cut away the clumps of darkness, a moon rises out of my face. It lights up the old canyon line of the jawbone. I am getting my face back. I lather up again and again and shave away the bristles until the skin is smooth as a newborn's—the red irritation spots where the skin has reacted to the unaccustomed blade seem a sort of diaper rash. When I am done, I look in the glass and my face itself is like a mirror, so polished and empty are the cheeks. I feel a little sorry for the tender boy-man reflected before me, his helpless features open to assault. The unguarded vacancy of that face! Now I will have to come to terms again with the weak chin, the domineering nose, the thin, sarcastic-pleading lips.

I look down at the reddish-gray curls in the sink. The men in my family have always been proud that our beards grew in red, though the tops of our heads were black. It seems an absurd triviality for Nature to waste a gene on, but it is one of the most tangible ways that my father has felt united to his sons and we to him. A momentary regret passes through me.

Never mind: I have taken an action. I grew the beard originally because I had been restless and dissatisfied with myself; I shaved it for the same reason. How few cut-rate stratagems there are to better our mood: you can take a trip, go shopping, change your hair, see every movie in town—and the list is exhausted. Now I will have to be contented for a while. It is summer, the wrong time to start growing a beard again.

Because of the hot weather, I also have a ready-made excuse for anyone who might ask why I gave up my beard. I know that the real reasons are more murky—they go the heart of my insecurities as a man and my envy of others of my sex. When I meet a man I admire and he is wearing a beard, I immediately think about emulating him. The tribe of bearded men have a patriarchal firmness, a rabbinical kindly wisdom in their faces. They strike me as good providers. They resemble trees (their beards are nests) or tree cutters. In any case, mentally I place them in the forest, with flannel shirt and axe.

So I join this fraternity, and start to collect the equivalent of approving winks from other beardies, fellow conspirators in the League of Hirsutes. It feels good to be taken for an ancestor or pioneer. Then the novelty begins to wear off, the beard starts to itch, and I realize that inside I am no more rooted or masculinely capable than before. I start to envy clean-shaven men—their frank, open, attractively "vulnerable" faces. Some women will trust you more if you are clean-shaven; they profess to see beards as Mephistophelian masks, hiding the emotions. Early in the relationship, this may be a good reason to keep a beard. At a later point shaving it off becomes tantamount to a giddy declaration of love.

Other women, on the other hand, will tell you that a kiss without facial hair is like a roast beef sandwich without mustard. *They* consider beards a mark of virility, trustworthiness, and bohemian sensitivity. Obviously, the image systems break down in the face of individual tastes. Nevertheless, it is still possible to say that beards connote freedom, telling the boss off, an attitude of "gone fishing"; men often grow them on vacations, or after being booted from the White House staff, like Ehrlichman. (Even Admiral Poindexter grew a mustache.) Clean-shavenness, on the other hand, implies a subscription to the rules of society.

A major division in the bearded kingdom exists between those who revel in no longer having to bother with maintenance, letting Nature have its luxuriant bushy way, and those who continue to keep a razor nearby, prudently pruning or shaving the cheeks every few days. A well-clipped beard on a kindly man looks as proper as a well-kept lawn on Sunday. On the other hand, there are beards with a glint of cruelty—beards trimmed to Caligulaesque exactitude. I had thought to be one of the pruners, but went too far, lacking the razor-sharp finesse.

Having shaved the beard off, I take my first cautious steps into society. I am dreading those who will ask why I did it, then settle back for a long soul-bearing explanation. What will I reply to those who are quick to say, "I liked you better the other way"? My impulse is to step on their toes, but we must not punish honesty. Once, when I was teaching in P.S. 90, I shaved off my beard, and the children, who were familiar with me as a hairy man, were so outraged that all through the first day of the new regime, they ran alongside and punched me. Children are good at expressing a sense of betrayal at change.

Those who are bearded for the long haul either tend to view the new me with something like a Mennonite's disapproval at backsliding, or are relieved that one who had appeared a member of the brotherhood was exposed in the nick of time as a turncoat.

A few friends, who pride themselves on their observational powers, make helpful comments like: You look fatter. You look thinner. You look younger. You look older. The majority say nothing. At first I think they are being polite, not meaning to broach a subject that might make me self-conscious. Then, out of frustration at their not having noticed, I finally call my naked face to their attention. They say: "I *thought* there was something different about you but I couldn't put my finger on it. Besides, you keep going back and forth, Lopate, who can keep up?"

# ONLY MAKE BELIEVE: SOME OBSERVATIONS ON ARCHITECTURAL LANGUAGE

As a layman with a dilettantish if persistent interest in cities and buildings, I often read architectural journals or go to lectures and exhibits on the subject. It intrigues me the way architectural discourse relies so constantly and, to some degree, unconsciously on metaphors. I am used to metaphoric thinking from writing and reading poetry; but whereas in poetry an analogy is made to enliven the ordinary by placing it in a strange and unexpected context, the architectural metaphor seems intended to do the opposite: to flatten itself out as soon as possible, so that it becomes a stale but cozy bit of white noise which may be interpreted by its professional audience according to what each wants to hear.

The most prevalent imagery in architectural discussion is somatic. We are all used to hearing the city described as a body; the parks are its lungs, the highways its arteries, the central business district its brain or heart, the slums its cancerous tissue. Buildings are also broken down into bodies, assigned circulatory and evacuative systems, a "skin," joints, skeletons, and so on. Beyond that, they seem to have a potential for romantic response: we read of an office building "embracing" its corner, or of facades curving "seductively" toward each other, of the "exquisite tension" between parts of a complex. Urban designers show a special concern for the sexual satisfaction of streets, hoping that they "climax" well at key intersections.

Architectural criticism is saturated, in fact, with this tone of longing for sexual economy and the poignancy of unmet urges. To read about the frustration of a clever design by an unenlightened developer, or the scotching of a university campus's original plan, or the failure to achieve the exciting possibilities of a public park, is to encounter the architectural equivalent of coitus interruptus—not surprising in a field where so many artistic dreams are left floating on the drawing board.

It is also interesting to note the influence of literary criticism, specifically narratology, on architectural writing: how often a spatial sequence is discussed in terms of a "narrative," a circulation pattern read as a "suspenseful scenario," a plaza referred to as an "event" or "denouement." There is something ridiculous about this tendency to speak of pieces of the built environment as though they were heroes and heroines of a novella—perhaps of one of those dry *nouvelles romans* by Robbe-Grillet that obsess over place descriptions. Still, you might ask, what is the harm in all this anthropomorphosing? The treatment of spaces and structures as autonomous needy beings can lead to Manifest Destiny, as specious a logical appeal in the realm of urban renewal as empire building. Beyond that, there is probably little harm, except for the promotion of fuzzy thinking, which keeps forgetting the chasm of nonidentity between the metaphoric halves.

Take, for example, a rather innocuous statement by architect Cesar Pelli. In an interview describing his Four Oaks and Four Leaf Towers in Houston, he said: "The buildings . . . end up in a flat top, although they have a gesture toward the sky." In what way they gesture we are not told, nor whether the gesture is an angry, tender, or neutral one. Animated cartoons, which often delight us by rendering a metaphor with literal exactitude, might dramatize this phrase by showing a building with plump arms extended, crying "Help, save me!" or "Come here, Blue Boy!" In Pelli's case, the architect seems merely to want us to know that he has taken into consideration a potential relationship between the apex of a building and the firmament, and that he has dealt with it, so to speak. If we were to decode this statement in terms of the architectural moment, we would probably find that this practitioner is trying to walk a tightrope between late modernism and postmodernism: he has broken, ever so gently, with the minimalist flat roof of the International Style, and, by designing a sloped plateau, has gone partway toward "meeting" the sky on friendly terms, as it were, in a gesture of conciliation. Now why a perfectly flat roof could not also be interpreted by the sky as a good-faith gesture, certainly as much as a poke in the eye could, I am not sure.

The word "gesture" in itself promises very little, which may explain why it has become so indispensable in architectural discourse. Gestures need not ensure that the intended communication is even received: one thinks of futile or empty gestures, for instance. Certain design gestures seem to me especially rarefied: I've heard a Manhattan architect speak of giving his building a blue facade because, while it was located five city blocks from the river, he wanted it to "refer" to the waterfront district. In the present climate of professional guilt about modernist architecture's failure to be sufficiently contextual, all this projection of gestural activity onto stationary buildings seems to imply a touching parental protectiveness, as though buildings were autistic children who were not expected to relate much, but whose every step in that direction must be celebrated.

A neoprimitive, mythologizing subtext is also invoked in these metaphors. One reads about design gestures toward the earth, the winds, the sky, the hills, the moon, the afternoon light, the ocean, the stars. The building seems a sort of aborigine placating elemental gods and the spirits of the site with its ritual dance. Avant-garde architecture, or at least one faction of it, seems to have taken on the burden of reconnecting secular man to the cosmos. Quite an ambition. Might one also detect a flight from urbanism and its complicated responsibilities in this nature-mythologizing process?

"Earth, sky, divinities, mortals"—I hear the tom-toms of the Heideggerian fourfold. Heidegger's essay, "Building Dwelling Thinking," with its advice, "The nature of building is letting dwell," seems to have greatly encouraged architectural thinkers to reimagine their discipline as part of an eternal cycle—which is all to the good. Where it becomes pretentious is the effort to locate phenomenological significance in banal design, as when one reads about the edifice's "presence" mediating chapel-like between heaven and earth, or about a new suburban house in the woods recapturing the pious vernacular simplicity of a forester's hut, only to see the project's spiritual intent so dismally subverted by the mundane photographic illustration.

Moving from the cosmic to the psychological realm, we find buildings judged as "narcissistic," for not having "responsible" lobbies or facades. Narcissism is a curious charge to level against an artifact that was not only intended to be beautiful, but which is incapable of beholding itself. I suppose this is professional shorthand for the ostentatious and unneighborly. However, real-life narcissists, whatever their shortcomings, are not necessarily vain or show-offy.

Perhaps the most problematic aspect of architectural morality, to an outsider like myself, is the notion of "honesty." It would appear that if a building "expresses" its structural elements—if its pipes, ducts, heating devices are brought out into the open, if its facade reveals the interior divisions of its floors, if its load-bearing columns are left exposed—it is somehow an honest fellow. This strikes me as an invitation to charlatanism: surely a building may unmask the Victorian decorum of backstage functions by exposing its pipes galore, while lying in its teeth on deeper matters of artistic integrity. What is missing in this excessively technical definition of honesty is any larger recognition of the degree to which architecture, like all the arts, must inevitably "cheat," if that is the proper word for creating a pleasing illusion.

In regard to ethics, let us also note the rationalizations of one architect who had accepted a building commission in a large project (Battery Park City, New York), the guidelines of which seemed to be encouraging "historical"—i. e., postmodernist—solutions. In the statement accompanying his exhibit maquette, James Stewart Polshek wrote: "While the composition recalls the architecture of Amsterdam South housing in the 1920s, its effect is made by the manipulation of basic elements, not the superimposition of decoration. In so doing, the design remains true to the ethical core of modernism. . . ." I am fascinated with that smug phrase "the ethical core of modernism." Would that all mortals could remain true to some ethical core in their daily struggle with modern life as easily, it would seem, as those in the architectural profession, who have only to eschew decoration to qualify.

I do not deny that there are serious moral questions implicit in architectural aesthetics; certainly there are profound problems regarding justice in the whole history of what gets built, and for whom. But these issues are often trivialized and deflected by a superficial moralism, which has more to do with visual trends and careerist maneuvers than anything else. Just as fashion magazine writing regularly tries to introduce the newest stylistic artifice as a more "natural" look, so does much architectural discussion seem an attempt to elevate wrinkles of taste into moral imperatives.

Let us consider the loaded phrase "human scale." This increasingly popular term would seem to have an obvious meaning, since everyone uses it with such confidence. Yet I wonder. I interpret the term cautiously to mean that a built environment should be sensitive to the biological requirements and psychological needs of its human users. (Elephants and other animals may have different scale needs, but theirs are not being addressed.) Since I do not see many buildings going up with ceilings only three feet high, I would assume that, except in extreme cases of height or girth, most modern architecture does respect the biological range of the human species. Therefore, the clamor for "human scale" must refer to some psychological idea about a desirable proportion between the individual and the structures that surround him or her. Is the idea simply that a building is a person writ large, and that, after a certain height or width, the metaphorical identification breaks down? We could start by imagining an optimum building height, beyond which a human being might feel unhealthily oppressed or dwarfed. Some would set this maximum at six stories, the limit of stairs one can tackle comfortably, and, for precedent's sake, the height of the tenements in ancient Rome. However, even most champions of a "human scale" would not press for so limiting a standard: they recognize both the invention of the elevator and society's need for centralized space as mitigating factors. Whatever the term "human scale" means from this point on becomes subjective and a bit mystifying.

Consider a realtor's full-page ad in the *New York Times* (January 23, 1984), which reads in part: "HUMAN SCALE: living the good life in today's New York is more a matter of careful scale and proportion than of expensive grandeur. On 22 floors, 309 East 49 Street has a total of only 86 homes. On many floors you have only one or two neighbors; on no floor do you have more than five." Is exclusivity of space accorded by social privilege the definition, then, of human scale? Conversely, does density imply a threat to what makes us human? Such a white middle-class view would surely not be shared in Jakarta, Bombay, Hong Kong, Tokyo. Are crowds inhuman? There are jammed public spaces, like Grand Central Station, that human beings navigate with a fair degree of assurance and even delight.

It seems curious that glass-box towers should be criticized for violating human scale, while the older, stepped skyscrapers, often just as large, now escape this charge. Does the terra-cotta detail on the Woolworth Building's admittedly lovely facade make it so much more "human" as to compensate for its immense size? Are older materials like stone and brick intrinsically more "humanistic" than concrete, glass, and steel?* For that matter, is

* We may intuitively think so, but architecture is full of exceptions—of "warm" uses of concrete and steel, and "cold" stone towers. In Jerusalem, a law was passed around 1935 by the British dictating that all future buildings use Jerusa-

there any truth to the idea that pedestrians, while they may be reduced to the size of ants from a penthouse perspective, actually *feel* like ants when walking on the sidewalk below? (And if man *were* humbled by the scale of the buildings around him, would this necessarily be a minus? It might bring him into a truer relation to his place in the universe.)

I realize I am playing devil's advocate here. I, too, believe there are good reasons for neighborhoods of smaller scale—more sunlight, less noise, greater variety of building type per plot, a more *gemütlich*, traditional atmosphere. I, too, fear that unchecked volume and density will lead to greater alienation, anomie, crime. Still, I cannot forget that what once seemed overpowering and intolerably ugly—the World Trade Center in Lower Manhattan, for example—now has a certain reassuringly familiar aspect. Given the remarkable adaptability of people to new technology, the term "human scale," with its static model of human nature, would appear in the final analysis to be presumptuous.

Up until now, I have been mostly discussing verbal metaphors in architecture; visual metaphors are another story. If verbal architectural metaphors often obfuscate in their blandness, visual metaphors run the contrary risk of esotericism. By visual metaphors I mean those physical hints that the architect may place in his or her buildings in the hope of raising certain specific associations in the viewer's mind—and, often as not, failing.

For example, I was listening recently to a flashily dressed South American architect explaining the symbolism behind his choices of color, material, and form in the community centers he had designed. These clues all added up, in his mind at least, to a

lem facing, the traditional yellowish limestone of the area. There could not have been a more enlightened statute, and it probably did preserve the harmonious character of the city. Yet the last of the thirties Bauhaus-style houses of concrete or stucco, built before the law was passed, often look a good deal more sympathetically contextual in Jerusalem today than do the monstrous new hotels with stone facades the thickness and chintziness of pressed cardboard.

"story" about the exploitation of the Indians by the Spanish, and the workers by the bosses. On the one hand, his color/politics equations were too bluntly programmatic, with a heavy-handed symbolism of the sort that most abstract painters would have rightly disavowed. On the other hand, they were too subtle: I doubted that any of the workers or Indian peasants who used these centers would possibly have grasped the metaphoric meanings behind his design choices, unless they had happened to attend one of his lectures.

I once had a dentist who told me he "signed" each of his fillings, so that any future dentist working on my mouth might recognize and applaud his handiwork. I wonder how many visual metaphors in buildings today are equally as hidden, waiting for some unknown colleague of the future to discover them, like the "Kilroy was here" calligraphies of my old dentist.

A practitioner might protest: Does it matter finally to the advancement of architecture as an art if the public doesn't "get" the visual metaphors? Can't people be touched subconsciously without knowing exactly why? After all, certain hermetic modern poets like Khlebnikov are read with understanding by only a hundred experts worldwide, yet they are still considered to have inched the art forward. Similarly, the more visionary architects of today, like John Hejduk or Aldo Rossi, seem to enjoy working with an abundance of private autobiographical imagery, quotations, dreams, imaginary cities, poetic texts, puns, all of which will soon necessitate the architectural equivalents of a reader's guide to *Finnegan's Wake*.

Unfortunately, only a master can get away with self-referential obscurity. Applied to lesser talents, "private imagery" is a term of criticism implying lack of clarity. I would guess that many esoteric visual metaphors or puns occur in architectural jobs of otherwise unredeemed constraint, where they are thrown in as an expression of powerless spite against the client's program, or as a tribute to the conceptual theory the young architect had learned in school and had optimistically imagined he was going to apply in practice.

At bottom, the fuzzy off-register quality of today's architectural language, verbal and visual, comes down to this: the field is going through a crisis, finds itself in a *cul-de-sac*. No matter which way it turns it seems to be merely replaying exhausted solutions, be it the no-longer-utopian geometries of modernism or the cynical, capricious recyclings of postmodernism or the folkloric naïveté of regionalism. It is an era for the minor if elegant refinements of an Isozaki or Richard Meier at the top, while in the trenches the vast majority of architects are preoccupied with the most squalidly pragmatic exercises of squeezing the maximum profit out of a particular building site. In the absence of any formal breakthrough or clear direction that might rally the ideals of the most gifted practitioners and the loyalty of the young, architectural professors and writers have cast an envious eye on the prestige of other disciplines. They have borrowed the vocabularies of structuralism, phenomenology, semiotics, the Frankfurt School, deconstructionist literary criticism, art history, and so on, until architectural discourse has become a sludge of intellectual intention. I am speaking of the brightest in the field; there is also a kind of architectural writing that provides as little overview as a snake crawling over a rock face and describing the terrain inch by inch as it slithers. Between the vague philosophical pastiche of the former and the myopically concrete style of the latter, a language has been concocted as much to evade as to confront the pain of the present hour, in which the architect finds his hands tied. It is then of necessity a metaphor-laden language, with the "as-if" equation signifying a longed-for union between dream and opportunity.

# HOUSTON
# HIDE-AND-SEEK

When I first moved to Texas in 1980 to teach at the University of Houston, I was struck by how many Houstonians asked me right away what I thought of the place; and then I would see their faces start to flinch in preparation for my not "getting it." Invariably I tried to frame a positive answer, to set them at ease, because I genuinely did like Houston, or the little I knew of it. I was, in fact, determined to like Houston. It seemed boorish to react like the all-too-typical New Yorker who keeps saying, "You call these bagels? You call this an Italian restaurant?" I knew I had not moved down to Houston in search of the perfect bagel. There would be enough local dishes and amenities to delight me, if I gave them the chance, and I quickly saw that when I expressed myself as even moderately well disposed toward their town, Houstonians would respond with a generosity, hospitality, and kindness I had not encountered anywhere else.

As I came to know Houston better, I began to get anxious watching visitors and new arrivals frame their own answers to the Houstonian's patient question, What do you think of our city? Often I was embarrassed to hear the newcomer's reply loaded with factual distortion, simplistic clichés, and superiority. But I was equally nonplussed at the Houstonian's grave, gentle nod of seeming agreement. The other side of the Texas-sized boast is a reserve, if not a kind of self-effacing modesty. One evening I asked a dear friend of mine—third-generation Houstonian, sixth-generation Texan—why she had not corrected the fatuous misstatements of several intellectual transients talking about her city at a dinner party we had both attended. Her reply was a weary, resigned "Why bother?" I wondered if this refusal to correct the newcomer's errors might be not just a case of good manners—native Houstonians have the finest manners—but something more aristocratically scornful as well. These people think we are fools, so let the truth be our secret and leave them to their own pitiful ignorance.

I have become enough of a Houstonian that now, when I go back to New York for a season, I get enraged listening to the idiotic stereotypes that Manhattanites have of Houston. I never fail to defend its high level of civilization; then I return to the Magnolia City and have to do the reverse when Houstonians start in on their New York-hating routines. During the Mets-Astros baseball playoffs a few years ago, my divided loyalties made me feel like a counterspy wherever I turned. However, this very perspective (bifocular, émigré, divided) may allow me to shed some light on the mysteries of Houston, since the city now has many residents like myself in its midst, people who originated elsewhere and remain on the fence of geographical commitment.

My arrival in Houston, during the record heat of July 1980 (you may recall the thousands of chicks who died in their incubators), occurred in the midst of an economic boom. It was a giddy, heady, can-do atmosphere; funding seemed to exist for every new idea; skyscrapers were going up by the dozen; the art world was flourishing; and the residential real estate market was so lush that people claimed even a retarded Realtor could make a fortune here. Every time the price of oil went up a dime a new crop of millionaires was birthed. Having fled New York, which had just escaped a bankruptcy scare by laying off teachers and other municipal workers by the thousands, I could not help but be enticed by this atmosphere of easy money. Not that a writer ever hopes to cash in on such wealth, but one can at least enjoy the good life by subliminal proximity.

At the same time, I was a little put off by all the boosterish rhetoric I heard. Houston was billing itself as the City of the Future, the one that all others would have to emulate. These were the days when the words "world-class city" were flung around like rice at a wedding. Either Houston had just arrived on the international stage as a "world-class city," or it merely needed a (fill in the blanks: first-class opera house/mass transit system/ new convention center/major Picasso from his cubist period) to become one. All this sounded, I'm sorry, rather dumb and yokel-like to me, because when a metropolis has achieved the status of a great world city—Paris, London, New York, Tokyo, Berlin, Beijing, Mexico City—everyone knows it and there is no need to keep acting as though one more item would push it over the top. Besides, this fuss to become a world-class city struck me as too outer-directed, too desperate to catch up, too futuristic without showing enough love for what Houston already had and was. (As it happens, Houston has since gotten its opera house, convention center, Picasso, and voter approval for a mass rail system —and the place still feels the same.)

Part of this hysteria to shed the city's more modest beginnings by trying to purchase "class" led to a kind of blue-chip approach in cultural decisions, a way of playing it safe that has, paradoxically, often resulted in Houston being taken for a ride. Again and again, the city has gone after the most established, distinguished names in the arts, with results that resemble every other provincial city on the make. Take, for example, Houston's public sculpture, entertaining in its way, but tame and predictable: one Henry Moore, one Dubuffet, one Miró, one Oldenburg, one

Beverly Pepper, and so on down the line. Need a big, prestigious corporate architect? Hire I. M. Pei, of course. Hence the boringly correct Texas Commerce Center. A sculpture garden designer? Who else but Isamu Noguchi? The result is an uneasy cross between rock garden "retreat" and corporate plaza, which almost no one uses, set on a site crying for human movement. Maybe it would have been better to commission a provocative younger artist on the rise than to have approached a master in his doddering years, or one whose practice is so big he farms out most of it to underlings. When the Museum of Fine Arts needed a new wing they went after the best architect money could buy, Mies van der Rohe. The first austere glass wall Mies designed may have been top-notch, I wasn't around to see it; all I know is that in the museum's next expansion, which swallowed up the first, they have gone to the Miesian well once too often. The curved, band-shell facade we live with today is not thrilling design, Miesian or otherwise. The interior is a different story; yet one becomes adjusted even to the lunkish exterior after a while, and to cherish it for its very familiarity.

This is part of what I mean by the bifocular vision I've developed toward Houston. My aesthetic response seems to consist in tenderness for what's there, chagrin for what isn't. Sometimes one can come to find lovable in Houston what in another context might appear less so. Several years back I was showing an English literary critic around town, and I took him to the Shamrock Hotel for lunch, since I loved their cheeseburgers. As the Shamrock confronted us, this very cosmopolitan, well-traveled gentleman said, "My God, what an ugly building!" I was pained. He did not understand—how could he?—the significance of that very building on that particular site. Not that I'd forgotten that my own response on first seeing it had been somewhat similar. But over the years I had become so attached to that improbable step-backed cliff looming up and anchoring the neighborhood around the Medical Center; so fond of its goofy lemon-and-lime color and faded-fancy lobby shops and Olympic pool amid cabanas and palm trees; so aware of its historical meaning to Houstonians—the hotel's wildcatter builder, Glenn McCarthy; its spectacular opening in 1949, the bands that broadcast from the Shamrock nationwide when it was all the rage; the rites of passage round the pool for generations of Houston adolescents (the girls whose families could not get into the restricted country clubs would form desperate crushes on the lifeguards, and then meet their safer future husbands; here also, Air France, which used to lodge its stewardesses and pilots, providing an informal beauty pageant, fondly remembered by the locals, of the latest maillots and monokinis, and the first shocked glimpse of men's bikini briefs)—that I would almost have died at that moment rather than see it go. Little did I anticipate that I would soon be marching in a futile protest rally to save the Shamrock. That's when you know you love a town, when you start mourning the way it savages itself.

But I'm getting off the track. The boomtown years of 1970–82 only speeded up a pattern of postwar growth that transformed Houston from a fairly compact, downtown-centered metropolis of 500,000 in 1950 to a 600-square-mile, Los Angeles–type sprawling, decentralized octopus gobbling up all the land around it, becoming the fourth-largest city in America, with a population close to two million. Suddenly it had turned into a city of transients, strangers lured by employment opportunities. Those who had been here five weeks gave tips to those who had just arrived.

We newcomers found it hard to put our finger on the essence of Houston. For one thing, it is a city without a symbol: you cannot conjure it up with a trolley car, an arch, an Eiffel Tower, an Empire State Building. Not that this was necessarily bad: it permitted the imagination to roam, and better the honesty of no symbol than a trumped-up logo rushed in to fill the void.

As temporary down payment on an identity, we newcomers were offered a congeries of regional clichés: chicken-fried steak and instant millionaires; king-sized cockroaches and giant potholes; country-and-western nightclubs like Gilley's; the infamous heat and humidity; rodeo parades down Main Street on Livestock Day. These folkloric simplifications were soaked up by *Times* stringers and the national media—not that you could blame them, since the city has been notoriously poor at projecting a more complex, truthful image of itself. One television station ran ads promising that its local newscasts would help you "get Houstonized," while the visuals showed people trying on cowboy boots, as though this equivocal place could be grasped by making such a stalwartly campy purchase. Besides, Houston is *not* a particularly Western town; if anything, it seems much more Southern in feeling, lying as it does just inland from the Gulf Coast, closer to New Orleans in vegetation and manners than to Fort Worth or Dallas.

When the boom ended, in 1982, people stopped talking about the need to demonstrate world-classness or to get Houstonized; the new idea was to get by. And, dare I say it, Houston is a calmer, pleasanter, more reasonable place to live in the diminished expectations of economic recession than it was during the boom years. I don't mean to minimize the suffering of the unemployed and homeless, but simply to appreciate the good-humored realism one encounters now. I would wager the atmosphere is more like the Houston of old (half sleepy, half go-getter), before the city was invaded by a million strangers like myself out to make our fortunes. The population is once again contracting (Philadelphia has regained fourth place), and the realization that there will not necessarily be an unbroken march of prosperity and progress, as Houston's drumbeaters envisioned for it, could prove salutary, even "character-building," as they say —provided the city uses this interregnum to reconsider what direction it should take when the economy picks up again; that is, to *plan* (traditionally a dirty word in Houston).

The next development I witnessed in the city's sense of self can be summarized by the down-but-not-out slogan, "Houston Proud." This defensive rallying cry failed to specify to what achievements or virtues our summoned pride should affix itself, while raising an afterecho of doubt in the listener's mind, suggesting some unaddressed inferiority complex. And for whom was this whistling in the dark intended? Whether meant as a civics lesson to socialize the immigrants, a morale-booster for the natives, or a warning to sneering competitors, like Atlanta, of Houston's plucky spirit in the face of hardship, it sounded a singularly tinny trumpet indeed. So often, Houston has fallen into a mechanical spirit of boosterism, like a sleepwalker inhabited by the ghost of the late Judge Hofheinz (the Astrodome's indefatigable promoter). Still, I don't want to run poor "Houston Proud" into the ground; let us accept it for what it is, a public relations Band-aid during a difficult transition period.

I am, if not Houston proud, then Houston fond. Must our chests swell with pride in order for us to love a place? The affection I have for Houston collects around certain street corners, landscapes, cicada sounds, atmospheres, many of which have nothing to do with civic pride *per se*. If I tell you that I am moved by the chastened afternoon light in February, on a day of scattered clouds, as it bounces through the crape myrtle trees and onto the white clapboard houses with their subtropical peeling paint jobs, it's not something I expect to see in a Chamber of Commerce brochure. Equally unusable is the fact that I love to ride my bike through the Vietnamese neighborhood downtown, around Tuam and Main, past the Saigon Cafe with its beaded curtain and extra-strong coffee and tables occupied by serious young Asian men in white shirts, past the upstairs nightclubs with their melancholy Vietnamese pop chanteuses, the apothecary shops and groceries with their consonant-clotted signs, all that homesick re-creation of Indochina mushrooming for a few blocks and then disappearing into the weeds, as mysterious as the old dry-cleaning establishment nearby that, for some reason, is housed in what looks like a Greek temple.

There is something funky and moody about Houston's allure. It has to do with the way surprises crop up in the middle of nowhere: a beautifully tended front garden next door to a tumbledown shack; a house made of beer cans; a stunning Mexican-style apartment court like the Isabella on decaying lower Main Street; a glass-bricked, art deco printing plant near deserted warehouses and railroad tracks on the outskirts of town. (Sometimes it feels as though three fourths of this city lies at the edge of town.) It's an aesthetic of grace notes amidst emptiness; mirage and discontinuity. No matter how much they build up Houston, it will always resemble to me a warm smile with missing teeth.

One reason is that it didn't grow up tightly and logically like other cities, which spread block by block in dense concentric rings, but kept jumping miles away from the center, establishing speculative outposts and overoptimistically expecting in-fill to come later. On the one hand, I regret Houston's refusal to play the game more like traditional European capitals, since there is a certain urbane synergism that can only be achieved when a metropolis is dependably dense, continuous, and citylike for miles and miles. On the other hand, as Kenneth Frampton has noted, "Given the distributive capacity of the freeway it is highly unlikely that we will ever return to the dense pattern of the traditional city." Besides, in an odd way I have come to enjoy the spaciness (in both senses) of this place. There is a weightless, eerie, floating quality about Houston, which comes partly from its decentralized clumps of skyscrapers rising with capricious verticality from the interminable flat horizon. Houston has the split personality of wanting to be both a big city and a small town, with backyard and lawn for every citizen; and the resulting schizoid contradictions of scale shouldn't, but do, form an oddly comforting meditational ground.

Driving along Kirby Avenue late at night—a nondescript nowhere corridor with billboards and fast-food stands and darkness, a way to get from one place to another but without much profile in itself—you are sucked in, as with so much of Houston, invited farther and farther along with no real opposition, nothing to bounce off of, until you notice that the place you're sucked into is your own inner self. Somewhere, always just beyond reach, is the city, all that flat, exploding, diffuse, strip shopping center galaxy, outside, but never bigger than, one's car window. The automobile is a moving monk's cell, it forces you back on your thoughts, while only marginally attending the vaguely urban streets. "Perhaps only through a kind of inattention, the most benevolent form of betrayal, is one faithful to a place," writes architect Aldo Rossi. If so, Houston invites fidelity; it is a strangely nonimposing environment.

Too much is made of the explanation that Houston lacks zoning, as though the presence of a saloon next to a private convent school could explain the weirdness of this place. All big cities have such surreal juxtapositions. No, what makes Houston so peculiarly itself is the alternation of being and nothingness. Driving around Houston, one grows conscious of that rhythm of negative and positive space, the lacunae, the gaps between teeth, the no-man's-land of vacant lots, speculatively held, which Nature has been busily reclaiming with high weeds and broken cars, rusting abandoned machine parts, mini-swamps, since, as we know, nature abhors a vacuum.

So do developers, but sometimes the economy is simply too sluggish for them to make their move, thank God. We owe to Houston's recession the continuing existence of the Fourth Ward, that amazing shantytown of shotgun wood-frame houses and churches and rib joints and poor blacks sitting on porches, a bit of Mississippi Delta that trembles just beyond the itchy paw of downtown. The Fourth Ward is historically important, the oldest black urban settlement in Texas, originally occupied by families from East Texas and Louisiana cotton farms who built modified versions of the old slave cabins, adding front porches for coolness and communal life. The city has been neglecting the area for decades, stingy with garbage pickups, sewer maintenance, nonpotable water pipes, as if hoping that the district will disintegrate of its own accord or that one good fire will clear the land for redevelopment. But the Fourth Ward obstinately holds on.

Houston became officially integrated only in the mid-1960s, through a coalition of black organizers, Texas liberals (a doughty breed), clergymen, and moderate businessmen who saw the writing on the wall. The change occurred without anything like the degree of ugly incident that took place elsewhere; Houston has a justifiable reputation around the state for tolerance and progressive politics. However, there is still a good deal of de facto segregation—or racial distance, if you will—in residential and recreational activity. Much of the vitality of Houston's nightlife, for instance, is hidden below the surface, in the barrios and ethnic neighborhoods, and you need a guide to help you explore.

Take the zydeco. I was first brought to a zydeco dance hall, the Continental Lounge, by my friend Lorenzo Thomas, a black poet. It was a big square barn with red walls and couples hugging in the middle. Somehow it reminded me of Renoir's paintings of country dance halls, except all the dancers were black. Many of the couples on the raised wood-planked dance floor were middle-aged or gray-haired: some dressed sharply in three-piece suits, others wore simple farm clothes; a few were in cowboy hats. Even the teenagers looked countrified, sweet-natured, and somehow from an earlier era. They danced to the music called zydeco, that haunting harmonic blend of sweet French Cajun and piquant Negro blues. The accordion-saxophone combination supplies the main spice; the rhythm section consisted of drums, a bass guitar, and, what struck me as most timeless, a man wearing an aluminum washboard vest over his chest, thumping himself to play.

We took seats at a table on the side and ordered beer and hot boudin sausages. The dance floor was packed, yet not claustrophobically so; the same swaying, relaxed motion passed from body to body. It was mostly touch dancing, and the strong rhythm more or less dictated what to do, as I discovered when my date and I (the only two whites) took the floor.

Individual styles gradually began to emerge from the dancers. One gray-sideburned, thickset man in a white suit and white tie rooster-strutted around his amused partner, inventing a little drama of attraction and rejection, working himself into a lather of romantic feeling, pausing only to take out a red bandana and dot his forehead. An intense young pair breezed through a slick, economical bunny hop. Nearby, another man, drunk, was dancing by himself with a half-grin that seemed to repeat the curve of the bags under his eyes. A black policeman took the mike and wished everyone a happy new year (it was mid-January) and announced that the police force was there to help so they should cooperate with the police in the coming year; nobody listened much, though they weren't rude to him either.

Having diplomatically left us alone at first, people now began coming over and extending hospitality. The white-suited man invited us to his home and to be his guest at other zydeco events. It seemed that zydeco moved from place to place every week like a traveling fair. There were no newspaper ads; you just had to *know* by seeing the Xeroxed handbills or belonging to the proper information circuit.

Since then I've returned on occasion to that strange, beautiful zydeco milieu, sometimes at the Continental or in the parish hall of a church out by the airport. It's just one of the many near-invisible worlds that make up buried Houston, the real Houston each resident seeks out individually, for want of a discernible mass focus. You end up putting together an interior city from the handful of locations that are charged with personal meaning. The milieu to which I mainly belong—the intelligentsia or "art crowd" —is another hardy scene that nevertheless eludes the world's image of Houston, maybe because intellectuals are less easily packaged into mythology than cowboy boots.

The art crowd consists of about two hundred visual artists, gallery owners, curators, architects, historians, writers, critics, musicians, dancers, patrons, students, hangers-on, and dilettanti who bump into each other year after year at the same art openings, performances, parties, and the same ten restaurants. There is much running around in packs, a hedge against loneliness as well as intimacy; sometimes two eventually pair off and marry, or friends quarrel and avoid each other, finally growing friendly again, because there aren't that many people to talk to, the cast of characters is so limited. Every once in a while a new curator or artistic celebrity moves to town and is feted, courted, scrutinized, privately dissected. Every so often, too, one of the regulars, like a Chekhov character who keeps sighing, "I must go to Moscow," actually picks himself up after years of threats to do so and moves to New York or Los Angeles or Washington, D.C. These defectors later return for visits, wistfully reporting that they have never been able to find elsewhere anything like the warm camaraderie of the Houston art crowd. On the plus side, the art scene here is exceptionally cohesive, supportive, and loyal; on the minus, this close-knit courtesy has so far stifled the development of honest, tough-minded public criticism, which means some local artists are never challenged to go beyond producing half-baked work.

One of the hallowed places for the art crowd is Brown Auditorium, in the Museum of Fine Arts. A splendid hall—and here I have only praise for Mies's handiwork—graced by perfect acoustics and sight lines, its scale allows for both intimacy and formality. With its ambitious program of repertory cinema, poetry readings, chamber music concerts, art history lectures, panel symposia, community meetings, and so on, Brown Auditorium functions as a truly democratic space, a sort of Town Hall for Houston's culture-hungry.

Another hallowed space is the Brazos Bookstore, which is surely one of the best literary bookstores in the country. For years it has been at the heart of the city's artistic life, an agora where one drops in expecting to meet friends, or to steal a few minutes' spicy if harried conversation from the impish, punning owner of the store, Karl Kilian, who will also tell you about the latest choreographic whiz or minimalist composer coming to town, for whose concert Karl happens to have a bunch of tickets to unload. We authors come by the Brazos to attend book-signing parties or readings, but also secretly to check where Karl has placed our own books and perhaps to bug him about it afterward.

The universities in town are of course great attractors and multipliers of culture. Rice University has an air of placid gentility; its Byzantine Revival quadrangle by Cram and Goodhue (who designed St. Bartholomew's Church in New York) is perhaps the most harmonious campus ensemble in America. The University of Houston exudes more of a nitty-gritty, messy, working-class atmosphere, as befits a state public institution. The University of St. Thomas, a small Catholic school with a strong Thomistic bent, has a trim, effectively severe campus designed by Philip Johnson in his Mondrian phase. All of these schools have played host to extraordinary cultural moments in the city's history.

The Rothko Chapel is another special place in my interior map of Houston. How many times have I trotted visitors from out of town over to that shrine and watched their differing reactions—some awed, some mildly impressed, others left cold—and with each I have tended to agree. I've sometimes allowed myself to think (blasphemously, in this town) that those paintings are not nearly as great as one might have hoped from Rothko. They are from his late, blackened period and do have a grim grandeur. My feelings toward them are as changeable as the natural illumination that filters through the chapel's skylight from hour to hour: I've gone there in the mornings when the building is empty, save for a long-hair meditating on a cushion; I've stared at a purplish-black canvas so long I was spooked when I looked down at my green Adidas and saw ebony shadows in them; I've felt peace and panic and pleasure and indifference and itchiness in that sacramental cube, wondering where the recessed niches led; in short, the Rothko Chapel plays back to me, for better or worse, my own mind. Then there are those "ecumenical" occasions when the chapel is packed, hosting a Sufi whirling dervish troupe, a Steve Reich concert, a human rights awards ceremony —or a memorial service. Each time the art crowd loses one of its own we pour into the Rothko Chapel to comfort each other. The occasion is sad, but there is some consolation in realizing that we are, in fact, a community still holding together. Precisely because Houston's art-making pool is so finite—unlike New York's or Paris's, where the inexhaustible riches of cultural life render it impossible for any one artist or writer even to meet all of his/her peers—this town values its creative people, and gives them a chance to play a larger civic role.

Houston is perceived by the outside world as a thoroughly modern environment, a sterile mélange of concrete and glass, so that people who have never been here are surprised when you tell them that, first, it is an exorbitantly verdant place, and second, that it retains much that is old. For myself, who am by nature attached more to the past than the present, this evidence of the old is very healing. I keep trying to root out the vestiges of old Houston, to understand what it was like before I came. My archaeological itch has taken me to the various cemeteries around town, where I stare at headstones and fantasize about the days when people routinely picnicked among the graves if the weather was nice; it has taken me through the charming old residential neighborhoods like the Montrose, the Heights, the Binz, Southampton, MacGregor Drive—which comprise for me the true heart of Houston, with their wonderfully diverse stock of vernacular bungalows, split-level ranch houses, and Bauhaus-style cottages made elegant or cozy by their owners' loving touches; it has taken me into the old tumbledown wards and the new ethnic areas in search of a polyglot, international Houston; it has taken me into the orderly, regulated suburbs like Kingwood, where clotheslines are forbidden and where the American Dream has been achieved to a degree that scares the hell out of me; and into the abandoned suburbs far beyond Loop 610,* where the American Dream suddenly stopped in its tracks and ran out on its mortgage. In a vain effort to grasp firsthand the city's economy, I have ridden around the obscure area of the Ship Channel, whose construction sixty years ago catapulted Houston over Galveston into one of the major ports in North America (a fact one so often forgets, even living here); out by the oil fields where mechanical grasshoppers paw the ground; and through the enormous Medical Center, a virtual walled empire of Disease (health care, not the oil business, is Houston's largest employer). But riding around and imagining can teach you only so much, and the history of Houston is not that easy to come by. This is not a city that wears its past on its sleeve. Quite the contrary, it is an amnesiac city, one that keeps forgetting its intriguing antecedents in a headlong rush to embrace the shock of the new (or the *schlock* of the new, like Jean-Michel Jarre's laser light show during Texas Sesquicentennial Year).

In the City of the Future, even native Houstonians fall into

* A belt highway, Loop 610 divides the older, inner city from the annexed suburbs. I am partial to life within the Loop, where the concentration of cultural institutions, downtown business district, and old neighborhoods connotes a life-style as well as an address—Manhattan might be a rough analogy—while what I would facetiously call Outer Loopovia refers to all that *terra incognita* (to me) of sprawling suburban subdivisions. Demographic figures show the population of Houston shifting more and more outside the Loop, which presents special problems for preserving and rejuvenating the old historical core of the city.

the habit of waiting expectantly for the Age of Culture to commence with the next new arts facility's construction (a necessary fund-raising stategy, I suppose), losing sight of the fact that the city has always had its share of culture, from the Ballet Russe de Monte Carlo and other major dance companies who have performed here, to Leopold Stokowski holding sway at the Houston Symphony, to locally developed writers like O. Henry, William Goyen, June Arnold, Donald Barthelme, Vassar Miller, Larry McMurtry. Streets have been named after the generals of the Texas War of Independence, but not in commemoration of the heroes of the common people, like Lydia Mendoza, the great Chicana singer who made her home in the Houston Heights, or Lightnin' Hopkins, the blues artist who lived and died here. Houston is profligate with its anticipations (the latest being a plan to snare a Disney operation for the Space Center), stingy with its memories.

Nowhere has this civic amnesia wreaked more damage than on the urban environment itself. In the last thirty years, the old, retail, walking downtown, a congenial gathering place with department stores, movie palaces, and eateries, was for the most part demolished and replaced by a colder set of freestanding corporate towers alternating with surface parking lots. One is no longer invited to dally, meander, window-shop. This single-use downtown closes up at six o'clock; at night or on weekends, it resembles nothing more than a huge deserted warehouse.

Interestingly, Houstonians are very proud of their new slab-tower central business district, which they see as a triumph of architectural up-to-dateness. And indeed, several of the new buildings are architecturally interesting, and—seen from a distance—there is something inspiring about the skyline of Houston as a whole; those chimerical salmon- and jade-colored reflecting glass surfaces vying for the eye's attention with the latest Mayan-topped or Dutch Guild Hall-inspired postmodernist skyscraper. It's not surprising that Houston became the sketch pad for Philip Johnson and other postmodernist practitioners. As critic M. Christine Boyer has written: "Architecture made to be

seen from the road demands an image which is immediately understandable to a public concentrating more on traffic than on a
building's details or structure. This architecture must offer a spontaneous theatrical spectacle manipulating images in simple com-
binations and patterns that are part of our collective recall. . . ."
This is sixty-miles-per-hour architecture, and the freeway offers
the best vantage point from which to experience Houston as an
urban place. The problems begin when one descends to street
level and finds oneself surrounded by such an unnuanced, im-
permeably monumental stage set. Since Houston's downtown
blocks are so short (250 square feet), a single contemporary office
tower will usually occupy a whole block: there is rarely any sense
of variegated, historically layered street wall; instead, one finds
that odd condition of constructional uniformity that architect
Jacqueline Robertson has called "the Hiroshima effect."

There are social as well as aesthetic drawbacks to the new
downtown. Regrettably, at the same historical moment that
Houston officially brought in racial integration, it converted its
downtown into a monolithically white-collar (if not white) universe, while redistributing its shopping and popular entertainment functions to outlying malls, where preexisting residential
patterns would reinforce de facto segregation. The only type of
entertainment that the city kept downtown was high culture: a
performing arts complex for opera, ballet, the symphony, and
repertory theater, whose ticket prices and cultural vocabulary
tend to exclude the working class and poor. The old social-mix
role of downtown was further diluted by an underground tunnel
system, put in with the new office buildings, which leached an
entire retail economy from ground level, taking much of the
area's street life with it. Whereas any stranger can happen upon
interesting shops while wandering through a city's streets, Houston's tunnels are a maze into which only those who work
downtown venture. In these minimalist corridors, slight
differentiations of material or lighting seem like giddy refinements, and the sudden entry into a radial underground "plaza"
becomes a thrilling event. Ultimately, though, it is a mole's life,

with torpor-inducing vista restrictions and monotonous duplications of retail offerings—soup and salad bars, travel agencies, novelty card shops—lopsidedly geared for a lunch-hour trade.

The tunnels are part of Houston's general tendency to avoid the street (i.e., the weather), a tendency that has yielded skyways between buildings and giant interiorized shopping malls like the Galleria, which have all the élan of an airport terminal. Actually, Houston's weather is not so terrible: our best-kept secret is that the city has one of the mildest and pleasantest climates of any North American metropolis—for about seven months. If the remaining five come close to being insufferably hot or wet, that average is no worse than those of London, New York, Chicago, or New Orleans, all excellent walking cities. In my view, Houston has overdone this business of climate control: in moving so much of its life indoors for "comfort" it has developed a kind of unhealthy phobia against its own natural environment. It was the city's misfortune, in a way, that its building boom coincided with the advent of new air-conditioning technologies, which sealed off buildings from the outside street.

I think I could more easily accept the self-cannibalization of the old historical business district, knowing that it came at a period (the sixties and seventies) when disastrous urban renewal policies were gutting downtowns all over the United States, were it not for the fact that Houston continues to dismantle its historical heritage, or what is left of it. In addition to the Shamrock, the distinguished Medical Arts Building, the old Lamar Hotel where the city fathers used to decide policy over poker hands, and John Staub's graciously designed Crabbe House in River Oaks have all recently fallen to the wrecking ball; the exemplary, small-scaled Allen Parkway Village public housing complex in Fourth Ward was cynically allowed to deteriorate by the Housing Authority; it is now half boarded up (though its defenders have just gotten it added to the National Register of Historic Places). The grand Rice Hotel, with its majestic portico, is on its last legs, also boarded up and vulnerable to demolition; and the Pillot Building, a handsome example of nineteenth-century cast-iron architecture, was first neglected and then, in a sloppy repair job, de-roofed, promptly causing part of the building to collapse. A "facadectomy" (the facade saved like a Hollywood set, the rest cleared for a new office building) became its only option for survival.

Whenever I am away from Houston and try to picture it, what comes to mind are the white concrete silos of the American Rice Company elevators that rise like Egyptian pyramids above the greenish waters of Buffalo Bayou. The rice elevators are a noble example of pure industrial architecture and probably my favorite Houston structure; now they, too, stand in grave danger of demolition. If they can no longer turn a sufficient profit, surely some other recycled use can be found for them—even as architectural ruins. All development proposals for Houston agree that the waterfront-park area along Buffalo Bayou will play a key part in the city's future, and when that day comes, how we'll miss the rice elevators, how we'll groan and tear our hair out, if we allow that chalky prominence to disappear.

It isn't just a matter of being sentimentally attached to old buildings, but of appreciating that cities need local landmarks to be spatially comprehensible, to be readable by their citizens. Whether it's an actual monument, or a commercial, industrial, or residential structure that stands out, by virtue of singular scale, materials, or design excellence, or a durable, gracious train terminal like Los Angeles's Union Station, landmarks create a sense of place around which memory and continuity accumulate. You need the big clock where the lovers rendezvous, and you need that clock to stay in the same spot for one generation after another. Houston is sadly short of landmarks. It *has* history, but it doesn't go out of its way to make it visibly apparent.

Take Allen's Landing, the very spot, tradition tells us, where the city was founded by our very own Romulus and Remus in 1836. Granted, the Allen brothers were two New York land developers out to make a bundle, but still it's thrilling to be able to point to a spot and say, Here's where it all started. I was living in Houston for years before I even found out about Allen's Landing, and when I finally did visit the unmarked site along the bayou, lured by an arts organization benefit, I was amazed at how pretty it was, how luckily close it was to downtown, and what an appalling highway bridge had been allowed to be built almost directly over it, obscuring and overwhelming what should have been the city's ancestral heart.

I am forever looking backwards, I admit it. Still, when I ask Houston to do the same, it is not to freeze the city in a static conservatism, or to prevent it from acting upon fresh visions, but so that, when it reaches for those visions, it can proceed from a more confident, mature sense of self, such as only comes from making peace with one's past. In order for a place to have a soul, it has to bear visible witness to a past. Without that manifestation of history, Houston will become what its detractors already claim it to be: a brash, thin-souled, postmodernist theme park. It is as necessary to create the past as to create the future. Again, this is not simply a matter of preserving what is already in our midst, but of coaxing from an analysis of the past those promising hints that were left undeveloped, and reforming the present defects accordingly. For instance, Hermann Park was meant to be our own Golden Gate Park or Central Park, but its original Olmstedian vision was blurred as acreage got nibbled away by hospital grabs, roadways connecting downtown with the Medical Center, and surface parking lots. It is still Houston's most popular and heavily used public space; the zoo is one of the few places in town where families of all social strata parade on a Sunday, and where the energy of urban life is both concentrated and mellowed. The Juneteenth blues concerts and Shakespeare in the Park at the Miller Outdoor Theater give us a glimpse of how lively this city could be. But Hermann Park needs nurturing, landscaping attention, and a retrieval of its initial "City Beautiful" impulse before its true scenic and recreational potential can be realized.

The Astrodome was once Houston's proudest achievement—"the Eighth Wonder of the World"—until domed stadia started cropping up everywhere. Built in the middle of Houston's love affair with the space program (and perhaps deriving its iconography more from NASA than from the sporting field), the Astrodome is like a flying saucer landed on a lunar landscape. There is no surrounding neighborhood to absorb or detain you here; once the game has ended, you have no alternative but to head for the parking lot and sit in your car until an opening presents itself in the exit lane. Compare this situation to Wrigley Field, Madison Square Garden, or the Boston Garden, where fans can spill directly into the streets and walk off their exuberance or disappointment, or crowd into bars and subway trains and carry on. There are few opportunities to linger *en masse* in Houston after an event, to savor oneself as part of an emotional crowd. It wouldn't be bad, either, if a city park were landscaped beside the Astrodome, so that people could play catch with their kids before or after a game, or have a picnic under shade trees. The glory of Houston is its trees. Yet whenever a new facility is built, it seems always to be aproned in harsh concrete.

Houston has a general lack of neighborhood parks, plazas, promenades, fountains—attractive public space where people can congregate to watch the spectacle of humanity and celebrate festivals and local rituals. In this sense, however friendly Houstonians as individuals are, the built environment wears a more hermetic face to outsiders, because there is so little effective public space to mediate between private homes and the impersonal workplace. It almost seems as though Houstonians have lost the habit of public space. One obvious reason for this atrophy is the privileging of the car at the expense of foot traffic and mass transit. Walking and public space have always been deeply intertwined: the great plazas and town squares did not bloom in a void, they were fed by rich circulation patterns of surrounding pedestrian streets.

In Houston, the rights of pedestrians are held in contempt. For example, outside of downtown, contractors are not even required to reconstruct a public sidewalk after tearing it up to permit new construction. Try walking in most neighborhoods of Houston, even along major thoroughfares. If you are lucky you will find a semblance of sidewalk, one narrow square of concrete, usually cracked, buckled, roiling, edged on both sides by grass plots that, after a rain, resemble flooded rice paddies; it is difficult to walk two abreast and carry on a conversation, but even single-file you cannot advance very far without being stopped by a ditch, an impassable puddle, a miasma of weeds and vines, someone's property fence, or a parked car forcing you into the roadway—down which most Houstonians choose to walk (if they walk) anyway, daring the cars. Should you swerve in the other direction, you find yourself crossing someone's lawn, with the awkward sense of trespassing. Houston's badly kept sidewalks give off the blunt message, "Don't bother, take the car," which is particularly hostile to citizens who don't have cars.

Not that all areas are so inhospitable to pedestrians. Among the most agreeable sections to walk are the parallel avenues of North and South Boulevards, with their double lanes of live oaks touching over a lovely brick promenade and forming a nave of sunlight. Even on the hottest days of August, one feels invited to stroll down the shady esplanade and peek at the old Edwardian and neoclassical mansions on either side on the street. These boulevards make one realize how breathtaking a city this could be, since its climate is ideal for supporting any number of live oak avenues. Lately, the local civic associations have pledged themselves to an ambitious tree-planting operation downtown and elsewhere, the fruits of which may take fifty years to be appreciated, but at least it is a start. Houston could certainly use a few broad landscaping or street design maneuvers, like real boulevards, to bring about a more harmonious whole. Until now, the town's wealthy benefactors have shown little interest in urban design; we are lacking not in millionaire-donated hospital pavilions or cultural edifices but in those gestures that would help to bring the city itself together more as a work of art.

Such synthesizing gestures need not be pharaonically expensive; they can also be quiet, subtle. We have a good example in the blocks around the Menil Collection, which the locals call "Do-ville" (after Dominique de Menil). First, all the cottages that the Menils owned in the area were painted gray, giving these blocks a uniform look. Then a museum was built that related with sublime contextual tact to the gray wooden houses, being itself a sort of oversized gray clapboard house. So something new is

created that completely respects the neighborhood and its past
—even, in this case, a partly manufactured past.

On the other hand, to cite a hellish example of lack of design, the Post Oak area around the Galleria shopping mall is
noteworthy for having the greatest concentration of buildings it
is possible to assemble without at the same time achieving anything like an urban texture. Today's architects are trained to build
freestanding objects; quite apart from whether the result is good
or bad architecture, what you get when you keep placing one
freestanding object next to another is a proliferation of objects.
What are needed are not so much objects as *places*. Much of
Houston suffers from floating placelessness. Of course, what I
am describing is not unique to Houston. It is only that Houston,
having been at the forefront, is sometimes blamed for the phenomenon, as when some architectural critic warns against the
"Houstonization" of his fair city. Obviously there are larger,
global forces at work that account for the increase in spatial
privatization and the decrease in the art of city-making.

In Houston, we have all sorts of wonderful excuses and rationalizations for our deficiencies in good public space and urban
design, which we trot out enthusiastically: the weather (though
many South American cities abound in lively outdoor plazas);
the lack of zoning (but zoning would not necessarily bring improved public space either); the rapid population growth (still,
Chicago grew from 300,000 to nearly two million between 1871
and 1900, and pioneered in urban design); the low-density
spread (then what to make of many Scandinavian cities? besides,
downtown Houston is hardly low density); the prohibitive cost
of public space in the present economy (was it ever cheap?); and
the free-enterprise, anti-tax climate in this part of the country
(perhaps this is beginning to change with the voters' approval of
a mass transit system).

Houston's resistance to city planning strikes me as partly a
way of putting off acceptance of its urban nature. Anti-city values
saturate the state's rugged-individualist, agrarian, Chamber of
Commerce religion, Texana; and Houston, as the largest city in

a state that has become predominantly urban but refuses to recognize the fact, has long been caught in the contradictions of that denial. The creation of public space is after all the most self-consciously urban act a municipality can undertake. It signifies a city's maturation, through the recognition of its responsibilities to the public to exist as a collectivity. Houston is often spoken of as an adolescent: the question is whether this immaturity is a phase (albeit a protracted one) or a permanent personality trait.

Some have argued that older cities had more of a need for good public space (as well as cafes, pubs, clubs, and community halls), because people's homes were generally less comfortable. In offering its citizens a much higher standard of domestic comfort, this argument goes, Houston represents a new type of suburbanized city where private convenience reduces the necessity, and the yearning, for public interaction. Perhaps, though I can't believe that the political vitality and conviviality of urban areas are not somehow diminished in the process. Still, most Houstonians do seem at peace with their city, find it reasonably easy to navigate, and don't seem to feel the same ache of placelessness that I, as a transplanted New Yorker, intermittently experience. For instance, I can't help noticing the oddity of two major thoroughfares crossing each other without anything more dramatic than a 7-Eleven convenience store and a gas station to mark the juncture. It seems to me that major intersections should be commemorated by an intensification of city life—a department store, a big movie theater, a dance hall, a public square or park, *something*—but Houstonians do not seem to share this uneasiness. Each Friday and Saturday night I look at the cars piling into the junction of Montrose and Westheimer streets, drawn by the magnetic attractions of these crossroads, and I think, Wouldn't it be better for these young people to have something to *do* once they got there, besides honk their horns and participate in gridlock? But no, they seem to like to sit bumper to bumper, perhaps entertaining the fantasy of picking up some cuties in the next car. Who knows?

The problem with looking at Houston from a strictly urbanistic perspective is that one inevitably falls into the trap of judging it by the cherished traditional values of urban form (real streets to walk in, real public spaces to be in). By these standards Houston must be seen as a failure, even while they ignore the degree to which it seems to work on its own terms. On the other hand, the proclamation of local champions to "Let Houston be Houston" has a smug Panglossian ring and dodges responsibility for correcting the very real deficiencies of the place. If you ask me, Houston will never become a great, "world-class" city. But it's an intriguing, evocative, comfortable, one-of-a-kind place with plenty of surprises. So it seems that once again I'm parked at the intersection between Tenderness and Chagrin, where I'll leave it alone for the present.

# CARLOS:
# EVENING
# IN THE
# CITY OF
# FRIENDS

$W$hen someone popular dies, it is human nature to be possessive, to try to assert a privileged status among the grief-stricken, to think: "They may have loved him, but I knew him better." This is particularly true with a person like Carlos Clarens, who was so vivacious and knowledgeable and attractive that we all wanted a piece of him—of his time, at any rate. And to an amazing extent he obliged, responding to the claims of who knows how many friends. Are there Casanovas in the realm of friendship? At Frank O'Hara's funeral, dozens of people testified they had lost their best friend—implying that he or she had been the poet's best friend as well. I make no claims to being Carlos's closest friend: in fact, I don't think he held with such a hierarchical distinction—or if he did, he was diplomatic enough never to tell me who it was. I know there must be many in this audience* who knew him longer and perhaps better than I, and whose Carlos Clarens may not be the same as my Carlos. I hope you will forgive me the silliness of even saying "*my* Carlos." But it is only by getting personal, by looking at our friendship, that I can begin to say something about this irreplaceable and lovable man.

It was characteristic of Carlos's openness to the possibilities of camaraderie that I now don't even remember the stages by which we became friends, except that there was none of that awkward testing behavior, no "He likes me, he likes me not." We met at a buffet-style dinner party, and by the time we had gone once around the table we were fast friends, conspirators. It facilitated things that I was already an admirer of his book on horror movies. Whether he knew my byline also, as he pretended, or was merely willing to give me the benefit of the doubt, doesn't really matter; we delighted in each other's company from the start, and that never wavered.

I was drawn to Carlos by his enthusiasm and wit and buoyant spirit, by his considerable personal charm—the twinkle-eyed, dimpled smile; the silver-templed curly hair; the Gilbert Roland mustache; the tall, rumpled-casual elegance—by his kindness, and by his tremendous cultural learning and worldliness. He had the sort of light touch in relation to intellectual culture that I think of as specifically Havanan (Havana, "the Paris of the Americas"). To me he was that romantic figure, a cosmopolitan, a Citizen of the World. With all the languages he spoke and the capitals he had lived in, that he chose to make New York his primary residence is a tribute to that city's internationalism; his unapologetic adoration of New York was not the least of the tastes that bound us together as friends.

A friendship between a gay man and a straight man is no easy thing. So often the initial rapport, based on shared tastes and

* This eulogy was given at a memorial service for Carlos Clarens at the Public Theater on March 9, 1987. The other speakers were Mary Corliss, Donald Lyons, and Susan Sontag. There was an overflow crowd and a showing of some of Carlos's favorite film clips.

values, may be jolted by suspicion: the gay friend may detect an air of majoritarian superiority or homophobia in his companion, while the straight one may recoil from what seems at times a too-hermetically encoded and excluding sensibility. It is so easy to inflame the wound—that defensive struggle rooted in adolescence over what it means to be a man. Each represents to the other the road not taken, the rejected possibility; and, with that awareness, it is hard to avoid entirely the sense of having one's own self rejected as well. Finally, if there should happen to be, as in most friendships, some erotic spark, it must be circumvented delicately or dealt with or laughed away.

Though I have had a number of friendships with gay men over the years, only with Carlos did these tensions completely evaporate. Why? First, in all frankness, I was probably more attracted physically to Carlos than he to me; I was obviously not his "type" (he liked them younger and cuter). Any good-bye hugs or casual touches were usually initiated by me, not him. Second, the graceful lightness that I have said affected his show of learning also governed his relation to homosexuality. It was not for him a sanctimonious religion but a matter of realistic self-appraisal and pleasure. He neither dwelt on the subject nor repressed it for my sake, thank goodness. Once, we were sitting in a Mexican restaurant, Rosa Mexicano, and Carlos was reminiscing about his youth, and I asked him when he first knew he was gay. He said it was while watching his first Disney cartoon, *The Three Little Pigs*. "All those bounding poss-tteriors!" he exclaimed in his Cuban accent, heavy on the consonants, and we both roared at the explanation.

Another factor in all this was Carlos's appreciation for women, particularly pretty ones—a taste we shared. He would say about one of his lovely friends: "If I were ever to go straight, she would be the one to make me do it." Or, "She is absolutely delicious, I could eat her like an oyster!" He was always promising to introduce me to some of these beauties. One night he took me to a birthday party uptown for his beloved brother Fernando, and, as good as his word, introduced me to two of the most bewitching women I'd ever seen. They were both absolutely infatuated—with Carlos. I watched him in operation; he was so very attentive with women, the gallant cavalier, a lost art (certainly one I never possessed).

Carlos had a great capacity for social life. He could fit in with the "beautiful people" on Park Avenue or with the MOMA moles. He would sometimes describe for me in Balzackian detail the previous night's gathering—from the food and ambiance of the latest restaurant he was championing, to the idiosyncrasies of the company. His fondness for his friends never prevented him from noticing their imperfections.

Sometimes I hankered for admittance into his *beau monde*. It had been twenty years since I'd stopped believing there was such a thing as a cafe society or bohemian circle worth coveting, but Carlos reawakened this fantasy. To find the center of city life, where it was *really* happening, it seemed I need only tag along with him. And he was generous in sharing his invitations. But invariably, Carlos himself would prove to be the most entertaining person at the gathering, the one whom the rest were waiting for so that the party could begin.

Why was he so in demand? What was his mysterious ability to enjoy life? He had an opportunistic zest for the present, which seemed to grow out of his comic awareness of how bad life could get. He'd obviously been through some grueling times, the splendors and miseries of the past, the youthful dissipations, the drugs. In recent years he had reversed that pattern and started taking very good care of himself. He barely touched alcohol; he ate moderately and well. Though he looked youthful and fit for a man in his mid-fifties, the references he made to old movies and theatrical performances he'd seen made you wonder. Part of the myth surrounding Carlos involved speculation about how old he really was. He seemed to have known *everyone*, from Visconti to Russ Meyer, and to have done a great many things, from studying architecture to working as a screenwriter, subtitler, and assistant director to Robert Bresson and Jacques Demy. Since he was not enough of a name-dropper, I would have to prod him: What was Orson Welles like? Agnes Varda? Edouardo Cozarinsky? Sometimes he would misunderstand my question: English was, after all, not his native language, and I think he was a little hard of hearing in one ear. When we walked together he always looked straight ahead, his eyes darting to take in the whole street, not turning to read one's lips. I now wish I had questioned him more systematically.

We each dragged the other to obscure revivals we would not have had the audacity to inflict on anyone else. We shared a passion for Mikio Naruse, and during the Naruse retrospective we would get together for a quick coffee at the Bagel Restaurant on West 4th Street and pore over the schedule to synchronize our viewings of "Mickey," as Carlos affectionately called the grim, neglected Japanese director. One time we had an hour to kill before a Museum of Modern Art screening, and went through the index of every film book in MOMA's shop for references to Naruse, like stagestruck teenagers. It is interesting how deeply Carlos was drawn to this filmmaker, whose cinematic craft is so restrained, whose attitude is so fatalistic and pessimistic, and whose whole sensibility is so un-campy. But then, Carlos was never that enthusiastic about camp: he had a taste for classical severity and psychologically mixed portraits. When he wanted to insult a picture he would say, "It's too heroic!" Maybe that explains why we both were so excited about Friedkin's *To Live and Die in L.A.*—the protagonist was a jerk who got blown away. Carlos's other attraction to that film was its kinetic energy: he liked it when a movie moved like a movie. Though he had a democratic attitude toward the genres, he judged each film individually by rigorous critical standards. I was always surprised by his unwillingness to excuse the many faults of a film if it had something good in it, as many of us do. "That movie is a dee-ssaster," he would declare. Though you could take issue with his opinions, he clung to his uncategorical sense of authority, about which he had no modest doubts. He once told me: "There are only three people in the world who really *know* movies: William K. Everson, *me*, and—" (the third was a Frenchman whose name unfortunately escapes me).

Typically, I would ask Carlos's opinion first about what to see, say, at a festival of Larry Cohen's horror movies at the

Public. He would answer instantaneously: "*God Told Me To*, a. k. a. *Demon*, is his *masterpiece!* Q is a lot of fun. . . ." and so on down the line. We both worshiped at the shrine of early Cronenberg, and went to see *The Fly* together with high expectations. During the film I could somehow sense from Carlos's breathing and chair-shiftings that he was disappointed. So was I, although I didn't want to admit it first. When the lights went up, we both looked at each other: "The script!" he cried. "It's a mess!"

We used to make plans to rendezvous at the auditorium of MOMA; Carlos liked to arrive at the last minute (because he was always rushing from a million other appointments) whereas I love to get to a movie house early and prepare myself, taking in the setting and the crowd. Carlos also preferred sitting in the front and I toward the middle or the back, so that sometimes I would arrive and begin marching up and down the aisles looking for him. If he had not yet arrived, I would twist my neck, scanning the newcomers for his ebullient face. I would fume, thinking I was being stood up, only to hear my name called out Hispani-cally just as the lights were dimming; Carlos would rush up with apologies about the subway. Or we would miss each other until after the film, when Carlos would grab my arm: "Where *were* you? I was looking for you; I came in early, I was down in the front row!" One time, however, he did stand me up, and the next day on the phone I gave him a hard time. He swore it was a misun-derstanding, that he had said he might come but had not made a definite commitment—in *his* mind, at least. On the whole, Car-los was very responsible about keeping dates, and reasonably punctual, for a Latin; but after that, I always liked to put him on the defensive about which of us was the more reliable, making him feel a bit guilty, if possible. "Phillip, you're worse than a Jewish mother!" he would joke. I think that underneath this touch-iness of mine was an insecurity about my importance to Carlos. If a man had so many friends, how could I be sure I could count on him? "If two called for help at the same time, which one would you run to?" (Montaigne, *Of Friendship*)

Fortunately, it never came to that. Besides movies, we had teaching and writing in common. Carlos had caught the teaching bug, and it was a pleasure to hear him speak so tenderly about his students at the New School or School of Visual Arts. He loved it when they reacted insightfully to a favorite film he screened for them, when they wrote an intelligent exam essay, or when he ran into them at offbeat movies after the course was over.

I regret to say that Carlos's interest in my own field, literature, was slight. He read film books mostly, for research purposes; fiction and poetry no longer interested him, though he promised to make an exception and read my novel when it finally came out. As a writer, Carlos had an elegant journalistic style, pierced by stunning insights and acute aesthetic judgments which made you realize what he could accomplish if he slowed down. His books on the history of horror pictures, crime movies, and George Cukor are essential starting points for any genre research. But they also seem written in haste, as though he had jotted down a few pages of galloping program notes before running off to a screening and a party. His brilliance made everything he wrote worth reading, but I often wished he would move beyond tantalizing summary and analyze the art of filmmaking as deeply as he actually saw it. In the last year or so, I had the feeling Carlos was becoming more serious about writing, more interested in perfecting the art of criticism. One night we went over, sentence by sentence, an article about Joseph Losey he was writing for the *Village Voice*, and I flattered myself that for once I was teaching him something.

In the last months before he died, he began making headway with his long-delayed opus, a history of art direction. The film stills rental business he had opened with Howard Mandelbaum, Phototeque, was doing well ("I'm rich!" he boasted, exaggerating), and at last he felt able to step back into the contemplative space necessary for good writing. I can't help lamenting that Carlos's best work as a film historian lay in the future—those books that would have tapped his uniquely rounded understanding of the subject. At the same time, I am tempted to subscribe to Robert Louis Stevenson's view that "All who have meant good work with their whole hearts, have done good work, although they may die before they have the time to sign it."

A week before his death, I called him from Houston to arrange a get-together. Since I had begun dividing my time between Texas and New York, I had gotten in the habit of calling Carlos first whenever I was coming into town, to find out what was going on. "Phillip! Where *are* you?" he would say with incredulous little-boyish excitement, as if I were playing some disappearing prank on him and might materialize any second through the phone's mouthpiece. "We *must* get together. What is your phone *number?*" He always spoke on the phone with Clarentine urgency, as though he were in the newsroom of *His Girl Friday* and I were calling from overseas and we were about to be cut off. This time I told him I was coming to New York for three days, for the opening of the Rudy Burckhardt retrospective at MOMA, which I had helped arrange. "Only three days? Poor baby! Just enough to get the honey on your lips."

"That's all right. I'm moving back permanently in May," I said. Indeed, one of the things I most looked forward to about returning to New York was getting to see Carlos on a regular basis.

"The city has been glorious this past week!" he said.

"Why? What's up? Any good retrospectives?"

"Nothing like that. The MOMA projection is a scan*dal*, we have all been complaining. No, I just feel happy with being in the city. It's been sunny, everything is going well. . . ." (I later learned from a mutual friend that Carlos had been worried in January about a lingering flu, and was overjoyed when he tested negative for AIDS. He would not have to die after all!) "So when am I going to meet your friend Peter?" he asked. "Arrange for the three of us to have a drink to*gether*, Saturday or Sunday."

"Fine, I'll call Peter. Which day do you prefer?"

"Phone me on Saturday and I'll know better. Meanwhile I hope to see you Friday night at the Rudy Burckhardt premi*ere!*"

That Saturday, February 7, the day before he died, I phoned him; he sounded chipper. "How was the Rudy Burckhardt showing last night?" he asked.

"A triumph. Where were you, you bum?" I needled him. Actually, I had half expected him not to show, since Carlos had never been an aficionado of nonnarrative, experimental cinema.

"I was helping them shoot a film all night, acting and who knows what till two in the morning!" he exclaimed. "Anyway, I am going to see the same Burckhardt program tomorrow at three, I promise."

"Good." I was mollified. "So, do you want to have lunch today?"

"Today is impossible because we are still shooting. But I would love to get together with you for brunch tomorrow! And your friend Peter, too, if he is available. And if he can't, it will just be the two of us, which is also a de*light!*"

"Where shall we meet?" I asked. "How about that luncheonette you took me to once, on Eighth Avenue?"

"La Bonbonnière? I *love* it. But in wintertime when you can't sit outside you come out smelling all greasy. Don't worry, I will think of the perfect rendezvous *spot*. Call me tomorrow morning and we'll talk."

"You're sure you'll be home tomorrow morning?" I asked.

"I'm positive!"

Sunday morning I called him at nine. There was no answer; I figured he'd gone out for a paper. Still, why wasn't he there when he'd promised? The memory of having been stood up that once at MOMA rankled me. I showered, made coffee, tried his number again. This time a stranger answered the phone. Did Carlos have a new boyfriend? I wondered.

It was Todd, Carlos's downstairs neighbor. He prepared me by saying he had bad news; then he told me Carlos had died that morning. No. I wanted to negotiate, propose a compromise, make Carlos be only ill in the hospital—anything but this definitive cutoff. Todd explained that Carlos had had an asthma attack around six in the morning and had phoned him for help; the difficulty with breathing had escalated into a massive heart attack. I knew Carlos had had asthma but hadn't guessed he could *die* from it. I began to explain that I had a luncheon date with Carlos that very afternoon, almost as if this important fact would cause him to reconsider his information. Todd said, "Yes, Phillip Lapont, he mentioned something about you . . ." and I could not tell whether Carlos had struggled to explain on his deathbed that he would have to break our appointment (so sheepish had I made him feel about these things), or whether he had told his neighbor about me at some other time.

I put down the phone and felt like a truck had run over me. No, I really don't want to describe my mood. It was awful. Mercifully, what I remember most from that time were a few inane, idiotic thoughts, amid the gloomy ones: (1) now Carlos would never get to see those Rudy Burckhardt films; (2) he would never read my novel; (3) I wonder if I should ask about renting his apartment . . . ?

An hour later my friend Peter called to find out where we were meeting, and I told him. He was stunned. "You're kidding. Is this for real?" When I assured him it was, he asked if I wanted to forgo lunch. I said definitely not, I didn't want to be alone. Peter picked me up in a cab fifteen minutes later, and I shall always be grateful for his sensitivity in proposing what I did not have the guts to ask for myself. "I think we should go by the house and pay our respects," he said. So we drove off to the apartment on Christopher Street above the Lion's Head Pub, that way station on the international underground railroad where Carlos had generously put up friends of friends from Madrid, Rio, Prague, etc. with a sort of disinterested hospitality.

As we hesitated downstairs by the doorbells, a young, very pretty Hispanic woman was leaving. "Excuse me," I said. "We're friends of Carlos Clarens, who lives here." She nodded gravely. "Yes, I'm his niece." It flashed through my mind that this must be the beautiful niece Carlos had once bragged to me about. When I had half jokingly asked to meet her, he had put me off. Now I was getting my wish, in this horrible manner. "Do you think we could go up?" I asked.

"Yes, please, the door is open, my father is there."

As I mounted the steps with Peter, I had a peculiar momentary sensation of cheerfulness, mysterious to me, until I realized that I always felt that way when I was going to visit Carlos. We entered the apartment. Carlos's oldest brother, Angel, whom I had never met, and several other relatives were standing around with red eyes. A page waited curled in the typewriter. Carlos's bookcases hugged the ground, and my eyes strayed across the titles of his film books, as usual. Several plastic garbage bags sat neatly tied in the corner, ready to be taken out.

I explained the purpose of our visit, and Angel, with the family courtliness, answered my questions promptly and helpfully. I wanted to know more about the circumstances of Carlos's death. He had been taken to St. Vincent's and they had been unable to save him. Do you think that the long hours of shooting the film may have tired Carlos unnecessarily? I asked. No, said Angel, Carlos knew how to budget his energies; he never overdid it; he quit when he was tired. That was true, but I still wanted to blame someone, something. If only there had been oxygen in the apartment, if only the emergency medics had gotten there sooner, if only . . . None of this speculation would alter the outcome one iota. No one was at fault, Carlos's brother in his dignified courteous manner suggested: not the medics, not the movie company, not Todd, not Carlos. Still, I wanted something more. I kept having the urge to peek into the other rooms—to see the body, even after I had been told Carlos had been taken to the hospital. I still had the sense that he was *there*, that they were hiding him from me. Or maybe I just wanted to explore his apartment one last time, walk from room to room, get closer to Carlos and feel him around me. But I could not bring myself to ask permission.

It was time to go. I felt sorry for Peter, who had thought to make Carlos's acquaintance and instead ended up in a mourning party. It was time to go. I said, "Well . . . I loved Carlos," and those words opened the floodgates. His brother burst into sobs, managing just barely to answer: "He was quite a guy." That odd American expression, spoken in a Cuban accent, somehow put the capper on the whole experience. We got out of there fast.

And ever since, every single day, I keep missing him. I wake up in the morning feeling happy, blank, or whatever, and suddenly realize, No more Carlos. You *did* stand me up, dammit. Do you hear that, Carlos? You stood us all up royally. So, wherever you are—and I'm sure you've adapted well by now, you who always managed to get the best out of cities, even if it has to be that most staid of metropolises, the City of God—I hope you also feel a little guilty for leaving us so indecently in the lurch.

IV

# UPSTAIRS
# NEIGHBORS

I am lying in bed listening to the upstairs party that began at midnight—just as I had almost drifted off to sleep. They are putting on that record for the fourth time, the space music with the heavy bass line, and there is considerable giggling and banging of furniture. My upstairs neighbor's stereo is right above my bedroom, making my walls vibrate like the insides of a washing machine. I am trying to work up the necessary rage to get out of my warm bed, switch on the lamp in the other room, and dial my upstairs neighbor's number for a most unpleasant phone conversation. Maybe if I pretend that I am having a dream about being kidnapped by a motorcycle gang I could manage to fall asleep.

Two-thirty. Should I wait until three to complain? Two-thirty might not strike most people as being the outrageous hour it does me, whereas "three in the morning" has a classical insomniac sound to it. It is important for me to imagine other people on my side, because any complaint I register has to have as its ethical centerpiece, so to speak, an appeal to the standards of "the community." (A vague proposition, at best, in my quick-turnover neighborhood.) Since I place little faith in my neighbor's sensitivity to others, I must conjure up a league of God-fearing, sleep-loving citizens and argue past her to this invisible gallery, hoping that this illusory consensus will somehow frighten her.

But I hate having to play the guardian of bourgeois proprieties. I understand, she's a checkout girl at an all-night supermarket, and she has invited some of her co-workers over. I'm not against young people having parties; if only she had told me in advance, a simple courtesy, I could have arranged to spend the night away. Too bad high school courses in neighborhood etiquette are not required; instead they just throw millions of strangers together and hope for the best. Nothing in modern urban life is more tricky than the code governing considerateness toward neighbors. We come up against the variable standards of those around us only when we are offended—or offend. I remember once unwittingly infuriating an upstairs neighbor by parking my car in what he took to be his space. He left a note on my dashboard saying he would smash my windows if I ever did it again!

Now that I'm awake, I can't help thinking about all the rambunctious upstairs neighbors I've had. There was the Polish family who clouted each other around while Granny rocked thump thump thump in her rocking chair. There was the law clerk who demonstrated she was a free spirit by stringing up the loudest wind chimes in North America. There were the people who left their dog locked in alone on weekends, causing the poor animal to race around the floor barking for hours. Or the man whose radio played loudly eighteen hours a day, until I thought I'd go crazy: when he answered neither his phone nor his door, I concluded he was dead. The landlord and I broke open the door, only to find the tenant had gone on vacation and left a timer on his radio to ward off burglars.

But all these remembered overlords tend to blend together, except for a particular couple, who shall always remain in my thoughts *the* upstairs neighbors. They lived above me on the second floor of a New York City brownstone, which became something like a rooming house above the first floor. Below me were my landlords, the Rourkes; above me these two, who were in their early twenties, though he still had the face of a scared adolescent boy. I think there was something "wrong with him," as they say. I would see him in the street arguing with himself, chewing his bottom lip furiously, pacing forward with a jerky, head-down walk. He was very slight—they both were—and he always wore the same black, greasy raincoat. I gathered he had a hard time finding a job. Still, it gave me a shock the first time I came across him selling umbrellas in front of the local train station.

Upstairs, they would quarrel fiercely. Footsteps would scutter across the floor, then I would hear him scream: "Come on, we're going to be *late!*" Such pathos he would wring out·of that word. "Why are we always *late?*" he would demand cosmically. She would start defending herself, saying it was his fault, too, and he would suddenly let out a wail, "We'll be *la-aa-aate!*" as though having a nervous breakdown. I pictured him falling on the bed with his head in his hands. "Come on, Johnny, stop," she'd coax. She couldn't stand his whimpering. I wondered if they might have even been brother and sister. Perhaps she was taking care of him as a favor to their parents. But when he let out a scream, "Where did you put my sweaterrrr?" it was with such dependent, accusatory anguish that I decided they must be lovers.

In the morning, when he went off, she would stay behind. She was a little mousy thing, almost pretty, with long, listless black hair she kept covered with a beret. Sometimes when I was at home trying to work I would hear her practicing the guitar and singing in an off-key, wavery, self-consoling voice the few Joan Baez songs she knew. I suffered with her when she started learning "Blackbird Singing in the Dead of Night." She would play a phrase and then stop, take it from the beginning again. I wondered what her system of self-correction was, since the last attempt sounded no more successfully in tune than the first.

I used to slap on a symphony record to drown out her practicing. But then I got used to thinking *through* it, so much so that I missed the dissonance on days she was away. As you can see, I am never satisfied: too much noise, too little. Sometimes I like nothing better than to listen to a person singing to herself. That pure release of soul from unthinking joy is a privilege to receive. I remember another neighbor on that block who would break into song—a pretty soprano voice whose owner I never met. Through the window would come a trilling, breaking off and starting again with the absentmindedness of a laundress humming as she ironed. Suddenly the taxing metropolis would seem melodic and humane, like the earthy, old-fashioned Paris of René Clair films. Life seemed simple, people seemed simple, we all wanted the same things.

Such tender fantasizing, fragile, difficult to sustain (probably because off-base), depended in my case on aural intimacy with an anonymous, unseen other. If I preferred the invisible soprano to my upstairs neighbor, it was not only because she had the better voice, but because I knew too much about the woman who lived above me. I knew, most of all, that she was unhappy.

It goes without saying that I felt sorry for the two people above me, which did not stop my being irritated at the noisy intrusiveness of their suffering. One New Year's Day, when I had a hangover, they started their worst fight. The yelling was so shrill that finally I decided to go upstairs and give them a piece of my mind. As soon as I rapped on their door—dead silence. "This is your downstairs neighbor," I began. "Please try to keep it quiet." I could have been the FBI or the KGB, so palpable was the terror inside. Then I heard him whispering vindictively to her: "You see what you did?" "Shh!" she hissed back. I waited a long while for them to reply to me but no answer came, except silence, the seemingly desired one. Holding the banister on my way down, I felt the hollow stomach that comes from having been a bully.

They moved soon afterward—were booted out, in fact, by Mrs. Rourke for nonpayment of rent. Shortly after that I moved, too, to Texas. In Houston, there were plenty of freestanding houses I could have rented for myself, but instead I ended up living on the first floor with neighbors above me. I chalked it up partly to habit, partly to my need to feel protected in a new environment by having other tenants around. And so I arrived at my present predicament, with heavy metal shaking the walls.

I stare up at the ceiling, thinking: "In my next rental reincarnation, I'll live on the top floor, I'll dish out the noise!" Yet even as I make the vow, I wonder if living below others signifies a pattern of choice. It could be my way of staying in touch with lives very different from mine; I am so self-absorbed much of the time, that the knowledge of other people's realities must be literally pounded into my head by that least distorting of modern media, the floorboard.

# WAITING FOR THE BOOK TO COME OUT

A year to fifteen months generally elapse between the time a publisher accepts a manuscript and its appearance in book form. Analogies between giving birth and publishing a book seem inescapable, but the process, which used to echo the nine-month human reproduction cycle, now resembles the gestation period of an elephant. During that year-plus of waiting, a writer may be visited by every emotion in the fun house, from rosy anticipation to exultation, megalomania, brooding, dread, cringing humility, avarice, guilt, and, finally, stolid acceptance.

Although nowadays a book can be rushed into print over a weekend if it is topical enough, publishers are inclined to follow a more leisurely schedule with most fiction, essays, and poetry. Around 1910, Edith Wharton complained to Scribner's that her novel was taking so long to come out—six months! Since the physical reproduction of a text has been speeded up, one must look elsewhere to explain today's attenuated production schedule: the fact that many publishers' editorial divisions are understaffed and overworked; the concern with avoiding competition with similar titles and fitting a volume into a publisher's overall schedule; the emphasis on gathering prepublication endorsements and pursuing book club and rights sales; the media's need for copies far in advance; and so on. At each step of the process, that sluggishness which infiltrates all bureaucracies, and from which the modern, conglomerated publishing industry is ever less immune, takes its little bite out of the calendar. The crux of the problem is that far too many books are published in America each year: most will fall into the sea unseen like Auden's Icarus, but each time the editorial and promotion staffs must at least pretend to gear up anew.

Suppose you have written a novel of serious literary intent and that a publishing contract has been offered. Let us say further that you are not in the elite of Nationally Recognized Names, but instead still belong to the majority faction, Authors Without Clout. I would not even presume to imagine what the waiting period for a Nationally Recognized Name is like, but I do feel sublimely qualified to speak for the majority.

After signing, there follows a grace period during which everyone is allowed to indulge his or her romantic optimism. The editor is rejuvenated by having championed a worthy attempt at fine literature and gotten his publishing house to acquire it. The editor's colleagues, who may be harboring secret doubts, are nevertheless prepared to gush in the hallways when the new author is taken around. And the writer—is on Parnassus. It is all one can do to keep from shouting: I did it! Nothing seems so singular, so improbable, as to have concocted a *book* out of thin air. (Later, nothing will seem so commonplace, but the first response is every bit as valid as the second.)

Next the editor goes over the manuscript carefully. (He/she may not be able to get to it right away, so we will figure a month or two for this stage.) The editor's suggestions may necessitate a few more weeks of revision; fine, you welcome the opportunity to demonstrate your cooperativeness, so long as the changes improve the book and do not compromise its integrity. Where there is strong disagreement, most editors will back off, eventually, allowing the author to have the final say on the book's artistic vision. Whatever clashes arise at this stage, it is still a honeymoon: both writer and editor are eager to bring the book as close to its perfected form as possible. How can the writer, who has struggled alone and so long, not be moved by all the attention the editor is lavishing on his manuscript? This companionable concern over the smallest linguistic choices, as though two medieval scholars with endless time were poring over a beloved text, constitutes the utopian phase of publishing.

But eventually that sweet duet ends, and the manuscript is turned over to the colder eye of the copy editor, whose job it is to police the text for grammatical, factual, and narrative errors. Copy editors are forced to play the part of humorless schoolmarms; perhaps because they hand out no gold stars but only *X*s, the writer may chafe a bit under this regimentation. I have known copy editors who tried to take away all my semicolons, dashes, italics, exclamation points, and ellipses, and break up every lengthy sentence and paragraph, because the publisher's post-Hemingway style manual had insisted the page would look "cleaner." But why quibble over a semicolon; if it makes them happy. . . .

By now, the writer is probably sick of looking at the manuscript anyway. It is time to "put the book into production"—that is, to ship the corrected text off to the typesetter. Attention turns to the cover design. The cover is a dessert the writer looks forward to in the long composing period—the hoped-for reward of someone else's creativity fashioning a perfect graphic image for all that you had intended to say; strengthening and protecting the vulnerable inside matter; enticing the distracted browser with a surface of Bonnard-like prettiness, yet suggesting the dignity of a literary classic; and, withal, embodying the sort of hip design idea that you have seen on the latest covers of Nationally Recognized Names. Not surprisingly, given these weighty expectations, the cover art proposed to an author is often a big disappointment. At this juncture, you can decide either to keep your mouth shut, saving goodwill for more crucial battles, or squawk. If you complain, however, be forewarned that in matters of cover design the author is usually treated like an idiot savant: just because you wrote the book doesn't mean you have any sense of how it should be packaged.

The author who requests a new cover will likely encounter the enraged ego of an art director. Art directors, too, are overworked; they farm out to freelancers their excess and are reluctant to antagonize their first illustrator or to find a second. Meanwhile, the editor tries to coax the author into compromise, since he is generally cost-conscious and needs to maintain good working relations with the art director. Whatever your importance as author in generating the product, you are essentially an outsider who enters the publishing workplace infrequently— once every few years, unless you are uncommonly prolific— whereas the editors, agents, art directors, rights people, and publicists are colleagues who work, party, and lunch together, move to the same industrial rhythm, and share a corporate mindset with bottom-line pressures. As such, they are inclined to treat the writer as a whining, unrealistic child, and to see themselves as the grownups. Perhaps, however, if you really insist, they will change the cover for you.

The proofs return from the typesetter, and now the overmasticated tale must be read again, for what the author hopes is the last time ever. You take it up with a proofreader's neutral eye, but before long you are giving it the anxious parental inspection. There is always some disillusionment; the divinity you had hoped would be conferred on your prose by its passage into type has not occurred; the strong parts still read smoothest, while the clumsy transitions remain so. It seems you have not written a masterpiece after all. It is too late to rewrite the book, attacking each sentence with the zeal of Flaubert; you must let it go. And you must forgive yourself, and be charmed by what is decent in it. In any case, you send back the corrected proofs; it is really now out of your hands.

For months you will probably hear next to nothing—perhaps a Christmas card from your editor. In that vacuum, you have an unmatched opportunity to brood. I once heard a famous author comparing his feelings about his work to a T-shirt: on the front it would read "Not Bad," and on the back, "Not Good Enough." Between these poles a writer lives out his life. You also brood about your literary status. You make mincemeat of every Johnny-Come-Lately and Short-Story Starlet on the literary circuit; you fret about your omission from newspaper roundups about novelists' favorite recipes or childhood books; you see a vast conspiracy, a network of mutual self-promoters at writers' conferences, art colonies, PEN meetings, all determined to exclude you and the other Authors Without Clout—in short, you become petty, bitter, and competitive, even when you know that all this careerist obsessing is nonsense, beneath you.

The problem is, you ought to be writing. Like Bellow's hero in *Dangling Man*, who marks time while anticipating the arrival of his draft notice, the writer waiting for a book to come out lives in suspended animation. Very few authors are able to use this time productively. They may do magazine assignments or book reviews, a short story or two, just to keep active, but rarely can they plunge into something ambitious, demanding creativity. Partly they are too burned out from having just completed a major project; at the same time they are too anxious and vulnerable. A book is an offering, the sum of what you have to say for a particular era in your life. Each book marks the end of a way of thinking, and it is hard to move on to the next thinking stage without having first undergone the ritual of reception.

One would think the prepublication process would get easier with each succeeding book, but the opposite is true. The first-time writer is carried along by ignorance, not knowing what to expect and half believing those celluloid myths about becoming a best-selling author and being summoned to Hollywood. With each additional book, however, one learns better how to read the telltale signposts of publishing. Just as a physician with hepatitis often becomes more depressed than a lay patient because he keeps taking his own pulse and diagnosing his stool, so a veteran writer looks for ominous clues in the size of his catalogue copy, the rapidity with which his phone calls are returned. Then, too, the first-book author has no track record and not much is expected of him. Publishers today are willing to take chances on new faces, whereas the veteran mid-list author is dogged by his past sales record, like a utility infielder with a .228 lifetime batting average. He knows that time is running out; he must have what is vulgarly called a "breakthrough book" soon, or the commercial houses may stop publishing him. The breakthrough book is that big, emotional, universal story your editor, agent, and relatives keep telling you to write (as though it were that easy) so that you can support your future shady proclivities for literary experiment.

There are certain prepublication events that help push a book into the breakthrough category: a book club adoption, foreign rights sale, national magazine excerpt, or television or film tie-in. Book club selection practically ensures vigorous sales, but book clubs are cautious, in general choosing titles for their membership that have popularity already written all over them. As for book excerpts, magazines tend to favor those writers who have appeared in their pages for years. The Author Without Clout will be told flatteringly that his or her novel is so tightly woven it is impossible to extract any portion without damaging the seamless whole. (Famous authors must write very loose, badly organized novels, because theirs seem to be quite excerptable.)

By the time the magazines, movies, book clubs, and foreigners have turned you down, desperation arrives. You realize that once again you have perpetrated a quiet uncommercial book, which must give itself up to "the Mercy of the Town" without the benefit of hype, advertising, or anything except the goodwill your tiny reputation has accrued. You fear this pattern of discouraging news less for your own morale than for its effect on your publisher. Publishing houses are addicted to Good News. They go from professionally ingenuous optimism to the cold-bloodedness of a stockbroker cutting his losses, with nothing in between. They are like hospitals that can treat only the most well patients; they practice strict triage, pouring all their energies into the promising ambulatory cases while finding it increasingly draining to think about the bedridden ones.

The curse of the veteran Author Without Clout is to foresee, clearer and earlier in the prepublication process, the commercial fate of his book. The first-time author thinks that everything will start once the book is officially published; the veteran knows the sad truth that most books are dead in the water long before their publication date. Your editor will tell you that this pessimism is premature, many good things can happen after pub date: positive reviews and that mysterious ally, word of mouth, can create a "groundswell." Historical examples are cited—*Catch* 22, or *Ironweed*. These Horatio Alger publishing stories are an evolving folklore, designed to buoy industry spirits in the face of statistical reality. To say that any book without prepublication advantages may make its way into the circle of success by merit and good press alone is about as true as it is that any American child can become president or a millionaire.

It stands to reason that if the company prints 20,000 copies of your novel initially instead of 5,000 it is more likely to promote it with ads and marketing attention, because no publisher wants to get stuck with 15,000 warehoused copies. (Similarly, if the publishing company has given you a big advance, it is more apt to galvanize into action in order to recoup its investment.) On the one hand, you fear that the audience for your book may realistically be no larger than those four thousand or so souls in America willing to pay the hardcover price for unheralded contemporary *belles lettres*. On the other hand, you can't help believing that if only your publisher got behind you and hyped the book, it would automatically sell. You retain a vast, perhaps credulous, respect for the ability of publicity and advertising to make any book into a commercial success, even the most farfetched (for example, *The Name of the Rose*). So you are on pins and needles to find out the size of your first printing.

Your initial print-run size will be determined by the early orders independent bookstore owners and chain-store buyers place after listening to your publisher's sales representative. Most of these salespeople have not read the book and are basing their pitch (along with those of twenty other titles for the season) on a page of catalogue copy, a cover mock-up, a fact sheet, and a four-minute sales conference briefing by your editor. On such slender supports stands the destiny of all your labor.

The prospect, you foresee, is one of dazzling self-fulfillment: the publisher's wait-and-see marketing attitude and low quotas set for its sales reps lead to cautious ordering by the bookseller, which leads to a low initial print run, which will lead to little or no advertising, since "there aren't enough books in the bookstores to justify taking ads now," which will mean disappointing sales. Your editor will argue that a small print run is not crucial, because it is easy enough to go back to press if great reviews and word of mouth generate demand. This is true. But even with superb reviews it may be too late: the publisher has moved on to the newer titles, those ingenues waiting in the wings whose fresh luster has not yet been dimmed.

The odd part is, you knew while writing the book that it would probably have limited commercial appeal, but you wanted to follow your quirky muse. Now that no miracle has stepped forward to rescue it from the nonprofit-literature ghetto, you look around in anger for someone besides yourself to blame. Your agent, your editor—have they really been trying hard enough? However accurate your analysis of the industry's self-defeating circularity may be, your legalistic eagerness to show the editor the holes in his publishing logic resembles the last stages of a love affair, when one partner cites verbal inconsistencies as though doing so could somehow compel the other into feeling what is no longer there.

The editor may still love the book, but naturally avoids these discussions, because there is nothing to be done about it. The writer's entreaties confront the editor with his own impotence, which is always disagreeable. Certainly the editor would love to be able to manipulate the company he works for and the apparatus of the literary world to make the book sell—not only this writer's book but those of the many other deserving, disappointed, and hungry authors under his care. It is easier to sign up a worthy book than it is to put it across to the public.

What is remarkable about publishing is not that it is a business—in the last analysis no more hypocritical than any other—but that its vestigial idealistic elements so persist. These vestiges tempt you to imagine your editor and your publisher as patrons of the arts, disinterestedly promoting contemporary literature (in the person of yourself), so that awakening to your suddenly devalued commodity status feels like a betrayal. Your first impulse is to reply in the language of commerce, to insist that you can be made into a more attractively packaged commodity. But this is a lost cause.

Part of the sense of betrayal may stem from the uneven contact between author and editor. In the beginning the writer is doted on; later, however immaturely, you may feel neglected, put on the back burner while your editor is acquiring or redacting the next crop of books. Some editors are much more sensitive than others to the writer's need for communication during the waiting period. Here, gender, I think, enters the picture. I have had three male and two female book editors, and it was the women editors who kept me informed, with friendly little notes or phone calls, whereas the men made a point of showing me how crowded their desks were, letting me know I could expect little in the way of hand-holding. Whether this was because women are trained more to think about the needs and feelings of others, or because editing a book is a kind of midwifery, an "acceptably" female role, or because of the particular sexual dynamic (the male editors might have nurtured their women writers more), in any case I noticed a difference.

A month and a half or so after page proofs, one can look forward to bound galleys, which arrive as much as six months before the publication date. Galleys generally look alike, with olive drab or khaki cardboard covers featuring standard typefaces. There is something reassuring about this anonymous, army-issue look, as though promising a democracy of literary reception. (In recent years, the practice of issuing a special reading galley with glossy, designed cover for breakthrough books has caught on, undermining this egalitarianism.) A dozen or so galleys get forwarded to other writers, soliciting favorable quotations for blurbs. I have mixed feelings about blurbs: the idea that every book must carry several endorsements from other writers is an invitation to literary back-scratching, praise-inflation, and cynicism, and I wish the institution would simply go away. But as long as the custom exists, I cannot be so high-minded as some writers (already established) who refuse to plug another writer's book—nor will I stop soliciting plugs. When you can plug an intelligent book with a clear conscience, it has the unselfish freshness of a good deed, and there is nothing so wonderful as getting the news that your peers or betters have come through with advance praise for your own work—never mind that most of these writers may be friends or acquaintances, and their views tempered by kindness.

As the time draws nearer for the final reckoning, the concern shifts back from the externals of publication to your own inner uncertainty about the text. Frequently at this stage I dream nightly of coming upon a review of my book: occasionally it extols, but more often it castigates me for literary sins whose precise nature evaporates upon waking, though the impression of shame does not. I steel myself for every insult, alternately defensive or contrite in advance. Apart from anxiety over the level of writing (it is never high enough), there is guilt simply because I have dared to have my say. The pleasure of writing is past; now I look ahead to a punishment for having spoken my mind. Isn't it presumptuous to have imagined that your thoughts were worth taking seriously? Or else you may worry that you may have revealed too much of your psyche, may have gone too far and violated your privacy or someone else's. You face guilt retroactively for the perversity of your writer's isolation: that desire to distance yourself from others and to be their witness, that effort to achieve a singular style, that compulsion to be honest, which suddenly seems monstrous, placing you out on a limb.

A year has gone by since your book went into production, and it is nail-biting time. Galleys have been forwarded to those magazines and review media that require a long lead period for articles. It is an eerie thought that, all over the media map, your text is being thumbed through, judged undeserving of review or assigned an appropriate critic—in any case, its fate decided, in the absolute stillness that precedes publication. And no one will tell you a thing; such is the ethical code of silence around review assignment. One time, a little before my publication date, I ran into a *New York Times Book Review* editor, a woman I had once met very briefly at a party. I reintroduced myself. "Yes, I know who you are," she replied with a little smile. We said good-bye; going down the elevator and for weeks afterward I tried to interpret that smile. Was it compassion for someone whose book was about to get it in the neck? Or the knowledge that I was in for a sweet surprise? Or neither?

Finished books have still not arrived, but, two months before pub date, the early reviews start to appear: *Publishers Weekly*, the *Kirkus Reviews*, *Library Journal*. The first negative critique hurts, really hurts. That old anxiety over your popularity, a high school obsession that you put behind yourself in order to write, unexpectedly flares up in the hour before publishing. Suddenly you want everyone to like you and your books, and don't exactly understand why they cannot.

One speaks of a book "coming out," like a debutante. Occasionally a little publication party is planned, which gives you something tangible to look forward to, since the actual pub date can be perfectly anticlimactic. In fact, as publication draws nearer and nearer, it becomes harder to locate the heart of the experience. A new ballet or symphony arrives at its premiere, a group of paintings at its gallery opening, but a book creeps on the scene like mist: a review here, then silence, another review.

I suppose the true sensation of having been published comes the first time you hold a finished copy in your hands. At that instant it all seems worthwhile, and you are wildly grateful. It exists; a tangible object; no one can take that away from you now. Of course, that moment precedes the book's arrival in stores by about three weeks, enough of an interval for hysteria to run amok yet again. But by now you feel, however tense, at least partly philosophical. The human psyche can take only so much anxiety before saturation occurs. A psychologist friend of mine pointed out that the series of emotional states I describe here as prepublication syndrome—anxiety, rage, megalomania, bitterness, terror, self-reproach, resignation, and acceptance—corresponds roughly to Elisabeth Kübler-Ross's stages of the grief experience. This insight shocked me, because I had not thought of having a book published as being analagous to getting over a death. True, the fact that you are no longer writing the book, that its potential for organic growth is finished, merits a kind of bereavement. Then, too, there is Hume's famous metaphor that his book "fell stillborn from the presses," which has haunted every writer to have heard it. But perhaps there is more fear of death in the waiting than grief itself. And something else: the anticipated birth trauma. As you and your book move ever closer to the womb's breath, prepare yourself for the slap of readership; bring on the primal scream.

# REFLECTIONS
# ON
# SUBLETTING

$M$y first night back in New York, I generally arrive from the airport just as the regular tenants are about to leave. An awkward changing of the guard takes place, initiation into the mysteries of pilot light and keys. They do not want to seem impolite by rushing off too soon, and I don't want to seem to be kicking them out of their own home, but the truth is, I am dying to be left alone. Finally they depart and I am alone. In fact, too alone; I roam around this strange apartment wondering where to place myself, like an actor feeling out a new stage set. Sounds from the street remind me how vast the city's business is, how little it knows or cares about my reentry. There is no place on earth that hits me with as keen and cosmic a loneliness as New York City on the first night back. I feel myself at the bottom of a steep concrete well. It is not just the monumental scale of the city, but the fact that New York really is my hometown, and lacks the adventurous camouflage of an exotic port that one knows in the end one will betray. I am homesick precisely because I have come home, but not to any house of mine.

Compulsively I begin to make phone calls. "I'm back in town!" I say to those friends I happen to catch in. "Great! Give me your number, I'm in the middle of something, I'll call you back around elevenish?" Wounded narcissism: they are always in the middle of something in New York; why can't they just rush over and embrace me? But even if they had offered, I would have shied away, wanting this first evening to myself, to experience head-on the excitement and the fear. How can I be afraid of a city where I've spent at least three fourths of my life? Mine is not the out-of-towner's dread that he'll be mugged or get on the wrong train, but the fear that this time New York will prove too much, that I've become soft away from the city, that I've already forfeited my place in it, like a latecomer to a game of musical chairs.

I start to unpack, laying claim to my new space. Animals piss on trees to establish territoriality; I unpack. The tenants have left me the requisite two empty dresser drawers and half a closet, storing their overflow in shopping bags on the closet floor. I hang up my travel-creased suits and shirts, spitefully shoving their hangered clothes tighter together to make more room for my own. (Why this spite? These people have kindly allowed me to live in their home.) I turn on the radio and fortuitously find a Mets game, which I listen to for a few innings while unpacking. Syllogistic comfort: I am still a Mets fan, therefore I must still be a New Yorker.

Finally I am ready to tackle the streets. My plan is a late dinner and a stroll around Greenwich Village. The streets don't alarm me; they are, in fact, what always lure me back. Prodigal son returning, I accept my patrimony of street life, this homecoming feast of gritty passing faces. What a privilege to be a member of a crowd again, wrapped in that downbeat anonymous sense of oneself. At the newsstand I buy a few papers and begin looking for a restaurant. There are five on every block; I can't make up my mind. I enter what seems a reasonably priced trattoria and am seated at a dark table by the rest rooms. Why are tables for one always shunted off in the blackest corners? It's precisely those of us who eat alone who need the best light to read by, while the romantic dates could use some chiaroscuro. "Sorry, it's too dim," I mutter to the waiter and abruptly leave, looking for another restaurant. Any one will do, I'm no fussy gourmet, and yet . . . the first meal back in New York is meant to be something better than a cheeseburger in the Greek coffee shop (admittedly brightly lit) whose window menu I study next. Finally I settle for an overpriced French bistro; its candlelight just enables me to make out the movie listings in the *Voice.* I start circling with a pen: Tuesday, the Film Forum; Friday, Japan Society. A regimen, a schedule, a life begins to suggest its trajectory above the ache of undifferentiated newcomer's time.

Back on the avenue, fed, I feel exhilarated, happy to be back in New York again. I follow the crowd's amoebic tropisms. Pulled along by the vortex of Sixth Avenue, doubling back to check the video rental store's display, edging past the teenage bikers and NYU show-offs, looking over the shoulder of the sidewalk portrait artist. . . . It is only when I turn in for the night that the panic returns: I am sleeping in another man's bed.

"There are roughly three New Yorks," E. B. White observed. "There is, first, the New York of the man or woman who was born here, who takes the city for granted and accepts its size and its turbulence as natural and inevitable. Second, there is the New York of the commuter—the city that is devoured by locusts each day and spat out each night. Third, there is the New York of the person who was born somewhere else and came to New York in quest of something . . . the city of final destination, the city that is the goal." To these I would add a fourth: that of the native New Yorker, self-exiled either through better job opportunities elsewhere or wanderlust, who now seeks to regain his paradise lost through a subletter's foothold.

Ever since I moved from New York to accept a teaching job in Houston, I have been sneaking back to the mother city for summer vacations or occasional leaves of absence. Since I had to give up my old Manhattan apartment when I first moved away, I've been obliged each time to find a sublet.

If a *pied-à-terre* is a foot on the ground in town, then a sublet must be a *pied-en-l'air,* the most tenuous of all claims to hearth and home. This is particularly true in New York, given the legally gray status of many sublets here. Sometimes the tenant's lease clearly stipulates the right to sublet his apartment (with the land-lord's permission), but relations between tenant and landlord have grown so antagonistic that the tenant is loath to ask for this favor. I have been assured via long distance that a sublet is legit-imate, only to be told on arrival not to put my name on the mailbox, "just to be on the safe side." In one apartment, where a tenant had no right to sublet except to a relative, I was asked to pose as his half-brother. I was once kept secret by a co-op apart-ment owner who had illegally walled off a section of his flat for rental income; threatened by a co-op board inspection, he said I might have to move out for a few weeks while he busted a hole in the wall again, "just temporarily." Fortunately, it never came to that. Still, unable to announce my citizenly existence in the standard manner, I started to feel vaguely on the run, like an outlaw or an illegal alien, although I was paying quite a hefty rent.

In the present avaricious New York market, it is certainly easier to find a sublet than a permanent apartment. Tenants now lease out their pads for slivers of time—two weeks, ten days, even a long weekend. They will always find takers: I have known fellow seekers who came to the city and, unable to secure an affordable apartment with a lease, have spent years moving from one sublet to another. In their own less extreme way, they are part of the city's homeless problem.

Each time I sublet, I land on a new box on the city's Monopoly board. My lodgings have gravitated from the Upper West Side to Tribeca to Stuyvesant Town to Chelsea to Herald Square to the West Village to Soho to the Upper East Side. I have learned the Sunday moods, dry cleaners, supermarkets, greasy spoons, slants of light, and vest-pocket parks of each. Streets I had only passed through as a visitor before, on my way to a restaurant or movie, have become, however briefly, my home turf. I have told myself that this vagabondage would make me into a more complete New Yorker, as I was learning the city—or at least mid-to-lower Manhattan—far better than when I lived here year-round. On the other hand, these relocations have left me uncentered, with no firm attachment or loyalty to any one section of town. I feel like an adolescent shifting from youth hostel to crash pad at a time when I should be settling into the householding wisdom of middle age. Maybe this subletting binge is my last-ditch attempt to forestall middle age.

Each time I have been quick to assure the regular tenant that I would not need much in the way of comforts. No air conditioner? No problem; the veteran subletter takes pride in his/her chameleonic ability to adjust. A worldly person can fit in anywhere, presumably: into a Scottish castle or a prison cell.

Yet once I have taken over a sublet, a tricky period of matching my sense of habitational order (or disorder) to the alien environment begins. It is part of the larger struggle to impose enough of my personality on the borrowed lodgings so that my spirit won't feel extinguished or overwhelmed. At the same time I am well aware that my main task is to adapt, not interfere. I may reverse the positions of couch and easy chair, but the objects remain obdurately themselves. Sometimes I become abnormally sensitive to light and lighting in these early stages: a long cavernous loft with windows only at both ends may give me a sense of wintry desolation.

Inevitably the practiced subletter develops both an ability to adjust and a finicky ideal of domestic space, based on accumulated awareness of one's peculiar little habits and one's discomfort when they are thwarted. For instance, I happen to like a hook or nail in the bathroom for my robe when I shower, and while we're at it, a nail or two inside the closet, so that if I should happen to come home at night too sloshed to hang up my clothes properly

I can always suspend them temporarily on a nail. But some designer purists consider it a sin to despoil their walls with anything so mundane as a nail. I have stayed in apartments that were as austere as art galleries, where I sensed a chilling frown of disapproval each time I left my socks bunched up on the hardwood floor.

There are sublets I have entered and felt immediately, gratefully at home in, and others that never stopped fighting me, like a transplanted organ the body keeps trying to reject. My feelings toward the people I am displacing enter into this, naturally. Whenever possible I sublet from friends: they don't profiteer by charging me more rent than they pay—the very definition of a friend in these dark times—and they are glad to have someone they know guarding their home. But even so, my sojourn is inevitably colored by the history of our relationship. If I am very fond of the regular tenants, I tend to delight in their little domestic ways. They become my ideal parents, taking care of me, guarding me, from afar. Conversely, if I have developed ambivalent feelings toward people who are subletting to me, living in their house only confirms prior doubts: a narrow squeeze between bed and chiffonier that condemns me to banged-up knees becomes a corroboration of their tight, unforgiving natures.

Subletting can be compared to that period of adjustment when a newlywed couple first sets up house and each begins to discover the little quirks and nesting habits of the other. The difference is that, in the subletting relationship, one of the parties is never around, while the one who remains on the premises still feels the tug of relationship, with its ups and downs, irritations, compromises, and insights. You learn more about a person by living in his house for a week than by years of running into him at social gatherings. This information is sometimes as tiny and precise as the dry goods kept in the pantry, which constitute his or her notions of emergency solace. I once sublet the loft of an admirable elderly couple, two artists who clung to a Spartan simplicity learned in their days of bohemian poverty, though they had become well-off recently. In the pantry were such homely, unepicurean staples as lentils, cornstarch, cocoa, a box of Mueller's spaghetti; when I ferreted around in their shelves, I felt empathic sensations of old age, a not unpleasant mixture of lumbago and historic memory rising in my bones.

Another time I sublet in Tribeca from a stylishly pretty woman: her silk kimonos, her peignoirs, her sachets cohabited with my undershorts and T-shirts in the limited dresser space. Not only did I have the pleasure of sleeping in this glamorous woman's bed, albeit without her, I also experienced myself for fractions of a second as a glamorous woman. The low angle of her showerhead, the scent of her oval bath soap, the pegboard arrangement of her pots and pans, all subtly feminized me: by going through her daily motions I was camping in her psyche, my muscles mimicking her reach, my eye level learning to emulate hers.

Trying on other lives is the privilege of the actor, the novelist, the schizophrenic—and the subletter. When I first started subletting I experienced this borrowing of identity only as a freedom. A temporary holiday from stewing in my own daily life. Both the subletter and the hotel customer have merely to lay out the cash to be absolved from the burdens of homemaking and repair. The hotel speaks more to our need for mediocre taste: conventional, consoling, the mass culture of travel. While the impersonal hotel bedroom conjures up a long parade of imagined licentious acts, erased as effortlessly in the mind as the squiggles on a child's "magic pad" when its plastic oversheet is lifted, the erotic relation to a sublet space is necessarily more tender, unrequited, prolonged. The subletter fingers day after day the combs, spoons, personal effects of another; the rooms he moves through are saturated with narrative; he has only to rest his absentminded gaze somewhere—like the detective in *Laura* falling in love with a portrait—to fantasize about the inner lives of the lady or man of the house.

With a mixture of stewardship, voyeurism, longing, and parasitic contempt, I haunt the rooms I have borrowed. As subletter I am the tamest of poltergeists, vowing to shake nothing permanently from its spot. Of course, I may temporarily remove the ugly nuclear-freeze poster from the hallway or the grandparents' pictures from the mantel, and store them under the bed, flaunting in their place some reassuring *kitsch* of my own. Or I may casually glance through the check stubs in the desk, or read the carbon copy of a letter left faceup, then the one underneath that. . . . But even if I bring myself to resist (as decent people should) the deplorable temptation to snoop through old diaries, to examine the shopping bags in the back of the closet for fetishistic clues, I may still experience guilt for having crossed some indeterminate line of privacy. Subletting revives psychologically the voluptuous shame of the child dressing up in Mother's clothes. One might say, in fact, that the subletter is a habitational transvestite, wrapping the self in decors that belong to another.

And, just as a drag costume insinuates an element of satire, however mediated by admiration, so, too, the first time I welcome a guest to my borrowed quarters and show him or her about, with the ironic pride of a nonpossessor, the urge to mock the taste of the original tenants is very strong. I detach myself from their follies, their pretenses, their art deco solemnities or country-quilt homilies, like a Peter Pan floating above nesting finalities. Not that I hesitate to show off the deluxe elements— the fireplace, the French doors—since they bestow status on me as well, prompting from my guests those expressions of apartment envy that in New York have become as much a conversational opener as inquiries about one's health used to be.

Subletting is a species of tourism, and offers opportunities to sample life-styles far above or below one's accustomed socioeconomic level. In the same way that a favorable currency fluctuation may suddenly allow a middle-class traveler to book a suite in the Grand Hotel, I once lucked into a light airy apartment with a beautiful art collection which I pedantically ciceroned for each of my visitors. On the other hand, I have sublet tiny sweatboxes in seedy, smelly, noisy, dilapidated six-story walk-ups. Since I grew up poor, "slumming" holds no adventurous novelty for me, only the sense of a nightmarish regression.

Rule of thumb: it is easier to expand into an abode larger and more luxurious than one is accustomed to than it is to contract into a smaller. I have found that the reduction of my normal

domestic space by so much as a room may induce a claustropho-
bic twinge, like the throbbing awareness of a missing limb to
which amputees testify.

Though I have had my share of fortunate sublets, somehow it is
the misadventures that linger in the mind. One time I sublet from
a rather short academic couple, whom we'll call the Lilliputians.
The rent was too cheap to pass up; the apartment, in an old
tenement building, had the quaint moldiness of a rabbit burrow,
with small, low, cell-like rooms off a main foyer. All the rooms,
including the narrowly passable foyer, were crammed with dou-
ble-stacked bookcases. To a bibliophile like myself, this looked
to be heaven, at first. I have always felt uneasy—no, threatened,
negated—in sublets with barely any books. Where books
abound, there is a particular thrill to that initial stroll through
the collection, discovering what rarities lie in store, what seren-
dipitous encounters with authors you had always intended to read
but never had got around to. As subletter, you have license to
eat of the Tree of Knowledge, to ravage the forbidden fruit of
your lessor's bookshelves. A scholar who might have hesitated to
loan you a prized volume now has no choice in the matter.

However, in this particular case, I found myself depressed by
the overwhelming number of books around me; moreover, the
collection seemed theory-greedy, leaning toward phenomenology, structuralism, ethnopoetics, Marxism, linguistics, and Buddhist philosophy. In fiction, which I always check out first, there
was Broch, Musil, Sarraute, Beckett, Pynchon, all laudable in
their way, but not exactly pleasurable old-fashioned stories with
which to while away a summer's afternoon. A certain puritanical
modernist taste was in operation here. So I took it upon myself
to become familiar at last with Musil's trilogy, with Husserl and
Polyani, with Scholem on kabbala, with Jakobson's poetics, but
most of it went way over my head: I would read a passage of
Scholem on the toilet, and dutifully pick up Habermas or Gram-
sci at the breakfast table, without finishing anything.

I always seemed to be getting a headache in that apartment,

partly because of the dense prose I was trying to riddle, and partly from the poor ventilation, but mostly, I think, because I kept banging my head. I am pretty tall and this couple, as I have mentioned before, were not: they had constructed an entire interior universe to suit their stature, so that I got shiners from cupboard doors and had to genuflect while washing dishes. The greatest menaces, however, were the loft beds, which seemed everywhere. It was the second marriage for both Lilliputians, and as each had several grown-up children from previous unions, their idea seemed to have been to encourage these young people to sleep over by offering them a plethora of lofts and bunk beds.

A further complication should be mentioned here. One of my subletter's tasks was to water the plants, of which there were some twenty-eight hanging, sitting, or potted, scattered around the apartment. This necessitated several trips back and forth to the sink with a watering can. But the real inconvenience came in reaching the plants on the upper windowsill, behind the bunk beds, in the woman's study. I would often knock my head against the protruding loft ledge while ascending the ladder, or else, having gained the upper berth and belly-whopped onto it with can tilted at an angle such that no water would spill until I had crawled forward to reach the geraniums, I would forgetfully straighten up and bang my head on the ceiling.

Now it should also be mentioned that these people kept a Buddhist altar at the front of this bunk bed. Various *chotchkes* of a ceremonial nature were carefully set on a prayer rug, below a framed portrait of their guru. I imagine they practiced sitting meditation there, though the one time I tried to get into a lotus position before the altar, just to see what it would be like, there was very little leg room. I also need to point out that this shrine was next to a window with an air conditioner—the only cooling device in the apartment. It was a summer of record heat; the electrical wiring in the building was very old; and I had been warned that if I did not hit the buttons on the unit at precisely timed intervals several minutes apart (each sequence increasing the cooling capacity), a fuse would blow and I and my neighbors would be plunged into darkness. Indeed, part of my subletter orientation session had consisted of a visit to the basement, flashlight in hand, to get acquainted with the fuse box. Since I had no desire ever to reexperience that urinous, rat-friendly catacomb, I quickly leaped up whenever the air conditioner sounded ready for its next cycle, usually knocking my head against the upper loft's ledge in my effort to avoid stepping on the altar and crunching its sacred objects, and I would lurch or corkscrew forward, gashing my hand against the torn metal of the air conditioner's facade, while groping in the dark for the right button. The whole apartment seemed to me a booby trap to which I never became accustomed.

I suppose the final straw was the place I sublet from a young investment banker who was being posted abroad to Paris. I had waited until the last minute, trusting to the network of friends' contacts, but this time they had turned up nothing, and the advertised sublets I dialed always seemed to be busy, and so I pounced on this place as a last resort. It was a grim white cube of a studio in Chelsea, quite expensive, decorated with various Francophilic touches like a Paris street sign and a tricolor baguette wrapper. When I discovered that the toilet was in the outer hall, not in the studio itself, I almost balked, but the young man assured me that this was very "European."

So I took it. Try as I might to imagine that I was staying in a continental hotel in Budapest, the indignity of not having my own bathroom at my age and in my own hometown kept eating at me. Moreover, I could never manage to relax in that apartment, to loll around with my clothes off late at night, because I was always worried that the call of nature would oblige me to throw on something before going off to the hallway toilet.

However, the toilet situation was nothing compared to the problem of the garbage trucks. The street was divided between manufacturing and residences—an enlightened urban practice in theory, but one that causes unexpected abrasions in practice. Among other things, mixed usage generates a lot of garbage, apparently too much for the city's sanitation department to handle. Instead of doing the logical thing, which would be to hire one truck to pick up for everybody, each building contracted with a separate carting firm. After midnight the street belonged to these private carters. The drivers would stand outside their trucks, joking and drinking from brown-bagged pints like the first guests to arrive at a party. Then the symphony of garbage collection would ensue. Being a native New Yorker, I do not mind a little city noise, nor am I normally an insomniac. But insomnia was the only possible response to the crash of upended dumpsters, the grinding of gears, the garbage masticated through the rumps of trucks hour after hour, until 5:00 A.M., when the last truck drove away and I was able to drift off. . . .

After a week of near sleeplessness, I had come to know the various beasts in the jungle. There was the high-pitched *breep-breep!* of the sea-green mastodon backing up in reverse; there was the dark blue dinosaur with its *jrowrr-jrowrr* gnashing mechanism; there was that mutant creature that went *garock-kikguh!* . . . Sometimes the drivers left their motors running for an hour while they went across the street to Lanza's Cafeteria (*vrip!* the metal grille of the cafeteria front lifting and closing) for a few rounds. Lying awake, I thought of opening sniper fire on the trucks; I thought of importing special Italian ear stoppers (the American ones did nothing); of buying thick drapes and rugs to deaden the sound (was it worth it for a three-month sublet?); I thought of organizing all the businesses on the block into a cooperative to pool their carter services; I thought of sleeping elsewhere and using this place as a daytime office; I thought of trying to become a night person by shifting my biological clock, or adapting to the noise through Zen mind control or sheer habituation; I thought of forfeiting my deposit and moving to another sublet. And I thought of Baudelaire's prose poem, "Anywhere Out of This World," about being contented nowhere. Surely it was partly my fault, my restlessness, the difficulty I had of living in my own skin. I am getting too old for this, I thought. One more sublet, I thought, will send me around the bend.

And yet, even as I finished off the season in this studio with the W.C. down the hall, as I went about shipping my books back to Houston and filing a change-of-address card at the post office, I experienced the usual wistfulness. I had been occasionally peaceful here, and productive at times; there was creaturely regret at being unseated from any nest, however uncomfortable.

It is the subletter's duty to leave no trace of himself. On the day before departure, I washed the dishes, scrubbed the bathtub, swabbed the floors, returned all photos to their original situations on the mantelpiece. Like a robber who makes sure to remove his fingerprints, I was destroying all evidence of my tenure. Like that of a lover who, in "possessing" a woman's flesh, possesses nothing in the end but a memory, my hold on the sublet was starting to evaporate. I noticed, however, that I had left a few bruises on the body of the place. Some little erosion has always taken place: a chip on a coffee mug's lip, a bureau handle that fell off and that I have clumsily Scotch-taped back in position. My subletter's calling card.

# SUICIDE
# OF A
# SCHOOLTEACHER

$A$ll this happened a while ago, in 1979. At the time I had been working for close to ten years as a writer-in-residence at P.S. 90, a public school on Manhattan's Upper West Side. My situation there was unique: unlike most writers-in-the-schools, who are sent into scattershot residences all over the map, I was allowed—thanks to the receptive staff of P.S. 90 and my sponsoring organization, Teachers and Writers Collaborative—to sink roots in one place and to teach anything I wanted. The children and I made films together, put on plays, produced novels and poetry magazines and comic books, ran a radio station. I became entwined with the life of the school, went to Parents Association meetings and staff parties, and felt for the first time in my life a productive member of a community.

If the elementary school world was far more earthbound, less glamorous, than the downtown literary/art circles (around which my career and erotic fantasies still revolved), it nevertheless felt warmer, more communal, richer in drama, and more willing to make a fuss over me personally. This dream of the grade school as maternally nurturing community may have been in part, I see now, a naïve family romance, or a narcissistic projection of my own need to play the favorite son. That not everyone who taught at P.S. 90 was so well served by, or contented with, the milieu was a fact I certainly took in but tended to downplay. In any case, my dream received a jolt of reality one night when Monte Clausen, the schoolteacher I was closest to at P.S. 90, phoned me at home.

"Did you hear about Jay Becker yet?" asked Monte, cautiously.

"No. What about Jay?"

"He killed himself."

I turned off the television. "How?"

"He jumped from his apartment window. The twenty-seventh floor, something like that, of the Amsterdam Towers."

"Jesus." All my life I had prepared myself for a phone call telling me that someone I knew had committed suicide. Now that one had finally come, I was at a loss. "The Amsterdam Towers, that's right around me."

"You knew he'd moved into your neighborhood . . . ?"

"Sure. We used to get off at the same bus stop together." This seemed so inadequate a claim of connection with the victim that I immediately felt ashamed for having said it. I pressed Clausen for details, and we had one of those *Dragnet* exchanges: What time of day did it happen? How did you find out? Underneath my sober tone I sensed a spark of excitement at the gaudiness of the news—perhaps survivor's superiority or simply the pleasure of sharing a choice bit of gossip, which did not seem real to me yet. It was almost as though, now that Jay had made his point, he could dust himself off and go about his business. Side by side with that reaction was the unwanted understanding, like a punch in the gut, that Jay Becker was gone forever.

Jay always seemed bigger than life. One simply didn't expect such a vivid person to die, period, much less kill himself. On the other hand, in some subterranean way, I had sensed this was going to happen. I didn't dare explain the reasons for this feeling to Clausen, not yet.

We talked for a few minutes, and I seem to remember mouthing clichés about the shallow relationships of people in the big city, where everyone rubbed elbows constantly but took no real responsibility for each other. This was bullshit: New York City was not to blame. In any locale I could have imagined, even a little mountain village, I would have kept my distance from Jay Becker.

Don't get me wrong, I genuinely liked Jay. I liked him, at the same time as I congratulated myself for being fond of someone who could be very hard to take. He had a shrillness about him that telegraphed a large hurt. One felt life's intensity in his presence, much as watching the dentist approach, drill in hand, quickens one's perceptual apparatus. Sometimes I was not in the mood for the challenge of his clangorousness, and had to steel myself before entering his orbit.

I had made an early attempt at describing Jay in *Being with Children*, the book I wrote in 1975 about my experiences as a writer-in-residence at P.S. 90. At the time I had changed Jay's name to Stanley Riegelhaupt:

> Riegelhaupt had the loudest teacher's voice I had ever encountered. Children ducked under their desks when they heard that voice; they held their ears like dogs whining at passing fire engines. The strangest part about his voice was that it was not malicious or cruel. Only loud. He seemed to enjoy demonstrating the power of the organ for the fun of it. While escorting his students through the halls he would unleash it, then turn around and smile at the cringing spectators. It did manage to keep the class in line; but only, I think, because they were irritated at the volume, not because they were afraid of him. Once they discovered that underneath that voice he was something of a softie and rather benign, they found ways of getting around him.
>
> Coming into that charged atmosphere as an outsider,

it was not always easy for me to know how to react to him. Every time I picked up the kids to go to the Writing Room, he would use my entrance as an occasion for a practical joke. One morning I came in wearing a red-flowered shirt; some kids complimented me on it. Stanley, picking up the murmur, demanded in his loud voice: "All right, class, who has the more colorful shirt on today, Phil or me?" He happened to be wearing an utterly bland tan wash and wear shirt. The kids cried over-whelmingly: "Phillip does!"

"What's that?" he roared. "All right, who wants to stay after school and get extra homework? You should know that I *always* have the most colorful shirt." He took another vote, and this time he won.

What embarrassed me was not the subtle hostility against me but the hostility against himself. But like all Dostoevskian buffoons, he seemed to imply that his time would come. On another occasion, he took the oppor-tunity to make me blush by announcing that I had just gotten married. As the kids crowded around me, offering handshakes and congratulations, I was covered in confu-sion and kept trying to tell them that it wasn't true! Fi-nally I had to run out of the room, with a few kids chasing down the halls yelling the news to everyone, and I got teased for days with that apocryphal story.

A love-hate relationship had grown up between Rie-gelhaupt's students and him, provoked by Stanley's own inclination to self-ridicule. Stanley liked to trade gross insults with his students. But often as not, he was the butt of his own jokes. The room was papered with com-positions which told of Riegelhaupt's animal genealogies and uncertain parentage, his lack of wit, his failure at every endeavor, his alleged nasty habits—and on top of each one he had written in red ink, "Excellent!" or "Very Funny, Great Imagination!"

In fact they were not so funny; they were a little hard to take. But the kids liked doing them. He had managed

to sell them the idea of creative writing by offering himself as a target. Every week he assigned "Creative Writing" for homework, and every week they came back with
pages and pages of sarcastic, juvenile fantasies about their
teacher.

I shudder when I read this now. In a book otherwise filled
with affectionate or at least diplomatic portraits of the schoolteachers I worked with, I had allowed myself a certain ridiculing
sport in Jay's case; even the pseudonym, Stanley Riegelhaupt,
was chosen for its comic, Jerry Lewis *shlemiel* sound. Not that
what I wrote was untrue, but the passage falsifies through its
cheerfulness; it denies an anguish I was trying not to see. Disturbing, too, is the ominous phrase, "he seemed to imply that his
time would come."

Jay Becker had a tight, compact body and an erect military
bearing, an impression furthered by his crew cut, which he wore
throughout the entire period when long hair was the male fashion. He had thick glasses with dark rims. His nose drew your
attention: it was always shiny, beaded with sweat, large-pored,
hooked, and aggressive. When he didn't like something his nostrils would pull in and the nasal ridgebone protrude. Sometimes
his nose alone would turn white or blush pink—dilate with pleasure or look suddenly pinched—betraying his secret emotion,
while the rest of his face remained frozen in geniality. He had a
ferocious grin that seemed partly intended to undercut the effect
of his vocal blasts. The edges of his mouth would tremble in
warning just as he was about to crack a joke, especially one at
the listener's expense.

Nowadays, there are many people who seem vague and wa-
tery, and whose search for identity troubles themselves and those
around them. Jay Becker was the opposite; if anything, he
seemed overdefined. Like a Harold Lloyd or Pee-wee Herman
assembling a recognizable persona from props and mannerisms,
Becker proudly displayed the barking voice, the Mr. Square costume, the towering, put-on rage before a malfeasant student—all
the while shielding his inner turmoil from sight.

Teachers are actors: little by little, like barnstorming Shake-spearians, they acquire exaggerated *shtiks*, routines to get them through. So what if some children regard them as battle-axes or grotesques? They know they still have within themselves the same complexities, the same youthful dreams. It seemed to me that Jay had become a victim of his overdrawn persona. By collaborating in your perception of him as a "character," he invited you not to take him seriously. When we say of someone "He's a character!" we disarm him; we don't expect anyone so categorized to be in such intense inner pain that he takes the measure of his own peculiarity and pronounces the death sentence, any more than we would expect it of a Dickens caricature like Mrs. Jellyby.

Yet there were times when Jay shed that overdrawn character. I remember particularly one relaxed June afternoon in 1972, a year after I had begun working at the school, when he and I took his class on a picnic to Central Park. We were sitting next to each other on the crosstown bus, and the kids were behaving well so there was no need to keep after them, and we settled into a quiet confiding conversation. He told me about his childhood. It seems his parents had operated a seaside hotel: he had never had his own room, and was forced to move to whichever one was unoccupied. It had given him a permanent anxiety about security, which was why, he thought, he had taken a civil service job.

After college, he told me, he had studied law at the University of Pennsylvania, and even gained his degree. But then the problem of military service arose; he did a stint in the air force. "Stay out of the armed services, Phil," he told me, grinning crookedly, "if you're anything like me." He couldn't take it, and was discharged, though I never did learn why the Air Force had been so harrowing for him. He was a good athlete, and, with his carefully creased pants and military posture and the value he placed on discipline, he almost seemed to belong in the service. Or else he had internalized a part of its training, even after it had proved inimical to him.

In any event, he became a teacher on leaving the service. I wondered if the relatively low status of elementary school teacher bothered him. He seemed to feel no regrets about not having practiced law. "I basically like teaching," he told me. And now he was getting married; he thought that might solve his problems of rootlessness and insecurity.

There was a beautiful, trusting sweetness in Jay as he spoke to me on the bus. I noticed it at other times as well, a tenderness that leaked out of his gruff mask in so pure and undefended a form it was almost jarring to watch. His return to "normal" a few hours later struck me as a kind of betrayal. While we were walking home across Central Park, I ran into an old acquaintance of mine, sitting on a park bench with her new baby. Since I had not seen her in some time, I stopped to chat while the group moved on. Later, when I caught up with them, I took a merciless ribbing from Becker. "Whose baby was that, Phil? Don't you think you ought to marry the lady? At least give her a place to live, so she doesn't have to sleep on a park bench!" Back to the armor.

Jay's marriage did not last a year. I never met his wife; when I asked him after the breakup what had gone wrong, he got a hard concentrated stare and a grimace around his mouth, as though he were eating some acidic fruit. He told the truth when he wore that expression, though he told the short version, shrugging between sentences. "There were problems with the in-laws. And she . . . she wanted to live in a suburb in New Jersey and I didn't like it out there. I felt more comfortable in the city. So now I'm a bachelor again." No doubt there were other problems, but Jay's telegraphic style did not encourage probing.

He moved into a high-rise apartment in the Lincoln Center area, not far from where I lived. One night I ran into him at Cherry's, a local diner that served Chinese food. He told me he was on his way to a Unitarian Church singles mixer. I could never go to those mixers or singles bars, preferring to do without rather than risk the humiliation of being rejected by a stranger. Jay, on the other hand, subjected himself regularly to the harshness of the singles scene. When he described the outcomes, he had a way of comically disparaging his capacity to attract and to hold. But behind the shrug, I imagine, was the ball of anger that grows in the stomach from being sexually rejected. "So how are *you* doing, Phil?" he would ask, quickly turning the subject away from himself. "You must be getting a lot of women."

He never told me what he thought about the portrait I had drawn of him in *Being with Children*. I wonder if it caused him grief. All he ever said was, "Congratulations, Phil. When are you going to write a best-seller? When are you going to leave us for Hollywood?" He always tried to give the impression that his life was unimportant compared to mine. At first I would attempt to compete with him in failure, but eventually I would rise to the flattery, and tell him a tidbit of recent literary fortune. "That's great! You're really going places," he would say, his sweat-coated nose quivering in what I guessed must be at least partly chagrin. But perhaps it wasn't: Jay read a lot and had a simple admiration for writers. Sometimes I would brag about the projects I was doing around P.S. 90, like the *Uncle Vanya* production, and again he would respond with unmixed praise. "Today Chekhov, tomorrow Shakespeare or George Bernard Shaw. Who knows? You can start your own repertory company here."

Did he ever boast about his own teaching achievements? Not that I remember. But he had a reputation for getting good results. One could always tell Becker's students' compositions because the grammar, punctuation, syntax, and spelling were generally on a much higher level than the other classes'. Becker would drill his class on the fundamentals: paragraph indentation, quotation marks, topic sentences. His creative writing assignments stressed fantasy over experience: boys often wrote about adventures in space, girls about raising Kentucky Derby winners. They had learned to exercise their imaginations glibly, but there were too few moments of true feeling or authentic observation for my taste.

Over the years, the written work that came out of Becker's classes had an odd thematic consistency. Besides the wish-fulfillment stories, there was that high quota of student attacks on their teacher, which I took to be a sort of guerrilla retaliation against Becker's efforts at embarrassing them. (For instance, he'd call a girl with dental retainers "Braceface.") There was also a surprising—for sixth graders—amount of toilet humor. Becker would consistently be flushed down the toilet, first having been suitably miniaturized, and would end up in a lady's apartment. I never could figure out what element of his classroom style prompted this obsession, but I do remember that getting a bathroom pass in that class was sometimes an ordeal, and cause for much smirking.

Even colleagues who found Jay's approach too strict or rote-based had to admit that the children learned under his command. When parents were dissatisfied with their kids' grammar, reading, or math skills, they would lobby for a transfer to Becker's class in senior year, as a sort of prep for the rigors of junior high school. If the child had not only learning but discipline problems, he would more than likely be assigned to Becker. Many successful young adults walking around today consider Jay Becker the teacher who changed their lives. Jay had always been a savior for certain kinds of kids—rowdy boys who lacked a sense of direction, shy intellectual girls who loved to read. But big rowdy girls, especially black girls, he rarely knew how to treat. His penchant for public embarrassment found a match in their sassiness, and often they would trade him decibel for decibel, their sense of dignity refusing to allow anyone to "yell at me that way" without equivalent comeback. It is safe to say that no teacher possesses a style that works for all students. But in the last year before his death, Jay began to get more agitated by the ones he couldn't reach.

One morning in June, four months before his suicide, I bumped into Jay inside a coffee shop on Broadway, where, a creature of habit, he ate his breakfast every morning before school. As we sat side by side on counter stools, I asked him how his class had gone that year. He started to stutter: "Some-some of these kids . . ." He stared off into space, searching for the right words. "Most of these kids are bright and want to work. They're good kids basically. I'm having trouble with a few of them. I don't know; I can't seem to get through to a few." His eyes glazed over. It was the pain of every teacher, the unsureness about ever doing a good enough, a thorough enough job. "I guess I've been teaching too long. I'm running out of solutions. Maybe I should get out of the profession."

"Look, no one bats a thousand."

"Sure, I know that, but I can't seem to get enthusiastic about teaching anymore. There's no kick in it for me. Anyway, we should probably get going before we're late," he said, picking up his check.

After learning of his suicide I remembered this conversation, but at the time it didn't leave much of an impression on me. I may have thought that Jay was suffering a little teacher burnout; 1979 was the year of "teacher burnout." It had become a catch-phrase; everyone was talking about the nagging frustrations that wore schoolteachers down, physically and spiritually, year after year, as though this common knowledge had suddenly become a scientific discovery. On the positive side, teachers could finally speak about their weariness as a systemic problem rather than a private, guilty secret. But "burnout," which had started as a useful shorthand for the complex of forces attriting schoolteachers, eventually came to possess an independent identity of its own, like a mysterious virus in a horror movie striking victims at random. Just as every decade turns up a new disease (mononucleosis, hypoglycemia, Epstein-Barr syndrome) to which not only its legitimate sufferers but all those afflicted with *tedium vitae* lay claim on the basis of having read a magazine article, so "teacher burnout" became the fashionable panacea of the moment, rationalizing all the unhappiness teachers were holding inside them in lieu of actually reforming the root educational problems.


The new school year was barely a month old when Jay Becker stayed home for a week. He was extremely conscientious; he had almost never taken a sick day; so we were all surprised when the week turned into an indefinite leave of absence. One of his colleagues, Cesar Gomez, called him at home to see what was wrong. Becker answered readily that he had "emotional problems." Gomez asked Becker whether or not he wanted people in the school to call him, and Jay, after a pause, said yes, he'd like to hear from them.

A teacher who did phone reported that Jay seemed to be getting his problems under control: he had invited his mother to move in temporarily to take care of him.

Sometime in the evening of Monday, October 22, 1979, Jay jumped out the window of his twenty-seventh-story apartment. One assumes his mother was out at the time. Did she return to find her son on the pavement? Many of these police-blotter details were never clarified, since no one at school felt he or she had the right to ask his relatives for the full story. Not that it is of any importance whether he jumped at eight or nine o'clock, climbed out the window onto a ledge or crashed through it. In any event, there must have been many curious strollers from Columbus Avenue gathered around the body on that warm October night.

I see two stories here. The first is about a man who couldn't take it anymore, which is of necessity a mystery story without a satisfying solution, since the motives and last thought processes of a "successful" suicide are for the most part denied us. I might speculate in my own way why he killed himself, but anyone else's guess would be as good as mine. The second is about a public school, and how everyone (including myself) dealt with the disturbing private challenge to institutional life that suicide proffers. Here at least I can record what I personally witnessed about the community's response to this crisis.

Around midnight, Eduardo Jimenez, the principal of P.S. 90 received a distraught call from Jay's stepfather telling him what had happened. By the next morning, the news had spread through the staff. A gloomy Tuesday morning; many teachers were in shock. "It can't be," they kept saying. "I just can't believe Jay is dead." Some students had begun to hear rumors, but when they asked for details they got little response. The adults seemed to be afraid of a panic breaking out among the children. One fourth-grade teacher, Kate Drucker, who often held long discussions with her class about the most serious topics (including death), and who herself is a very analytical, honest woman, told them evasively that she wasn't sure what had happened. She admitted later that a truthful discussion would probably have been the best approach, but she didn't feel like talking about it just yet, she was too shaken up. (That night, Kate told me later, she called everyone she knew, people she hadn't spoken to in years, to see if they were still alive.)

The other staff members were equally reticent, as though they were waiting for a policy statement from the main office about how to phrase it—or, even better, an expert opinion from a developmental psychologist on what amount of truth the children could absorb at each grade level.

Becker's own class, of course, would have to be informed. Mr. Jimenez went into Room 234, along with the Parents Association president, and told the students that their teacher had died. When they asked the principal how, all he would answer was that it had been an "untimely death," which was tantamount to telling the kids that he had died of death.

An emergency lunchtime staff meeting was called to discuss the crisis. Ed Jimenez, somber on the best of days, seemed especially grim, as well as uncharacteristically subdued. He admitted that he was at a loss, and solicited the advice of his staff. To those who had watched Jimenez laying down the law at staff meetings over the years—sometimes judiciously, sometimes wrongheadedly, but always forcefully—his uncertainty came as a surprise.

A parent suggested that we bring someone in from the nearby Columbia Teachers College or Bank Street School of Education to do a workshop on handling death and grief in the classroom. Someone else remembered that Dr. Myra Hecht, the director of the New York Center for Learning, had once given a valuable talk on this subject. Perhaps she could be prevailed upon to deliver it again, this time with special attention to suicide. "For the kids or the staff?" it was asked. "For both, maybe," came the tentative reply. "You mean two separate workshops?" Someone volunteered to phone Dr. Hecht and see what she was amenable to doing.

After the meeting, Kate Drucker commented: "How screwed

up we are that we have to bring in someone from the outside to tell us what we should be feeling and how we should respond at a time like this."

It had taken honesty for the principal to admit that he could not be the leader, the Father-knows-best figure, that everyone seemed to want in the situation. The cause of death may have had something to do with his hesitancy. Jimenez was not at his best when on the receiving end of strong emotional display; given to temperamental outbursts himself, he was nevertheless made profoundly uncomfortable by others' eruptions. He once told a female teacher, who burst into tears after he had severely scolded her, that if she cried one more time in his office he would put a letter in her file for unprofessional behavior.

The second reason he had trouble leading the school in its grief was that he and Jay Becker had been on opposite sides politically for many years. What had begun as an educational difference of opinion had taken on the nuances of a personal feud. But to understand their quarrel, it is necessary for me to backtrack a bit and explain some of the school's history.

The trouble goes back to the big citywide school strike in 1968, during John V. Lindsay's mayoralty. Though any veteran of New York City's "school wars" will tell you that it started long before that, I prefer the 1968 cutoff date because that strike, the bitterest and most interesting of recent decades, left deep ideological scars. It was a strike, as you may remember, that pitted the teachers' union against the ethnic minorities, liberals against radicals, one half of the civil service bureaucracy against the other. It started when black and Hispanic parents, who felt their children were getting cheated educationally, demanded more community control over their schools, and gained it in a few experimental areas; then the United Federation of Teachers (UFT), the most powerful teachers' union, rose up and said that the integrity of the teaching profession was being undermined by community interference. The minority parents accused the largely Jewish union of racism, the union replied with charges of anti-Semitism, and the battle was joined. In that quarrel, leftists crossed picket lines for the first time in their lives and volunteered to keep the schools open as teachers and principals (the Association of Supervisors having taken the side of the striking teachers). It was a period when some reputations were damaged for good (including Mayor Lindsay's), while others rose astonishingly swiftly. When the dust settled, the union had gained ground from the community groups; both kept long memories of who had done what to whom.

On the Upper West Side, however, the concentration of reformers and community activists helped to produce results that were different from those in the city at large. A coalition of minority parents and white progressives installed three "community principals" chosen by the community school groups rather than taken from an approved list of potential supervisors. One of the three men was Eduardo Jimenez at P.S. 90. The unorthodox selection process was disputed, and led to a court case in which Jimenez and a black principal successfully challenged the Association of Supervisors list as racially unfair and an instrument to inhibit minority principalships.

Ever since, P.S. 90 had been divided into two camps: the traditional or "more formal" (as they were called on the organization sheet) teachers, who had sided with the union in the strike; and the neo-Deweyite or "open classroom" teachers, who had allied with the community forces. The dominant philosophy of the school and its principal was the open classroom. Jimenez is an educator immensely sympathetic to creative ideas. A tall, bearded man with thick glasses and an electric-socketed bush of hair, he had studied painting in his youth, and he brought to the school an almost artistic vision of a dynamic educational environment. He set about recruiting like-minded staff and ensnaring outside resource programs. In very little time the school became an experimental laboratory in which science museums, theater troupes, philosophers, opera workshops, and artist-in-residence programs (such as my own Writing Team) all tried out ambitious curricula. P.S. 90's open corridor and bilingual programs became models, drawing visitors from all over the country and abroad. Convenient to the downtown television stations and newspapers, the school also became a media favorite. It was no surprise to see a TV crew hanging around the colorful open classrooms on the first floor when a visual filler was needed on children's reactions to a holiday or current event.

Understandably, the traditional teachers felt bitter about what they perceived as second-class treatment; and in terms of resource allocation—the open classrooms had parents' committees that raised funds for special materials, as well as an adviser from Dr. Hecht's Center for Learning—and the boss's positive approval, they were right. Most of the traditional teachers had been on staff prior to Jimenez's appointment in 1970; they were the old guard, and the principal made no secret of his desire to be rid of them. His very appointment had entailed a fight, he was embattled from Day One, and it was his personal style to struggle against, rather than to accommodate, those he took to be his enemies. There is a certain kind of humanistic activist whose values are impeccably compassionate but whose own human skills at handling people leave much to be desired. The teachers frequently complained that Jimenez ignored people's wants and needs and rode roughshod over them. Since he did not, according to contract rules, have the right to fire teachers he disapproved of as long as they were functioning adequately, he tended instead to make life hard for them, with the hope that they would eventually leave of their own accord. They reciprocated by plotting against him and undermining him whenever possible.

The traditional teachers' stronghold was a corridor on the second floor where Edna Jacoby, Jay Becker, Harriet Ullman, and Millie Brown all had classrooms. These four teachers shared resources, co-taught subjects, and kept their strength up, as good friends and allies will. Harriet Ullman and Millie Brown usually taught classrooms that combined third and fourth grades, while Edna Jacoby and Jay Becker handled the "big kids," the eleven-to twelve-year-olds in fifth- and sixth-grade classrooms. It was the bitter contention of some of these teachers that the children in the open classrooms were not getting a good education, that their teachers were too permissive and were thus harming the children's chances for advancement at a later date. Conversely, the open classroom teachers accused the traditionalists of being stodgy, unimaginative, lackluster "lifers" who would never get involved in schoolwide activities, and who punched out at three o'clock on the dot. Though I myself felt closer to the open classroom philosophy (and was perhaps even seen in the school as one of Jimenez's boys), I made a point of working in both settings; I could see that each side had misjudged the other. I knew that Jay Becker stayed late many afternoons, tutoring students who needed help, and I knew that the open classroom teachers ran a much tighter ship than the traditionalists had assumed.

In any event, to return to their personal feud, Jimenez and Becker would go at it during staff meetings. Both were capable of violent self-righteousness, though from different directions: Jimenez was a revolutionary who bullied those around him "for their own good"; Becker was a stubborn stickler for procedure who had been in the school system a million years and knew "the way things had to be done." To add to the tension, Becker was elected UFT chapter chairman. In his vigilance over the potential erosion of teachers' privileges, in his advice to colleagues on filing grievances against their principal, he often came into conflict with Jimenez. Between them, they revived again and again the acrimony of the 1968 strike.

When Jay's term as chapter chairman ended, he was ironically faced with having to ask the principal for a favor. He wanted to take a rest from his regular assignment, to give up the running of a classroom for a year and become a cluster teacher. A cluster is someone who goes around from class to class, spelling the regular teachers during their prep period breaks and presenting a short lesson in some specialty of his or her own. Jay's would have been history, a field he knew better than anyone at P.S. 90. Jimenez reviewed his available personnel in the face of extensive budget cuts that year—and ruled against the request.

Each year there were teachers who complained about Jimenez's assignments, claiming that he gave preferential treatment to his favorites. Others, like Monte Clausen and Doris Friedman, both open classroom teachers, were quietly of the opinion that as principal he had the right to make whatever assignments he saw fit. But in the days following Jay Becker's suicide, even Jimenez's staunchest supporters felt resentful retrospectively over the denial of Jay's cluster request. The temptation to blame someone for the tragedy (other than the perpetrator himself) was strong, and who better to point the finger at than the boss?

By Tuesday afternoon, around the lunchroom and the schoolyard, the kids' rumor mill was already in full operation. Some children thought Mr. Becker may have been hit by a car. Another rumor, unfounded but tenacious, was that Becker had been suffering from skin cancer, and that he had decided to kill himself rather than prolong the incurable disease. The cancer rumor had probably been started by a well-meaning adult who had sought to justify Becker's suicide (as if unbearable emotional suffering were not enough justification). Some of the parents who knew the circumstances of Becker's death let their children in on the facts; but the next day, when their children told other kids, many of these kids refused to believe them, thinking it a wild, made-up story. Gradually, they would approach their teachers and say, "Somebody told me this crazy thing that Mr. Becker jumped out the window. That's not true, is it?"

Meanwhile, the school continued to handle Becker's suicide in the way they would a death from natural causes. On Wednesday morning the usual public address messages were canceled, and instead the announcement was made that the school had suffered a great loss. Mr. Becker, a man who had taught and helped children for fourteen years, was no longer with us, and the classes were asked to observe a minute of silence. It was the first of many such moments of silence, a ritual that became almost droll in its ecumenical utility.

What fascinated me was the *denial* of suicide, the reluctance to speak its name publicly. It put me in mind of another situation I had encountered at the school. In 1976, after the debacle of Senator Eagleton withdrawing from the vice-presidential race because of previous psychiatric treatment, I thought of doing an educational unit on mental illness. How did the idea of "crazy" differ from society to society? What was the historical evolution of insane asylums? What about Freud's ideas? I could see the creative writing possibilities, using literary models like Gogol's "Diary of a Madman." It seemed a rich subject, one which afforded a chance to reduce the children's fears of their own deviations from the norm. So I was a little surprised when everyone at school—even Clausen, who usually indulged my zaniest notions —reacted with discomfort and total resistance. Since the idea would never work without my colleagues' cooperation, I abandoned it.

I kept thinking about this earlier constraint in connection with the adult reticence to tell the kids about Jay's suicide. How far did the taboo extend? Were we still so close, I wondered, to the barbaric medieval stigma attached to suicide? Perhaps the theological and legal sanctions that continue to surround the deed, such as refusing to bury the victim in hallowed ground, or requiring hospitals to file a police report, accounted for some of the reticence. But not all: no, there was something unique about suicide, I began to feel, that made a public school singularly ill-equipped to handle it. Schools are dedicated to helping children find their way into life, and an adult self-doubt so deep it denies the worth of life itself cannot help but threaten that environment. Since little children often regard their teachers as semi-parents, and since the offspring of suicides have a greater tendency than others to follow that self-destructive path, the suicide of a schoolteacher could seem a dangerous model. Beyond that, suicide is a defiantly private expression, a dissonance jamming public discourse, like a monotonously insistent burglar alarm that no one can shut off. The radical nature of the suicide act is that it both draws attention to a distressing problem and simultaneously obliterates the possibility of ameliorating it. By rejecting all human assistance, by announcing in advance that any relief will have arrived too late, it negates the whole *raison d'être* of those in the "caring professions": teachers, nurses, social workers, psycho-therapists.

Implicating his or her survivors in guilt, the suicide (strange

how the word fuses doer and deed) mocks the shallow understanding of those who thought he or she was doing all right, who
mistook a calm scornful smile for adjustment. Revenge, spite,
anger, stubborn willfulness all have their part in suicide. The
suicide insists on having the final word. No wonder people at the
school found themselves unable to talk freely.

The most frightening part of suicide is its reminder that we
are none of us so far from it. Suicide has a suggestive, contagious
dimension, as Durkheim showed long ago with his charts, or the
suburban teenagers in Texas and New Jersey more recently. But
why go so far afield? I had only to look within myself to know
my own vulnerability.

At seventeen I had tried to kill myself with pills, and, botch-
ing the job, had landed in a locked psychiatric ward. Though
this was my only bona fide suicide attempt, it began in me a
lifelong relationship with that temptation. It seemed to me I had
a "virus" inside me like malaria that could flare up at any moment,
and I needed always to be on guard against it. On the other
hand, I would court it, even in times of seeming tranquillity. I
seemed to derive creative energy from the assertion of suicide as
an option. This morbidity left me freer to act or write as I
wanted, as much as to say: No one understands me, I'll show
them. It also became my little secret that, while going about in
the world, and functioning equably as expected, several times a
week I would be batting away the thought of killing myself. How
often have I thought, in moods of exasperation or weariness: "I
don't want to go on anymore. Enough of this, I don't want any
more life!" I would imagine, say, cutting my belly open to relieve
the tensions once and for all. Usually, this thought would be
enough to keep at bay the temptation to not exist. So I found
myself using the threat of suicide for many purposes: it was a
superstitious double hex warding off suicide; it was a petulant,
spoiled response to not getting my way; and it was my shorthand
for an inner life, to which I alone had access—an inner life of
furious negation, which paradoxically seemed a source of my
creativity as a writer.

Added to this was an element of loyalty to youthful positions.

Just as a student protester might vow never to become conservative in middle age, similarly, after they released me from the psychiatric ward and people said to me, "Now wasn't that a stupid thing to do?" I swallowed my pride and nodded yes; in my head, however, I swore allegiance to the validity of my decision. If nothing else, I vowed that I would always respect the right of an individual to kill himself. Whether suicide was a moral or immoral act I no longer felt sure, but of the dignity of its intransigence I was convinced.

In any event, I came to believe, rightly or wrongly, that I had a sixth sense in these matters, which is why Clausen's phone call with the news did not entirely surprise me. I had started seeing a look of constant pain in Jay's eyes; I knew more or less what the look meant. I think because he could not bear to have another person see him that way—hunted from within—his eyes fled mine. Whenever our gaze did lock for a moment, it was odd and unbearable. A sympathetic vibration exists between "suicide-heads" that is dismaying, to say the least. After Jay killed himself and everyone kept saying how astonished they were, I felt isolated by having had a presentiment along these lines. It's hard to tell whether the uncanny shiver that comes from sensing, after an act of violence, that one may have foreseen it is mere vanity or something more valid. The matter was complicated by a memory fragment that suddenly surfaced after Jay's death; I was not a hundred percent sure whether it had actually happened this way, whether this was a hallucinatory vision, or a combination of both. Here is what I "remembered," from the previous spring:

We had been standing by the time clock, where we often bumped into each other at the end of a school day. Jay was getting ready to punch out. (As a consultant I was not required to, but I hung around the time clock out of solidarity and a need to imagine myself in the regular teachers' shoes.) I asked him: "How goes it?" He said: "'Not so good." "Why, what's the matter?" Then I remember that twisted smile of his, as he faced the time cards, and his saying, "Everything," and adding under his breath, "I'm even thinking of killing myself." His tone had just enough of that pessimistic New York irony for me to try to dismiss it as hyperbole. "Cheer up," I said, patting his shoulder, trying to make light of it, "hang in there. Death comes soon enough on its own."

I next remember fleeing the schoolhouse, shaken by what one might call the paranoia of empathy. I had had a glimpse at a pain so palpable it could not be denied, and was revulsed by my patronizing pat on the back, as though a colleague's reassurance could somehow assuage it.

This sensing of Jay's suicidal capacity went no further than species recognition. I did not feel impelled to warn those close to him, or to speak to his therapist if he had one, or even to draw him out about the fantasy, as one is supposed to do with suspected suicides. If anything, I'd been scared away from him. In my defense, we did not have the kind of relationship that could have easily permitted my extracting other confidences; he told me exactly as much as he wanted and then clammed up. Beyond that, I did not really consider myself to have the power to change his feelings. It was his decision to make, to live or die. All I could do was be a witness, and file away my impressions for a later date when I might be able to help him more, if the situation arose. Was this a cop-out? Does it show the error of my frequent position of detachment? Or is it megalomaniacal now to horn in on his death and act as though it was up to me to alter the trajectory of his history? I don't know what my responsibilities are to alleviate the suffering of others. Let me add that barely a day goes by without my picking up uncanny hints of someone's urgent misery beneath the social mask. I am never sure how much of this "intuition" is trustworthy and how much is projection, a distortion for the sake of promoting melodrama or feelings of superiority. I have sniffed suicide in the air a dozen times or more and been proven wrong. This time, however, I was right, and it spooked me.

The funeral was on Wednesday, around noon, and some of the teachers who had been closest to Jay switched their lunch hours with other staff so that they could attend. They piled into taxis and rode the twenty blocks down to Riverside Chapel, on 75th Street and Amsterdam Avenue.

As usual, tabs were kept on who showed up. The principal's absence was duly noted. On the other hand, some of Becker's traditionalist allies, who were very protective of him, made caustic remarks about certain open classroom teachers who did attend. "What's she doing here? She always gave him trouble when he was alive."

The funeral lasted fifteen minutes.

Jay's mother and stepfather wept. The rabbi spoke of the special relationship between the mother and her departed son, which was unusually close and devoted; of the deceased's having helped children; of his years of dedicated service to the community; his love of fresh air. Not a word about suicide. True, it was a religious service, and since Judaism views suicide as a sin, the rabbi perhaps felt unable to mention it. Nevertheless, it seemed ironic that Jay, who had finally spoken of his pain in a manner impossible to ignore, was still not getting through.

After the funeral, most of the teachers returned to school. A few, who had student teachers covering their classes, went out for coffee, along with some ex–P.S. 90 teachers who had been notified of the service. Two of these "alumnae" were now teaching in other schools; several had gone on to downtown jobs like copywriting or bank-telling, which seemed elegant to them compared with working in an elementary school. They defended their decision to leave teaching.

"Let's face it," said one ex-teacher bitterly. "Kids are takers, not givers."

"No, kids can give you a lot," said a woman still at P.S. 90. "But you have to know how to receive it from them."

"And if you know that, you're probably secure enough not to need their support in the first place," replied the first woman.

Lilly Chu, a more formal teacher who was on sabbatical that year, spoke to me with feeling about how good Jay had been to her. "Once there was a mouse running around the classroom and I was scared stiff. He came in and took care of it. His door was always open. He was such an important part of that school! He was like a rock, always there when you needed him. I'm afraid I got more from him than I ever gave him. . . . If only I had reached out more."

"But he made it hard to reach out," I answered. "He never asked for help. There has to be something in the person that you can grab on to."

"That's true, but still I think we could have done more. Everyone's in their own world, their own problems. So much sadness in him. Nobody pays attention." Lilly's eyes began watering.

There was much talk, after Jay's death, about "reaching out." As one teacher put it, "To work in the same school and not know he was suffering like that . . . and all he needed was a little friendship." Everyone took it as a given that Jay had died of loneliness, that his death could have been prevented by more human contact. I was not so sure. P.S. 90 is not a particularly cruel, unfeeling environment—quite the opposite. Most suicides have people around them who do say a kind word, offer a helping hand, but it seems to come from a great distance away, and they don't know how to read the gesture. Often they don't want to. The suicide has to screen out or misinterpret a great deal of the kindness that comes his way if he is to get on with the business at hand. He must concentrate all his energies on keeping the tenuous flame of suicide alive inside and feeding it day by day. Sometimes it is not loneliness so much as the need to act decisively, for once, in one's uncontrolled, errant life.

The words "reach out," with their telephone-commercial sappiness, began to get on my nerves. In contradistinction to that line from *Under the Volcano*, "No se puede vivir sin amor," I believed it *was* possible to live without love. Many do in this world, and we mock their endurance by pretending otherwise. Of course it could be argued that I am using the word "love" in too narrow a sense. There are many kinds of love besides human companionship: love of place, love of work, love of culture and beauty, love of God. In my view Jay had known some or all of these. I guessed that he had gotten fatigued, exhausted from some unremitting inner struggle, or from a tormenting superego that told him he could do much better, and that somehow he had crossed the line between the tolerable and the unbearable. Yet even as I balked at the kitschy explanation, "All you need is love," what if an important truth did lie under its sentimentality? Perhaps my old need to defend suicide as a valid action was getting in the way of my understanding the obvious: that Jay Becker had not been cared about or loved enough.

After the funeral I went back to school. In the teachers' lounge, where Jay had so often held forth, loudly and raucously turning innocent remarks into double entendres (he had, by his own cheerful admission, a "dirty mind"), he continued to dominate by his absence. As we discussed him, I had the feeling that each of us was fingering a private guilt.

"I was so surprised about Jay Becker," said the elderly librarian, Sophie Arens, who shook with palsy. "I couldn't help thinking about it all night. I mean, he seemed to be doing all right, he had a girlfriend—"

"What's that got to do with it?" I said testily.

"Well, you figure if someone has a girlfriend or a boyfriend, they're a little happier. These days, you don't have to get married. You can live with your girlfriend or your boyfriend and no one says anything about it anymore," Sophie noted, with a trace of shock.

"Wasn't Jay living with someone?" asked Debby Trabulski, a younger teacher.

"Yes, but she moved out."

"Well, maybe that's what did it," said Sophie. "He got depressed about the breakup."

*Cherchez la femme.*

"His girlfriend did not break up with him," informed Frieda Maura. Frieda was big as a house, slow-moving, shrewd, with thin gray hair dyed red: her beady little eyes set in her fat, canny face reminded me of a Politboro functionary. I could never figure out what Frieda Maura's real job was; she seemed to just sit around drinking coffee and *kibitzing* all day. Frieda had probably gotten closer to Jay Becker than any of his other colleagues; in the last two days she had become a *maven* of Jay-ology. "His girlfriend moved out when he got too despondent. But she was on the phone with him every day."

"Then what was he unhappy about?" asked Sophie Arens.

"There were all kinds of things. He didn't like what was happening to the school, with the administration," said Frieda, lowering her voice significantly. "'When Jay fought, it was good. This year he didn't fight."

"It was three years ago when *he* started in on me. And that was when my tremors started," said Sophie. In a public school, whenever an unidentified *he* or *she* enters the conversation, it is always understood to be the principal.

"I remember how, when I came back after my illness," said Frieda Maura, "Jay came over to me and offered to pick up my kids at lunchtime and have his monitors run errands. Because it was hard for me to climb the stairs."

"When I filed my grievance," said Sophie, "Jay wrote a very strong letter in my behalf against Jimenez. He stuck his neck out for me. And I know I wasn't the only one he did that for."

"I don't know if you know this: Jay had an earlier breakdown. But he went to a shrink and he got over it," said Frieda.

"I had no idea."

"Sure," Frieda continued, shifting her remarkable bulk in the chair. "I knew he had this illness for years. He spent a fortune on psychiatrists."

Kiko Fuzuwa, a petite Japanese-American who taught third-fourth grades, volunteered that she thought Jay had great difficulty relating to women.

Everyone nodded, each mulling this over in his own way.

It seemed strange, I thought, that Jay, whom everyone was diagnosing as starved for the love of a woman, should have worked in such a female environment. Of the thirty-four classes in P.S. 90, only four had male teachers. The rest were women, many of them as lonely as Jay. Yet the "logical" solution of getting together with one had never seemed a possibility—for him any more than it had for me. I suspected Jay's suicide had touched the single teachers in a rawer way, reminding them of the fragility of living alone.

"I spoke to him just last week," Kiko Fuzuwa was saying. "He told me that when this emotional problem was over he would go on a hike with me. We both belonged to the same hiking club, you know. I'm being honest, he sounded pretty good!"

"You know, I keep thinking of something his mother told me at the funeral," said Frieda Maura. "She told me that all during the last week of his life he kept saying to her, 'I love you, Ma. I love you.' His mother said to him, 'I know you do, honey.' He was just being considerate. He didn't want her to feel guilty after he did it."

"Isn't that nice."

"I wonder what will happen to his pension," said Sophie Arens. "Will the money go to the state, or . . ."

Doris Friedman, a veteran teacher who had been in a sad daze all this time, awoke and answered: "His beneficiaries will get it."

"I don't think the union will try to claim it."

Long silence.

"It takes guts," said Debby Trabulski.

"No it doesn't. It takes desperation," Doris Friedman replied with conviction.

"You don't think jumping out of a twenty-seventh-story window takes strength?"

"The strength is to go on living. All it requires is desperation."

A brief argument followed on the subject.


That day I saw two girls I knew in the hallway. They were from Becker's class, and I asked them how his students were taking it. They giggled and said most of the kids were glad! Then they did an imitation of the adults: "We should all talk about this. Mr. Becker died yesterday. Now on to math." They mocked the public address announcements, the solemnity of the principal, everything. These were both fairly sweet, sensitive, and intelligent girls, for the record. Their merry refusal to grieve, chilling and unfeeling as it was, bespoke a survivors' will to be themselves in the face of what they perceived as adult intimidation. I asked the girls if they knew how their teacher had died. "We don't! Someone said—he *killed himself,* but that's probably wrong." They giggled at the scandal of it. I listened without answering: I was too intrigued by their response to reprimand them; besides, I needed to think about it more.

On Wednesday night the annual bake sale was supposed to take place at the school. Some had argued that it should be canceled in deference to the recent tragedy, but others answered that the children and parents had gone to a lot of effort, and why should they be punished? So the bake sale was held in the school cafeteria as planned.

A large crowd swarmed around the tables and bought cake slices and cupcakes, the proceeds of which were to go for the school's legal battle to get back its Title I funding.* It was a happy crowd, with the children running around the cafeteria and the parents chatting, and everyone waiting for the judges to award the prizes. Before the judging began, the new Parents Association president, Dave Naumann, a friendly shaggy-bearded man with a huge belly, rose to make an announcement.

He said that the school had suffered a deep loss. "And I don't mean the loss of our Title I designation. A teacher who had served in the school for sixteen years—"

"Fourteen years!" corrected several pedantic children.

"—Jay Becker, who had been suffering from an illness . . . died of that illness on Monday night. Now I'd like us to have a moment of silence—a minute is a long time, I know, so I'm only asking for a moment—to honor the memory of Jay Becker."

---

* For years, the federal Title I monies, earmarked to support compensatory education programs for disadvantaged children and desegregation, had provided Jimenez with the discretionary funds to improve the educational product. They paid for, among other things, the cluster teacher positions of the sort that Jay Becker had wanted. As P.S. 90 stabilized and improved, the neighborhood around it started to gentrify, at which point the government decided that its disadvantaged population had dipped slightly below federal guidelines, and cut off its Title I funds.

Everyone stood at attention, facing different directions, perhaps wondering how long a moment was in Dave Naumann's mind. I thought it a shame that, having gotten everyone's attention, he had waffled at the crucial moment. But later I agreed with others that Naumann had done a brave thing under the circumstances. After all, many had opposed his making any announcement, on the grounds that it would mar a festive event.

Several parents spoke to me that evening. They were worried about the kids in Becker's class. No one seemed to be talking to them, working through whatever problems they might be having with the tragedy. Some of the other teachers had held honest discussions with their classes by this time, but Becker's kids had only been treated to a succession of substitute teachers, starting with his leave three weeks before. The mood in that class had grown anarchic. Becker's kids were being avoided, almost like pariahs contaminated with the unpleasantness of suicide. Maybe, in some unconscious way, people blamed them for what had happened, or—and this, the parents stressed, was particularly dangerous—the children felt themselves to blame. Meanwhile, Jimenez had gone away for a few days on business, and, due to the budget cuts, there was no assistant principal around that year to deal with the problem.

I decided that it was up to me to go into Jay's class the next morning and level with the kids. Over the years I had developed the conviction that it was wrong to shield children from the truth; to the extent that we could even know the truth (and in this case we did), we must tell it to them. What worried me was the thought that this high-minded position might have also satisfied some sadistic impulse in me—the side of truth-telling that takes pleasure in pulling the mask off hypocrisy and disenchanting innocence. Also, I hesitated because I was not a trained psychologist or counselor, only a writing teacher. But this qualm finally seemed cowardly to me: What else was being a teacher but trying to respond as humanly as possible to problems that would not wait for an expert? Besides, I would get them to write.

On Thursday morning I came into school early. I was shaking, as though I were about to teach my first lesson at P.S. 90. I ran into Monte Clausen in the main office. I told him that I would probably be criticized like hell for this but that I was going to discuss Becker's death with his class. "Why criticized?" he said. "It's about time someone did. People will most likely be grateful to you. What are you afraid of?"

I couldn't explain my fear. I had the sense that I was about to touch something very explosive and dangerous, partly because my own feelings about suicide might not be under control. "Oh, I guess I'm worried that parents will write letters protesting my exposing their kids to such ugly matters. . . ."

"But you have a role in this school of articulating feelings that no one else will come out and say."

"I do?" I felt relieved that what I thought might be interpreted as provocation had come to be considered approved behavior— my "role," in fact. Articulating the unspoken feelings of a community seemed a much more interesting function for a writer-in-the-schools than the narrower one of imparting writing techniques. I thanked Clausen for saying what he had said, and he wished me good luck.

I spoke to the substitute teacher and asked if I could take over her class for about an hour to discuss Becker's death. She said they were in the middle of long division, but if I came back in half an hour, they would be ready for me. I went down to the teachers' lounge and had a cup of coffee, and when I came back I was shaking a little less.

First I introduced myself to the class, said my name, and reminded them that I was the writing teacher. A third of the kids had worked with me in previous classes; the others recognized me from the halls, or in any event acknowledged my right to be there. I said I wanted to "clear the air" about Mr. Becker's death. When something important happens like that, you just can't sweep it under the rug. You need to bring it out into the open, talk about it, not let it stay bottled up inside. (I heard myself resorting to cliché after cliché, but I clung to them for support; these trite, soothing figures of speech seemed to be absolutely necessary to get me started.)

"First of all, how did Mr. Becker die?" I asked.

A few hands. "My father told me he committed suicide."

"That's right. He did."

"How did he kill himself?" several kids called out.

"He jumped out of a twenty-seventh-story window."

There were several gasps. "See, I told you!" one boy cried as he smacked another.

"Was there blood on the sidewalk?"

"Get outta here!" cried David, a sensitive blond-haired kid who was embarrassed at his classmates' gory curiosity.

"I didn't see the spot where he fell," I answered.

"When did it happen?"

"Monday evening."

"What time Monday evening?"

"I don't know, about eight or nine, thereabouts. . . ."

"Somebody said he had cancer."

"To the best of my knowledge, he didn't have cancer. He killed himself for emotional reasons."

The students began talking loudly among themselves.

"What kind of teacher was Mr. Becker?" I asked over the noise.

An explosion of hands.

"He was funny," two girls said, laughing together.

"How, funny?"

"He would always tell corny jokes like—if a boy was talking to a girl, he would say, 'Flirting with the girls, Damon?' And one time he said that Julie shouldn't worry about Damon liking her, because Damon liked only dogs!"

"No, he said Damon only liked girls who looked like dogs!"

"And he brought in a picture of a collie and said that was Damon's girlfriend."

"And he used to say, 'When I talk about my two friends, I mean Danielle and Julie.' And they would get embar-rassed."

"He liked the girls better than the boys."

"No he didn't."

"Hold it! Quiet. One at a time. What else about Mr. Becker?" I asked.

"He screamed at you."

"Yeah! We had to put our fingers in our ears and dive under the desks. And one time he yelled at Tracy and Tracy yelled right back at him. He hollered *'Aren't you doing your assignment?'* and Tracy hollered back *'No!'* "

Tracy beamed with pride. She was a cute black girl who had a reputation for fearlessness and trouble.

"What did he do when he wanted to reward you for being good?"

"He would let us go to the park. He would give us extra recess."

"And how did he punish you for being bad?"

"By screaming at us!"

"That's all?"

"That was enough! He would scream till you were sick to your stomach."

I paused a moment. So far, the kids seemed to regard their teacher as a one-dimensional figure. As yet they showed no feeling that a real man had died.

"How did he seem in class?"

"He seemed happy!"

"Did he ever seem not happy? Did he ever do anything that seemed strange to you?"

One little black girl near the front said softly: "Sometimes, when everyone was doing their work in silent period, he would stare out at nothing and look real sad."

"Yeah, he would stare out the window. But only during reading period."

"Or he would look down at his shoe and sorta frown."

"Uh huh," I nodded encouragingly, but there was nothing more forthcoming on the topic. "Why do you think someone would want to kill himself?" I asked.

"Somebody said he was married and his wife divorced him."

"That's true, she did, but that was many years ago."

"Somebody said his wife was still bothering him, even after the divorce."

"I wouldn't know," I said. "But lots of people get divorced. Why would someone go so far as to kill himself?"

"Can't take it anymore," one boy shrugged.

"Uh huh. . . . Why not?"

"Maybe he's depressed," said one child.

"Maybe he has emotional problems," said another.

There was something glib, almost disinterested in the tone of their responses. I've taught certain lessons with children that attained a deep spiritual quality, where each of their answers sounded forth like a bell in a thoughtful silence. This was where I had hoped to bring the discussion, but for the most part the kids were extroverted, noisy, too impatient to listen to each other or take the pain of the subject seriously. I understood there must be a terrific need to avoid that pain at all costs. I was torn between pushing further into it and letting them get away.

"I knew a girl, she hung herself because she got an F on her report card," mentioned the same soft-spoken little black girl in front.

"I once wanted to kill myself," said a boy in the middle rows, "because I did something wrong, and I thought my mother was going to kill me!"

"*She* tried to kill herself!" Tracy pointed happily at a plump white girl across the aisle from her.

"Shut up, Tracy," muttered the girl.

"How?" someone else asked.

"She took a whole mess of pills."

"You and your big mouth, Tracy," said the girl, looking daggers at her supposed friend.

I asked the class how many had ever thought about killing themselves. About ten raised their hands (including the substitute teacher!). It was odd how they could admit to suicidal feelings in themselves but still not identify enough with Becker to feel very sorry for him.

One boy said disenchantedly: "Mr. Becker always told *us* to be good and then he went and jumped out a window!"

"I don't think that it's like 'being bad' to kill yourself," I said. "It's a tragedy, it's a sad thing, but I don't think it's a crime or a sin."

"It *is* a sin," said a tall Hispanic boy in back. "It's breaking one of the Ten Commandments."

I quickly went through the list in my mind, not having remembered any against suicide. "Which one?"

" 'Thou shalt not kill,' " he answered.

"But doesn't that mean you shouldn't kill someone else?" asked a boy near him. "Not: you shouldn't kill yourself?"

"I honestly don't know," I said.

"What does 'adultery' mean?" asked one of the girls.

"It's . . . when you're married and you sleep with someone who's not your husband or wife." I turned to the substitute teacher apologetically, as if to say: Well, they're getting an education at least. Then I went to the blackboard, out of some pedagogical instinct (or perhaps to shift the subject from theologically hazardous waters) and showed them the etymological breakdown of the word "suicide," along with homicide, fratricide, parricide, and regicide.

Some children wanted to discuss what happens to a person when he dies: the worms versus heaven. There was a lot of cross-conversation at this point, not all of it germane; those with short attention spans were getting impatient with the strain of a long discussion and tried to sabotage the focus.

"When someone is dead—" I began to phrase the question.

"Don't use that word!" cried a girl.

"Why not?"

"It sounds awful! Gives me the creeps. Use something else."

"Which would you prefer?"

"Passed on."

I began to make a list on the blackboard, based on their suggestions, not sure where this was leading: passed on/retired/into the blue/on vacation/gone but not forgotten. To these, at the bottom, I added my own word: dead.

"Do you think Mr. Becker is in heaven, or in the other place?" asked a boy whimsically. This got a big laugh.

"I don't actually believe in heaven or hell," I answered, "but everyone is entitled to have his own ideas on the subject."

I had noticed that there was a group of children who had been silent for most of the discussion. Just out of curiosity, I asked how many children had had Mr. Becker in class all of the previous year as well as this term. Most of the silent ones, sixth graders, raised their hands. I asked how many of the children had had Mr. Becker only since September. This time most of the noisiest students raised their hands. It was clear that the children who had been in his class the longest felt most complexly about him, and as yet were unable to put their feelings into words. The taboo against sentimentality in this age group may also have deterred them.

"Of those who had Mr. Becker last year," I asked, "do you think your attitude toward him changed over time?"

Yes, several volunteered. One Chinese-American boy explained how he had come to like the man because, when Mr. Becker explained things, he made sure you understood them. He was strict but he really cared if you learned. *He,* personally, had learned a lot from Mr. Becker.

"Some of the teachers in this school let you get away with murder," said another sixth grader. "But Mr. Becker really taught you. He was the best teacher in the school."

Now the tide seemed to be turning.

"I liked him because, even when he made fun of you, he always knew if he hurt your feelings," said a scholarly girl with glasses. "And then later he would try to cheer you up. I *liked* having Mr. Becker as a teacher, only I didn't like being in this class because of the other kids who spoiled it for me, like—" Her recitation of names was drowned out by the classmates' boos.

I asked them whether they thought that, overall, Mr. Becker was a good teacher, a bad teacher, or in between. For some reason, this question made Becker's critics most uncomfortable. They were unwilling to say out loud that they thought he had been a bad teacher, although some obviously felt it.

I told them I didn't think there was a single teacher who worked well with all kids. There were bound to be some kids who would thrive under one teacher while others would do better with someone else.

"What about Mrs. Reilly?" asked a boy. "I had her in the first grade and she was good with all the kids."

A little wide-eyed girl begged to differ: "She *hits* kids."

Rather than get into a discussion of the merits of Mrs. Reilly, I asked them how they had felt when they heard that their teacher had died.

"I was shocked!" said Danielle, one of Jay's favorites.

"I felt sad the way I would if any man had died," said a fifth-grade boy soberly, "like if someone had been shot on the battle-field. But I didn't really know the man."

Many of the newcomers to the class agreed. They had barely known him, how could they feel much about his death?

I explained that it was not a question of right or wrong feelings. Feelings were like the cards you were dealt in a game; you just had to go with those cards. Sometimes everyone might be crying at a funeral and you might be feeling nothing; that was the card you had been dealt that time. Sometimes a person died and you felt angry at him for leaving you. The important thing was to be honest and know what you were feeling. There was no point in faking it.

I told them I wanted them to write, a request that was met with the usual groans of protest. I threw out two suggestions: One idea was to write a portrait of Mr. Becker as they remembered him, a truthful portrait, not making him look either better or worse than he did while he was alive. The second idea was to write about how they felt and were still feeling about his death.

Paper was handed out, the children set to work. Some worked in pairs, most wrote singly.

I approached the substitute teacher, who had helped maintain some order during the discussion, which was not always easy. She had technically supported my efforts, but at the same time I had sensed something like disapproval in her—not exactly disapproval, but a scowling, hard-bitten quality, an angry wall. Substituting does that to some people.

"How has this class been?" I asked, under my breath.

"Rough," she said. "It's a tough situation."

"I'll bet it is."

"I wouldn't have been able to get that much out of them. I didn't think it was my place to talk to them about it."

"Were you surprised," I asked, "at the . . . amount of indifference they expressed at first?"

"I'm always surprised by their amount of indifference. I've been teaching for years and I've never seen a group of kids like this. They're cold. They have no hearts."

"They're avoiding a lot," I countered.

"Maybe you could excuse them that way. To me they're just cold. The other day we were at gym and I said at the end of the period, 'Aren't you going to put away the mats?' 'We didn't take them out, so we're not going to put them back!' I tried to explain to them that if you do something nice for people in this world, it will be better for you in the long run. 'Don't you believe in helping others?' I asked them. They all said, 'No. It's every man for himself.' "

What bad luck these kids had, I thought: on top of everything else, they had ended up with a rather narrow-minded substitute teacher who could see no farther than their manners. Oh, I knew what she meant; I've felt that way about kids at times. But this class didn't seem so extraordinarily vicious. A little rowdy, perhaps, having escaped the strict disciplinary hand of Mr. Becker. A class that starts to get a maverick reputation often takes perverse pride in confirming its notoriety; something of that "bad seed" swagger was detectable here.

About half of the children wrote short pieces, a few generalized, perfunctory sentences that were followed by a drawing of their former teacher. I don't know if our discussion had already exhausted what they had to say, or if the challenge of judging an authority figure objectively on paper was too threatening, or if they were just being lazy. The other half wrote papers that were more interesting—at the very least, shot through with revealing flashes. I offer these examples not so much as gems of children's creative writing, but as documentation that may shed some light on the various ways children come to terms with an unusual situation:

*On the first day of school, all my friends and I were waiting to see what classes we were in. After about fifteen minutes, everybody in my class went to their new classes, all except me. I was not on the list. I told the principal, and he went to all the classes to see if I was listed. Finally one of my friends came to tell me that Mr. Becker had called my name when he was calling roll. I was a little disappointed that I had Mr. Becker because he had a bad reputation of yelling so much. When I got into the room and of course he was yelling, I said to myself, "it's going to be a long year." After about a week of school I liked Mr. Becker, and I thought that everybody was wrong about him. Then he started coming on strong with his yelling. I once heard that he was a little deaf, that's why he had to yell so loud. When Mr. Becker died I felt sad but not too sad because I didn't know him that well.*
*—David*

*At times he acted very strange. When he walk he puts his hands in his pockets and looks down at the floor like if he was very very sad.*
*He was a very good teacher. He knew when he was going to be absent. He was absent every day and Mr. Jimenez said he'll be back next year and then 3 weeks later Mr. Jimenez came in with 2 parents and said that he died but he didn't want to tell that he committed suicide.*
*—Lorraine*

*Mr. Becker was much more different than the other teachers I had and know about. He was very positive. He had a special touch to make kids like himself. Mr. Becker had no right to kill himself, he should have been proud of his work. Many amount of kids since the last 14 years have gone to fantastic schools. His pupils had a lot of liking for him.*
*Mr. Becker might of yelled a lot but the kids he yelled at deserved it. Every kid in school except for kids in his class think he's a loudmouth but he really isn't what kids think he is. He let us do things that no other kids got.*

*We went outside and every time we went out we went to the park! Personally
I liked him.*
—Jonah

*When I heard Mr. Becker died I was really surprised almost shocked. I
couldn't believe it. Mr. Becker will be gone forever. You won't hear him yell
or scream again.*

*Most people didn't like him. I admit I didn't like him that much but not
enough to hate him or be happy he died.*

*I'm very unhappy he died. I wish he hadn't.*
—Kim

*Mr. Becker was a very strange man he always wanted things done his
way. When we had a spelling test if you made a certain mistake like if you
added a s he would count it wrong. And he always squinted his eyes like he
couldn't see and he always put his hands in his pockets. And yelled like he
couldn't hear his self.*
—Wendy

*When I heard that Mr. Becker died, I was very surprised because he had
been with this school for 14 years, and now when I come into this class he
jumps out the window. Last year when I was just going into fifth grade, Mrs.
Goldstein got hit with a block. The girl that threw the block, meant to throw
the block at a boy named Donald, but he ducked and it hit Mrs. Goldstein
and she fell off her chair and was knocked out. Mrs. Goldstein went to the
hospital and never came back to our school. And the girl that threw the block
was in lots of trouble and got transferred to another school.*

*So the same thing happened this time but Mr. Becker jumped out a
window.*
—Damon

*Mr. Becker is a very good or you could say was a very good teacher. It's
a shame that I could not have written is, but I hate to say I had to write was.*

*I wish he did not kill himself because he was the best teacher in the school.*
—Ian

*We felt surprised and upset cause something died. We never expected it
but in a way we appreciated it. But it was very interesting, cause if it were on*

*the 100th floor that would be more interesting, cause then he would die before he reached the ground. But even though Malina is so sad, and Mrs. Hoffheinz cries, we on the other hand clap, clap, clap, while Malina is saying boo we're saying Yeah and we mean YEAH!*
—Dara and Michelle

Chapter 1: *The truth about Noodlenose Greasy Fingers!*
This may be a strange name for Mr. Becker but if you saw him you'd agree. Noodlenose stands for his noodle shaped nose. Greasy Fingers means that when he thinks he puts his index and middle finger up his nose and pushes his nostrils up. So this makes his fingers greasy because snot gets all over them.
Chapter 2: *In the beginning of the year*
When I came in the first year in his class I was glad to sit in the back. Because he screams so loud. When he screams nobody seems to listen.
Chapter 3: *His looks*
Now he is a very odd looking thing. His hair looks like toothpicks. His nose is so big that it weighs more than his body does and it makes him walk hunched over. His mouth can open as big as an ocean when he yells, but still big when it's closed tightly.
Chapter 4: *Our thoughts of him*
Sometimes we get so mad at him, that we wish he gets hit by a car on his way home. So he'll have to stay in the hospital with 2 broken arms, legs. And he'll stay in the hospital for the rest of the year.
—Tanya and Danielle

When I heard that Mr. Becker died, I was sad at first. Later on I decided it wasn't so bad. That night, I just stared at my bedroom ceiling over my bed. As I was lying there, I thought about all the jokes he always made.
I really do miss him. He was mean sometimes, but usually, he knew that he had hurt your feelings, and he would cheer you by making jokes. He was a nice teacher.
—Julie

When I heard that Mr. Becker died I thought he died of a sickness in a hospital. Then I heard rumors that he commited sewerside. Then when I heard that it was true I felt pretty shocked.
—Jason

*I felt like I was going to cry but when I heard he killed himself I was mad because they said he died of a sickness.*
*—John*

*When I heard about Mr. Becker I almost fainted because it happen all of a sudden. When I heard he committed suicide I said shut your mouth because my mother said that he jump out 27 floors. Mr. Becker was a nice and mean man but he was a good one. I am glad I was in his class.*
*—Sonia*

*Mr. Becker was a very nice teacher when I was in the class for the first 7 days. Mr. Becker showed me how to fill out my label and he showed me where to put my Glossary in my spiral notebook and he yelled at me only 5 times.*
*—Pierre*

*When I heard that Mr. Becker was dead I felt so surprised that I had to go to his funeral. When I went to the funeral it was the saddest funeral. I never could go in and see other funerals cause you need to be a certain age.*
*I thought they were going to open part of the coffin but they didn't. In the funeral a Jew was preaching and some ladies started crying.*
*—Nikola*

All in all, I felt pleased with the way the lesson had gone and told myself I had risen to the occasion. My chronic need to be the hero of my life story had resulted in making myself take action, which temporarily silenced my frustration at the *fait accompli* of Becker's suicide. So we console ourselves with having "done something" by turning out a well-phrased eulogy on a friend, or seeing that his obituary gets in the *Times*.

Myra Hecht said no to a workshop for us; she had lost a sister to suicide the previous year and wasn't sure she could conduct it without breaking down. Dr. Hecht did advise Jimenez on the phone that they could not afford to look at suicide as an isolated aberration—in other words, getting rid of it by putting it in a category. We had to realize, she said, that we were all quite close to it a dozen times a day. On the other hand, she thought that in this jittery period we should emphasize "continuity and connection": both Jay's connection to the school through his good works as a teacher, and the ongoing life of the school community itself.

This word "community" began to seem more and more abstract to me each time it was invoked as a worthwhile counterweight to Jay's self-destructive act. Is one alone or in a community? I was not so sure anymore. And what was so special about this "community" that it could absorb any number of human sacrifices without having its ongoingness disturbed? Apparently I was not the only one visited by these thoughts.

On Friday, amid the brown-bag lunch eaters of the teachers' lounge, Kate Drucker voiced in her usual skeptical manner the doubts she'd been having. "Everyone says, 'Life must go on.' But what's so good about life going on as always? I feel there's something terribly wrong about this business-as-usual attitude. Couldn't the factory be stopped for just a little while? Shouldn't this tragedy be acknowledged in some way?"

"We need a ritual. Come on, Phil, think of a good ritual, you're the creative one around here."

"Bullshit," I said.

"At least some sort of memorial service," muttered Kate Drucker.

"That's a good idea. Who'd take charge of it?"

"I don't know. Not me, I feel shot," Kate said.

"I think we should put a plaque in the library," said Doris Friedman, "and buy history books and donate them to the library in Jay's name."

"Yes. And we should celebrate the birthdays of Claude and Jay every year!" suggested Cesar Gomez.

There had been another death in the P.S. 90 "family" a few years before: Claude Hardwick, the beloved assistant principal, a young man who played jazz and loved a good time, had died of cancer at age thirty. Out of that death came annual memorial evenings and a Claude Hardwick scholarship fund; his photo was cheered during the graduation exercises' slide show; his black-bordered portrait hung permanently by the main entrance door; and there was even a movement to rename the school after him. One sensed that there would be none of that groundswell of iconographic devotion in Becker's case. As Monte Clausen, my P.S. 90 guru, explained later: "There are two complicating factors why it won't happen. The first is the manner of Jay's death, which some people feel very turned off by. The second is that Jay was not exactly the most popular teacher with kids in this school." Still, it seemed the least we could do was to go ahead with a memorial service.

On Sunday afternoon, Ed Jimenez called me at home. It was a surprise, since he rarely phoned me at home; on the other hand, our paths crossed often enough outside school. I would run into him around town, usually at gallery openings or book signings, and once every few years we would meet for a colleagual drink. I really liked Ed, and admired what he was trying to do, though I was well aware of his difficult, moody side, which rubbed people the wrong way. I figured he must have needed to talk with someone who could sympathize with his point of view. Irrationally or not, I had been angry at him since Jay's death, making him out to be the villain of the piece. Therefore I welcomed the chance to hear him out.

Over the past week I had been keeping fairly lengthy diary entries about everything connected to Jay's suicide; I took notes while Ed spoke on the phone.

"Thank you for going in and working with Becker's kids. I checked with one of them on Friday and he said the discussion with Phil Lopate really cleared the air."

"I'm very glad to hear it."

"This morning, it hit me," he said, sounding tired. "It must have been a delayed reaction. I was making French toast and I started to cry. Now I can't remember when I did that last. I didn't even cry when my father died. But it must have been linked in my mind to my father's recent death and Claude Hardwick's. It was like that extra water in the glass that makes the whole thing overflow."

We talked about his father's death for a minute, and then I asked why he hadn't told the kids the facts about how Jay died.

"I got the news from Becker's stepfather, who was so hysterical over the phone I wasn't sure whether to believe him even. I mean, he wasn't making any sense. Also, I didn't know if the stepfather wanted everyone to know it was suicide. Tuesday I consulted with everyone: the teachers, the parents, the district office. No one had much guidance to offer. I read a book on death for young people, but there was no advice on how to handle suicide. I told his class it was an 'untimely death.' I figured it was enough of a shock for them to deal with that and it would be too much of a shock for them all at once to know it was suicide as well. . . . Some of the reactions of people, particularly the parents, were so weird. This one parent grabbed hold of me and she said her son was a potential behavior problem and she had placed him in Becker's class because he needed a strong traditional male teacher to stabilize him and could I guarantee a replacement? This woman knows the school staff and she knows there isn't any other male traditional teacher at the fifth-sixth level. Some of the other people's reactions were so selfish. It was hard having to play the role of the calm person consoling everyone. I had to go out of town for two days, to a minimum competency conference in Philadelphia. I was glad to get out because the atmosphere around the school was so depressing. When I came back on Friday the atmosphere was still depressed. Monte Clausen confirmed to me that everyone had been down."

I asked Kate Drucker's question: Then why encourage business to go on as usual?

"I didn't want there to be business as usual. I was against holding the cake sale. I figured, who would want to go to a festive occasion after what had happened? But the parents insisted. Most of the traditional teachers respond with business as usual because they're trained in that authoritarian manner. But we have a humanistic school here, with concern about the individual, so it doesn't make sense. If someone else had died, let's face it, Becker would have gone on with business as usual. He was a very rigid guy. I'm not saying he wasn't a dedicated teacher, because obviously he was. He would tutor kids after school on his own time. If a kid came to him and said, 'I really care about learning,' he would go all out for him. But if a kid cut up and seemed indifferent to learning, he had no use for him. I don't like to have to say this about the dead, but I'm trying to be honest. Often Jay was nasty, he was abrasive, he was rigid. He would have recurring periods where he was feeling bad and then he would take it out on me. He gave me a tough time with union matters. In the ten years or so that I've been principal, I've gone through several of those phases with him. After his marriage broke up, and after the breakup of another serious relationship. . . . But you had to be a prophet to know when these phases would recur. . . . He had asked me for a cluster position, and because of the budget cuts I couldn't. So I designed a class for him that would be easy, with no troublemakers. That's why they've held together so well."

"Do you feel guilty now because you denied him the cluster request?"

"No, I don't feel guilty. It was the only decision I could have made. I had to balance the good of the institution with the available staff."

"I don't know how to say this without making you angry," I plunged in, "but sometimes people feel that your administration overlooks the needs and wants of individual staff, and usually makes decisions for the good of the institution rather than the person. Eventually someone has to pay the price."

He was silent. "Look, who knows what it takes to push someone over the edge? Maybe if there hadn't been those budget cuts . . . maybe if we hadn't lost Title I he could have become a cluster teacher, and maybe gone on to find a new lease on life. On the other hand, maybe none of it would have made any difference. The last year or so, I knew something was wrong because he was finding it increasingly harder to handle troublesome kids. The kind he used to handle easily. After he took the first three days off, he came back and he was depressed. But sweet. Not nasty like usual toward me. Frieda Maura was the only one who knew how sick he was. Look, it's a closed society. They don't tell the principal who's having severe emotional problems, who's in therapy, who's under stress. Can you blame them?"

We talked for a few minutes more. I was touched by Jimenez's willingness to listen to whatever challenges I threw his way. On the one hand, who was I to sit in judgment? On the other hand, I wanted to use the opportunity to mediate a little between him and his enemies, by expressing their point of view in the words of someone he respected, and I wanted to clear up my own resentments. By the end of the conversation it was impossible to hold a grudge against him. What struck me, in fact, was that Jay, Jimenez, and I had been the three bachelors of P.S. 90. We were each peculiar in our own ways, each a solitary, and now one had quit the ranks and the two of us were left to commiserate.


The following week, Cesar Gomez emerged as the natural leader to organize the memorial service. In many ways, Cesar—young, handsome, outgoing, married, a bilingual open classroom teacher, and gung-ho organizer of the kids' basketball tournament—seemed Jay's antipode; but he had succeeded Jay Becker as the UFT chapter chairman, and this transfer had established a bond between the men. "Let's stress the positive!" Cesar told everyone now. "His life should be the topic of the service, not his death."

Cesar called up Jay's relatives and confreres and invited them to the service, which was scheduled for the evening of November 7. A strange listlessness, no doubt a secondary symptom of grief, was affecting everyone else, however, to the point that even getting the stencil for the memorial program typed began to seem a Sisyphean effort. Then there was the stalemate over which budget to use for the cake and cookies. Jimenez pulled forty-five dollars out of his pocket, settling the bureaucratic tangle with his characteristic brusque impatience, and sent his assistant off to the bakery. Still, there seemed none of the usual last-minute competition among parent volunteers to make the coffee. The community was not pulling together; people began to express fears about an embarrassingly poor turnout.

Myself, I had other anxieties: I had been asked to deliver one of the eulogies. I could appreciate that the decorum of memorial services dictated a stylization of virtues and that any alteration of that genre might prove offensive to some. On the other hand, it always seemed to me a mockery of the dead person's complexity as a human being to portray him or her as a flawless saint. If there is, underneath all, comfort in hearing the truth, would not a balanced description prove more healing?

As usual, I talked things over with Monte Clausen. "The one thing you can't do," he told me, "is to link pathology with behavior in the classroom. People won't stand for it." In other words, I could not so much as hint that the emotional distress that made Jay kill himself might have carried over, however slightly, into his professional conduct. For this reason, Clausen even advised against my reading the Riegelhaupt passage from *Being with Children*.

Sophie Arens, the librarian, wasn't sure whether to tell the story of how Jay went to bat for her as UFT chapter chairman. Specifically, she wondered whether she should use the word "grievance"—whether it would be too divisive, or would violate the spirit of the occasion. I told her I thought it would be all right.

A few kids from Becker's class were supposed to read the portraits they had written for me. Word had come down that Jimenez was worried I might let them get away with "inappropriate" observations; he wanted to take a look at their pieces before the program. I was becoming annoyed at the spirit of censorship, or self-censorship, that seemed to be descending on the memorial service from all sides. So I refused to turn the kids' compositions over to Jimenez—not by arguing him down, but by lying low and staying out of his sight.

A hundred people showed up, a respectable crowd. They settled in the first ten rows of the school auditorium. The memorial service began with a reading of the Emily Dickinson poem, "After great pain, a formal feeling comes." Frieda Maura served as M.C. She introduced Ed Jimenez, who spoke briefly, stressing how much Becker had cared about children. "He was connected to our school. He was connected to our children. He was connected to all of us. He became isolated, and he went away from us." In these words I heard Myra Hecht's advice to Jimenez somewhat gingerly and formulaically applied.

Harriet Ullman, a traditional classroom teacher, spoke touchingly about Jay's sense of fairness, his wanting everyone to be treated with justice.

Sophie Arens, the librarian, said, "I came to him with a problem and he treated the problem as if it were his own" (a nice end-run around the g-word).

Cesar Gomez gave a flowery oration in the Latin American mode, emphasizing Jay's moral stature, dedication, and love for what he did, ending with: "It is up to us to make Jay Becker immortal—through continuing his work! Let us not mourn his death, let us simply celebrate his life."

Then a serious-looking fifth grader, Jessica, played a classical violin piece. She played it so well that one's adult indulgence, held in readiness for any mistakes she might make, proved unnecessary. Her music reverberated in the auditorium, giving me goose bumps.

I was next on the program. I read aloud the two-page statement I had written in which I described Jay physically, analyzed the rather stereotypical persona he had developed as a teacher, and then went on to show his contradictory aspects, concluding:

> One could see a secret tenderness in him, which was not only his vulnerability to hurt, but his sensitivity to other people's suffering minus the usual protective screening device. And one could see an anger which he worked so hard to control, popping out with surprisingly harsh reproach or malice in public situations. This anger was his other secret. Manfully he wrestled to subdue it, and in the end, perhaps also manfully, he turned it against himself.

One of his students, when I asked them to write about their teacher last week, wrote a sentence that stuck in my head: "He talked so loud like he couldn't hear hisself." He couldn't hear his *self*. If Jay's death tells us anything tonight, on the eve of winter, it is that we need to listen more patiently and lovingly to the chaos in ourselves, and we need to attend more carefully to the pain in others.

I was not at all sure what I meant by this pious last sentence, but it had a rhetorical ring, so I let it stand. "Children from Class 5-6/234" were listed next in the program, and strangely, none of the delegated student readers had shown up. Perhaps they were ashamed of what they had written, perhaps they simply couldn't be bothered to come at night. In any case, I breathed a sigh of relief. We proceeded to Dave Naumann, president of the Parents Association. "He has touched many lives," said Naumann. Specifically addressing Jay's mother in the first row, he said, "I congratulate you on a remarkable, remarkable son."

The final speaker was Virginia Cramer, a first-second-grade open classroom teacher who had written a poem for the occasion. It was Virginia who had pointed out to me earlier the typo on the program:

IN MEMORIAM
JEY BECKER
1935–1979

"If I die, check the spelling, Phil," she said, with her dimpled smile. A woman of great heart, with the matronly soothing appearance of a veteran first-grade teacher, Virginia had turned out to be one of the most prolific poets in the writing workshop I had given for teachers and parents the year before. Now she began reading her three-page poem:

*Goodbye, Jay.*
*I never said goodbye to you before;*

I always said, "Hi, Jay!"
Or "Have a good weekend, or holiday, or summer."

Goodbye, Jay.
Goodbye to running into your room for a signature
Or an opinion, or to borrow a window pole for gym.
Goodbye to the erect way you sat up close to your desk
And the sensitivity I watched in your hands and fingers
As you received a paper from a kid,
Or returned one.

Goodbye, Jay.
Goodbye to your loud voice and your abrasiveness
At staff conferences and UFT meetings.
Sometimes you grated on me; I'd get annoyed, impatient, aggravated.
Sometimes I'd think, "I wish he'd shut up!"
And sometimes I'd think, "Good for him! He said what we were
All thinking but couldn't say straight out."
And goodbye to your laughter.
To the boyish, rascally way you sometimes kidded
And exaggerated a funny idea or a line of sarcasm;
Laughing and talking fast with the excitement of saying it all
Before it got lost.

Goodbye, Jay.
Goodbye to seeing you in the district office corridor every day
Coming from leaving your class for lunch,
Walking your usual pace, hands in pockets,
Head slightly tipped, glasses glared by light.

Goodbye to your medium size, middle age, thinning hair;
Your rough, tweedy sports jackets
And dark shirts.
To the tempo at which you always moved
(I never saw you rush or run).
Goodbye to the question drawn across your eyes
That never came out when you talked.
Goodbye to your positions from which you rarely bent;
To all the statements of conviction I heard and knew you believed.

*Goodbye to your professionalism*
*That protected a space in this school*
*For kids and staff;*
*A space I never worried about; I knew it was safe;*
*You kept it so.*

*Goodbye, Jay.*
*Goodbye to the little I knew of you*
*And to the larger part of you I missed.*
*You were here for fourteen years*
*But you're not here now*
*And your not-here-ness is heavy, hard and palpable*
*In my chest, stone-like behind my sternum.*
*The back of my head stings at the words sharply reminding me:*
*You were one of us; as thick and richly colored and strong*
*As any of the fibers in the fabric of this school.*
*We go on, school goes on, life goes on,*
*The cloth holds.*
*The tears are repaired, the lost threads replaced;*
*But there is memory.*

*Goodbye, Jay.*
*Goodbye to your physicalness;*
*To your sounds, your shapes, colors and movements.*
*And Hello to you as a member of my memory,*
*A membership I clutch closely now,*
*Some solace amid the disarray of death.*

*Hello, Jay.*
*Goodbye, Jay.*
*Hello, Goodbye, Hello.*

I was proud of Virginia. Yes, her poem included lines I might
have wanted to edit out or strengthen; but she had caught a piece
of Jay in it. I was moved by her deciding in the first place that
her own fledgling poetry could be the proper vehicle for responding to his death. As soon as the memorial service was over, I
went up to her and we hugged.

At the reception afterward, I went up to several strangers who introduced themselves to me as Jay's neighbors, "part of the Amsterdam Towers family." They hadn't known Jay much, he rarely spoke in the elevator, but they had wanted to come because they felt "involved somehow." (Indeed, he had jumped from their building.) Someone from the Appalachian Mountain Club, who had led hikes with Jay, came up to me. He said Jay and he had clashed at times, but they'd shared a love of nature. Denise Loftin one of my favorite P.S. 90 teachers, remarked that my speech had been "hard-hitting," which made me wince. "What do you mean, hard-hitting?" "Just—hard-hitting," she said, looking me squarely in the eye: "It was good and honest but it was a little close for comfort."

There was far too much cake left. No one seemed in the mood for noshing. I hesitated about introducing myself to the family, in case they had taken offense at my portrait. But Jay's younger brother Roger (handsome, curly-haired, a successful attorney, I had been told, which made me wonder about their sibling rivalry) was very gracious, asking for a copy of the speech. "You really caught him, down to the shiny nose," he said.

"If you don't mind my asking, why do *you* think he . . ."

"Jumped? Jay didn't believe in halfway measures. That's why he chose that way. He never did anything half-assed. He was very thorough: he left two notes, one to me, one to our mother. And he left all his bank statements and effects perfectly taken care of."

"He always had a sense of order."

"There's something else you might not know," said the brother. "Jay was on antidepressant drugs, and he'd had an adverse reaction to them shortly before he died. Maybe, with a different drug, he might still be alive. I'm convinced these things are partly chemical."

In the next few days, I heard some indirect negative feedback about Virginia's and my eulogies, all of it originating from the "more formal" teachers. Among other things, they were particularly outraged, it seemed, with one detail of our physical descriptions, which they thought we'd misrepresented: "Why did they both say he was medium height? Jay wasn't medium height, he was tall! I remember seeing him and Mario standing next to each other, and he was as tall as Cesar, not counting Cesar's Afro. Why do they go out of their way to belittle the man?"

Had I really meant to belittle Jay, unconsciously or otherwise? I didn't think so. . . . As for his height, it was hard for me to summon an exact physical impression of him any more. Perhaps I'd gotten that part wrong—and if that part, who knows what else.


Slowly the ache began to recede.

A month after his suicide, people had stopped talking about Jay. Everything had been said. And resaid. What was the point of dwelling morbidly on it? seemed to be the general sentiment. I could see their point. When all was said and done, the school staff had done everything that could be expected and more.

Still, Jay's suicide continued to preoccupy me. By now I had begun to wrestle with Becker—to identify with and argue with him. If he had waited longer, things might have gotten better for him. What arrogance, to assume it would all stay the same. I kept trying to enter his consciousness to understand why he did what he did. How does one arrive at a final conviction that there is no hope? What part of the decision was rational, mental, and what part physiological? I imagined a psychic pain growing inside him (myself) that demanded some physical outlet. Suicide must have been his attempt to give Pain a body, a representation, to put it outside himself. A need to convert inner torment into some outward tangible wound that all could see. It was almost as though suicide were a last-ditch effort at exorcism, in which the person sacrificed his life in order that the devil inside might die.

At the simplest level, I imagined Jay a victim of a screaming inside his head. When the screaming grew too intense, he jumped.

I had no such inner scream, but a continuous subvocal nattering, and at times I pretended to turn the volume up on it so that I might experience what Jay's distress would have been like. With the cold weather and shrinking of daylight, I felt a contraction of hope. That fall I decided to go to Yom Kippur services; the main sin I confessed to on Kol Nidre night was despair. (Didn't Catholicism also consider it the sin against the Holy Ghost?) I was experimenting with suicidal consciousness, walking for a while in Jay's footsteps. From the outside everyone saw me as tranquil, productive, satisfied; I had so tricked them into believing my confident act that they could not perceive the suffering underneath. Was suicide the only way I could ever get them to take my pain seriously? I wondered melodramatically. Of course, part of the reason people could not "credit" my misery was that it didn't go that deep, compared to others'. Yet I supposedly had all this friendship and good fortune coming toward me, and then I would turn the corner and not feel it.

Why did I, who, if I wanted to be honest about it, had a much wider support network of love and admiration than Jay, keep trying to minimize the difference between us? Perhaps if he and I were equally bereft, then I no longer had to feel guilty about being more advantaged; my debt would be cleared toward him. In part, my flirtation with suicide was also a way to absorb the shock of his passing. Sometimes we mime on a minor level the death of someone we know—take to our beds with a lingering cold when a friend has died of AIDS. I also needed to manufacture grief (or sorrow, which kept turning into self-pity) because I felt bad about not being more upset by his not being around. Maybe I was also competing with Jay Becker on some unconscious level, jealous of the attention he had gotten by killing himself.

Though I preferred to think of Jay as in some sense my opposite (shrill, inflexible), he kept turning up in my head as an undesired aspect of myself, an alter ego I was trying to push down. His self-contempt held up a frightening mirror to my own tendencies toward self-dislike. I suspect, too, that, because he was older and stronger-voiced than I, I was projecting onto him some of my feelings toward my older brother. Though in daily life I get along well with my older brother, we have had at times a very troubled, treacherous, competitive relationship, and in dreams he still often threatens to harm or kill me; the obverse is that subconsciously I have wished him dead on occasion. Who knows whether there was not some disguised relief experienced at Jay's (my brother's) death, for which I felt doubly culpable?

Preoccupied by all this, I tried my usual method of coping with distress, which is to write about it. I had in mind an objective reportorial essay, with myself kept firmly in the background, for some magazine like *The Atlantic* or *The New Yorker*. But as soon as I put pen to paper I felt my insides shaken up. I couldn't find the right entryway into the story, I couldn't get enough distance from it; everything was so interconnected mentally that hundreds of possibly irrelevant details begged to be written down. I was also disgusted at the idea of capitalizing on Jay's suicide, making something opportunistically, journalistically "topical" out of still open wounds. So I put away my notes for a little while, until I could feel calmer, more objective. That little while stretched into eight years; and it is only now, at forty-four—Jay's age when he jumped—that I am at last ready to take it up again.

I think there was another reason for my having been unable to write the essay then. I had come to a decision, around the middle of the school year, to leave P.S. 90. Running the P.S. 90 project for Teachers and Writers had been the best job I'd ever had, maybe ever would have, but after ten years of doing it, I felt "burned out," if you will. I had exhausted my pedagogic fantasies; I couldn't think of any new projects. On the one hand, I needed to break away from a place in which I felt almost cloyingly, undeservedly loved, and try new risks; on the other, I was tired of being so poorly paid, getting less after twelve years as a consultant than a starting teacher's salary. It was time to "graduate" to a university post.

Jay's death had seemed a warning sign to get out—of P.S. 90, of New York City, of my solitariness, if possible—before it was too late. I heard from a poet friend, Cynthia Macdonald, about a job that had opened up in the new creative writing department at the University of Houston; I applied for it, was interviewed in March, and was accepted. Knowing I would be leaving, I did not feel I could in good conscience write about P.S. 90 as though still an inside member of that community. I had already said good-bye to it. Like Jay, I, too, was walking out on the kids, the school. Any attempt to write about my connection to that ongoing institution would be dogged by elegy and guilt.


A permanent teacher had been hired to take over Becker's class. Hildy Weiss was young and pretty, an ex-stewardess, I was told. I said hello to her in the halls; she had a pretty smile. Before I got around to trying anything, the grapevine informed me she was getting married.

Sometime in the spring, we had a long chat. Hildy Weiss (now Korman) told me how she'd been recruited for the job. She had done some pinch-hit teaching at P.S. 90 several years before, but had left to become a stewardess. Apparently the administration had liked her and had kept her résumé on file. After Jay's death, Jimenez's assistant, Marian Morrone, phoned her repeatedly to ask her to come back. "I wasn't sure I could teach again," she said, "because I'd been away from it so long. But Marian kept saying, 'These kids *need* you.' Finally I went into my Pan Am supervisor's office and told her I was thinking of going back to teach school. 'You're crazy!' she said to me. 'You have to live your own life. In two years they won't even remember you. You should be having your own family, your own children!' I was torn. I loved flying more than anything, and I kept changing my mind about whether I could give it up, until finally Jimenez told Marian I was probably too immature for the job anyway. The next morning he called me on the Coast: one last time, yes or no? I said I would do it. On the flight home that night I was crying. I thought, 'I'll never be in a plane again, this is the last time!' But when I walked into that class, I couldn't leave them. They were my class.

"At the beginning, I didn't feel comfortable. I didn't know

whether I was supposed to do an extension of Jay's curriculum or start my own. I felt very insecure. I was doing what my parents or the principal wanted, I was being a 'good girl.' Then eventually it all came together."

"You should be proud of having done such a good teaching job," I said, thinking of her having stepped into a difficult situation and gotten the class to cohere, with a lively production of *Oliver.*

She shrugged off the compliment. "I'm not a good teacher. I'm a good human being, but I'm not a good teacher."

"At that age level maybe they need a good human being more than a pedagogic whiz."

"I still wish I knew what I was doing more. Half the time I'm bluffing."

"What do you think the net effect of Jay's suicide has been on the class?" I asked.

"The kids don't talk much about Jay. At first they were angry because they were the last ones told how he died. But then they stopped talking about it. Around December, a social worker from Mount Sinai Hospital started coming in. I think the administration hired her because they were worried about buried feelings and traumas. It may also have been to protect themselves legally, in case parents said later on, 'My child suffered a deep emotional scar.' Anyhow, by the time she started visiting it was probably too late. This social worker had a very psychiatric approach. She'd sit there and say, 'What's bothering you? How do you feel? What do you want to talk about?' There were great silences. The kids really resented her. She visited the class once a week for forty-five minutes or so—three or four sessions, all told. In between her visits, the kids would say, 'Why does she have to come again? We don't want to talk about it anymore! That happened so long ago.' It would take the kids an hour to settle down each time after she left.

"Anyway—I get a real kick out of this—the last time she came, she said to them in the final minutes, 'Are there any questions *you'd* like to ask *me?*' One kid raised his hand: 'Are you pregnant?' And she was! Somehow they'd guessed it. That's what they were interested in. Meanwhile, Jimenez was pleased: he wrote her a rave letter about the great job she'd done. . . .

"I think for the most part they don't brood about his death. A few of them probably feel guilty because they didn't like him when he was alive. I have to say I didn't like Jay that much myself. He was strange. A few years back, when I was student-teaching here, we would be in the subway and he would talk really loud, the way he did to the kids. Maybe he had a hearing problem. I would move two steps away to show that it was too loud. He never seemed to notice. There was a rigidity about him that transferred to the classroom. It was stark. Bare. When you're a teacher you collect all sorts of junk through the years. But when I took over his class there was nothing. A few books lined up. Nothing on the walls. There was an emptiness."

In May I told Jimenez I was leaving. But the program would continue: Teachers and Writers would replace me with another writer.

In Tolstoy's *Death of Ivan Illych*, one of the noblest works of fiction, the protagonist is "redeemed" by his mortality. Before dying he learns what he was put on earth for, and by extension, so do we, the story's readers, at least for a wrenching, consoling moment. But I keep forgetting the Tolstoyan point. What *is* it that we are put on earth for? After all these pages, I can redeem neither Jay Becker's life nor his death.

That June the school was featured on the cover of *New York* magazine under the headline "Twelve Public Schools That Really Work." The photograph, which showed every kid in class with his or her multi-ethnic hand straining to the bursting point to answer, had obviously been staged. To me there was something ludicrous about a city magazine's consumerist mania to find the twelve best of everything, be it late-night rib joints or neighborhood schools. But while we took the compliment with a grain of salt, knowing how inaccurate such media hype can be, we also acknowledged that P.S. 90 was a pretty good public school, all things considered. Typical was the defensive pride of one speaker at graduation exercises: "We didn't need *New York* magazine to tell us we were special. We knew that already."

At graduation, Ed Jimenez said in his principal's address: "This school prides itself on being a caring community. That's one thing that never changes. We care about the children, we care about each other. We continue to hold a belief in humanistic education, the importance of the individual in the learning process." True, but on the other hand, I mused (in the way one has of framing objections to any speaker's rhetoric), what about the vitriolic tensions among the staff, or an individual like Jay, who slipped between the cracks of our caring?

Nine months after the warm October night of Monte Clausen's phone call, a staff party was thrown to celebrate the end of the school year. Jimenez, with his ill-at-ease attempts at facetious banter, was trying to circulate, play the gracious boss, though his very presence made certain staff members deeply uneasy. They had not even wanted to invite him. He had, however, been so kind to me at graduation exercises, reading aloud one of my poems and wishing me the best in my new, post-P.S. 90 life, that I made it a point to chat with him for a long while, conspicuously distancing myself from those who were getting their revenge by cold-shouldering him at the staff party. By the same token, making small talk with Jimenez could be an arduous affair, and some of my friends on the Malcontents' sofa were giggling at me, and I longed to join their bitchy confab.

By the time I finally did make it over there, the mood had grown quiet.

Kate Drucker was saying what a hard year it had been. The staff hadn't organized anything like the previous year's fun activities: no Vest Day (when everyone had dressed elegantly and worn a vest), no lunch-hour volleyball game for teachers. Somehow the spirit just hadn't been there this year.

"Why is that, do you think?" I asked.

"Because there were no prep periods," said Kate. "Once the budget cuts eliminated our preps, we didn't have any time to visit each other's classes or talk during the day."

"And then everyone in *our* crowd got assigned different lunch periods. Not unintentionally, I might add," said Denise Loftin, with a significant arch of the eyebrow in Jimenez's direction.

Judy Hoffheinz, one of the few cluster teachers left, said: "It was just a very rough year. Hard. Grueling. Relentless. Grim. I found it that way at least."

"Do you think," I asked, "it might have had something to do with Jay Becker?"

Kate Drucker seemed surprised to hear that name from the past. Then she answered, with her sad ironic little smile, "No, I honestly think it had more to do with their taking away the prep periods."

Reproduced baldly, her remark may sound callous, but in that living moment it felt the opposite—warm with the perplexed gallows humor of truth-telling—so much so that we all laughed. It was an uncomfortable laugh, to be sure. We were all thinking of Jay at that moment. Like the group's bad conscience, I had forced us to, but having done so, a bit self-righteously, I had no more to say on the subject than any of the others. I had hoped *they* would come up with the right, miraculously eloquent response. Someone had passed away whom we had known, liked, and worked alongside for years, and yet—how can it be that a man's death does not matter more? It could have been a leaf falling in the background. Was it because of Jay's exasperating nature, or our own impotence to mourn? Leave it alone, I thought. Beneath our rueful collusive chuckle lay a plea for forgiveness and a recognition that this is finally how we do deal with the death of someone not central to our lives: we absorb it, we hurt over it, we forget it, we move on.

*About the Author*

Phillip Lopate is the author of *Bachelorhood, The Rug Merchant, Being with Children,* and *Confessions of Summer.* He is on the selection committee of the New York Film Festival, and is a recipient of Guggenheim and National Endowment for the Arts fellowships. His works have appeared in *Best American Essays, The Paris Review,* Pushcart Prize annuals, and other publications. Mr. Lopate is an Associate Professor at the University of Houston and also teaches at Columbia University's graduate writing program.